Science and Sentiment in America

Other Books by Morton White

THE ORIGIN OF DEWEY'S INSTRUMENTALISM
SOCIAL THOUGHT IN AMERICA: *The Revolt Against Formalism*
THE AGE OF ANALYSIS (ed.)
TOWARD REUNION IN PHILOSOPHY
RELIGION, POLITICS AND THE HIGHER LEARNING
THE INTELLECTUAL VERSUS THE CITY (with Lucia White)
PATHS OF AMERICAN THOUGHT (ed., with Arthur Schlesinger, Jr.)
FOUNDATIONS OF HISTORICAL KNOWLEDGE

Science and Sentiment in America

PHILOSOPHICAL THOUGHT
FROM JONATHAN EDWARDS TO JOHN DEWEY

MORTON WHITE

OXFORD UNIVERSITY PRESS
London   Oxford   New York

To Lucia

Preface

I have so often expressed my appreciation to my wife for helping me write my books that I find it almost impossible to find new words in which to thank her for her part in the composition of the present work. Once again she has given me indispensable assistance in the course of my research, greatly improved my prose, and helped me maintain the strength to see a book through to completion. For all of this and more, I express my appreciation by once again dedicating a book to her, a better book, I hope, than the one I dedicated to her thirty years ago.

I also wish to express my gratitude to four friends. Professor Kenneth Lynn of The Johns Hopkins University, Professor Israel Scheffler of Harvard University, Professor Arthur Schlesinger, Jr., of The City University of New York, and Professor Margaret Wilson of Princeton University have very generously given the manuscript the benefit of their sympathetic yet searching criticism. The manuscript, I should add, has been typed with extraordinary diligence by Mrs. Patricia J. Fenner, to whom I am also grateful for checking the accuracy of quotations and for calling my attention to a number of awkward expressions in an earlier draft.

I am indebted to Harvard University's Charles Warren
Center for Studies in American History for helping me de-
fray the expense of taking leave of absence from teaching
in the spring of 1967–68 so that I could work on this book.
The Warren Center also provided funds for research assistance in 1966–67, as did the Harvard Program on Technology and Society in 1967–68, and The City University
of New York while I was Visiting Professor there in the fall
of 1968–69. The Widener Library at Harvard, the Fire-
stone Library of Princeton University, and the Speer Library of the Princeton Theological Seminary have all put
me in their debt by allowing me to read many books that
are hard to come by.

In 1968 I wrote much of this book while I was a visiting
member of The Institute for Advanced Study in Princeton, New Jersey; and I would not have finished it when I
did if I had not had the good fortune to become permanently connected with the Institute in July of 1970.

In another volume I have gathered together several important selections from the writings of American and foreign
thinkers discussed in the present work. That other volume is
entitled *Documents in the History of American Philosophy:
From Jonathan Edwards to John Dewey* and is to be published by Oxford University Press shortly after the present
one appears. The two books may be read independently of
one another, but it may be of interest to readers of the present work to know that the volume of selections contains
many of the sources referred to here.

Princeton, N. J.   M. W.
February 1971

Contents

Science and Sentiment in America

Prologue: Philosophy, Science, and Civilization

This story revolves around what I think is the most important and most interesting strain in the development of American philosophy—its response to the challenge of modern science and scientific method. From Jonathan Edwards to John Dewey, American philosophers have felt obliged to meet that challenge. Some of them responded by defending their common-sense beliefs or their most firmly held theological, metaphysical, and moral convictions against what they took to be the unjustified incursions of science; whereas others, assuming a more offensive posture, tried to use science and scientific method in an effort to reconstruct common sense, theology, metaphysics, morals, and even society itself. In the period from Edwards to Dewey, this desire to respond to the challenge of science was part of a broader tendency that is typical of that period: the tendency to think that philosophy is obliged to deal with the more general problems of civilized life and not merely with technical questions of interest to philosophers alone. Because I think that after John Dewey, American philosophy entered a new phase in which it altered its conception of its responsibilities, I have ended this study with a discussion of Dewey's thought, hoping to turn to his successors in a sequel to the present work.

American philosophy's earlier concern with the impact of science on the rest of culture may best be understood by thinking of all philosophers as roughly divisible into three classes that merge into one another like the bands of a spectrum. At one end, we find theorists of knowledge who specialize in inquiring into how we know that this cow is brown and that penny round, and who concentrate so intensively on what we mean by words like "this", "cow", "is", "brown", "know", and "perceive" that they have little time or inclination for anything else. Such concentration not only precludes their having a serious interest in broader aspects of civilization like art, religion, morals, education, or politics, but it even prevents them from reflecting on the foundations of science and mathematics. Therefore, they are at the opposite end of the spectrum from pundits and sages who immerse themselves so deeply in the spiritual issues of their time that they make hardly any effort to reason systematically. The pundits claim to know important things about God, freedom, and immortality and to have feelings that are especially exalted and especially revealing, but they rarely argue, they never use logic in a serious way. In the middle of the spectrum, however, between highly specialized epistemologists and great-souled sages, there are philosophers who have their epistemologies all right, but who keep them warm by linking them to reflections on the great disciplines and institutions of civilization. They try to discourse intelligibly on the nature of mathematics, natural science, metaphysics, morals, history, art, law, politics, education, or religion; they advance views on man's condition and his fate; they offer analyses and assessments of their times; they are technicians but not mere technicians; they are seers but not madmen.

It is not difficult to give examples of these three bands of thinkers. The first extreme is strikingly illustrated by many

American philosophers of the generation that followed
Dewey. The other extreme is well represented by mystics of
all the ages as well as by pseudo-philosophers who mistake
pompous obscurity for profundity. The middle band includes
the most influential American philosophers who lived in the
period treated by this book, notably Edwards, Emerson,
James, Royce, Santayana, and Dewey. These Americans chose
to apply their technical conclusions to some of the main spiritual problems of their times, and one of the ways in which almost all of them did so was by responding, as I have said, to
the challenge posed by natural science.

For some the sword of science created anxieties that they
could resolve only by blunting it, while others let the chips of
common sense and high culture fall where they might. Some
tried to circumvent the effect of Newton's or Darwin's theories on their most cherished beliefs, whereas others tried to
apply such theories in areas that may have seemed utterly in-
accessible to experimental observation and to inductive inference. But whichever of these stances they adopted, they were
led to ask questions like: What is the nature and scope of scientific method? Can we apply it to theology and, if so, with
what effect? Can we apply it to metaphysics? Can we apply it
to morals, law, and politics? As we run over the works of the
more illustrious figures in the library of American philosophy, we can see that almost every one of them wrestled with
such questions. Jonathan Edwards was greatly influenced by
John Locke, that self-appointed philosophical spokesman for
modern science, but because Edwards was a Calvinist who believed that Protestant saints had a power to transcend the cognitive limits of natural men, his "Sense of the Heart" was a
device for escaping from what he thought were the limitations
of Locke's empiricism. Although Emerson respected science,
he was keenly concerned to protect the rights of poetry and
morality, and so he used Coleridge's distinction between the
lowly Understanding and the exalted Reason, claiming that

country poets and moralists were blessed with the latter whereas city empiricists and calculators were not. Charles Peirce managed to extract a scholastic metaphysics from his pragmatic theory of scientific meaning, and William James' "Will To Believe" in a supernatural order was a spirited response to what he regarded as the bullying tactics of scientific agnostics. By contrast, John Dewey was eager to see the scope of science extended as far as possible: into metaphysics, morals, education, and politics.

Having made explicit my plan of concentrating on American philosophy's efforts to come to terms with science, I should also make explicit another principle of selection. In order to avoid the impossible task of treating all American thinkers who have dealt with the impact of science, I have resolved to limit my attention primarily to the most distinguished American philosophers, diverging from comparatively high intellectual standards of selection only when considerations of social, political, religious, or literary influence send me off on what I think are interesting and justifiable tangents. Such forbearance yields time and space that may be used on more interesting matters. For one thing, it permits me to deal in greater detail with the American philosophers I choose to treat; for another, it permits me to devote attention to the relationship between American philosophy and the world around it, both intellectual and social. From the beginning, of course, American philosophy has been deeply influenced by European philosophy, and because it has been predominantly what I have called middle-band in character, it has been seriously affected by scientific, religious, political, and educational thought in ways that should not be neglected by its historians.

By concentrating mainly on first-rate American philosophers, by expounding the views of foreign philosophers where they are relevant, and by turning for illumination to other aspects of the American mind, I hope that I can do something to make this a somewhat unusual study of the history of American philosophy. In the same spirit, I shall also take the liberty of making critical comments on certain views when I think it may be helpful. In all of these ways, I hope to prevent this book from resembling a milk train that stops at all and only the familiar philosophical towns of America under the direction of a yawning conductor; and if the conductor does not yawn, the chances are greater that the passengers will not either. The passengers—if I may continue with that figure—need not be philosophers. Since I write mainly about thinkers who had their eyes on more than the problems of technical philosophy and since I try my best to present their views clearly, I hope that this volume will be of use to philosophers and to all readers interested in the history of American thought and society.

I · The Legacy of Locke: Intuition Versus Enthusiasm

In the beginning, American philosophy was a colonial philosophy—as derivative and unoriginal as one might expect it to be in an outpost of civilization. In the seventeenth century a scholastic version of Aristotle had been expounded in most Puritan textbooks, and in the eighteenth century colonial thinkers simply found themselves new foreign masters. Americans went on working in the shadows of minds greater than theirs, often revising imported theories to make them applicable to the peculiarities and exigencies of American life, and this continued to be the pattern of American philosophy from the time of Jonathan Edwards, born in 1703, to the days of Chauncey Wright, who died in 1875. The era of philosophical subservience encompassed the eighteenth century, when John Locke so powerfully influenced the philosophical thought of Edwards and that of Jefferson; and it lasted at least through the first decade after the Civil War, when Chauncey Wright was working within boundaries almost wholly determined by the biology of Darwin and the epistemology of John Stuart Mill. From the beginning then, American philosophy was dominated by transatlantic philosophy, until pragmatism, the first original American philosophy, emerged in the writings of Charles Peirce and William James.

Because our story begins with American thought in the eighteenth century, it is desirable to treat in some detail the most important transatlantic factor in its background, John Locke's philosophy of science. For more than a century—from the time that Edwards as a young man pored over Locke's *Essay Concerning Human Understanding*,[1] through the revolutionary period when Jefferson was accused of copying from Locke's *Two Treatises of Government*,[2] and up to the days when Emerson was dismissing Locke as a prosaic mind [3]— that deep, sober, thoroughly honest, and often inconsistent Englishman was at the center of American philosophical attention. He provided Americans with views to be canonized as well as views to be condemned, and he constructed a framework and a language within which much of their thinking took place even when he did not make converts of them. Most importantly for our purposes, he developed a theory of scientific knowledge that had enormous impact on American thought about religion, morals, law, and politics. That theory greatly helps us to understand one of the dominant features of American philosophical thought—its celebration of, and frequent appeal to, a power of the mind called "intuition". One of the most striking characteristics of American philosophical thought in this period was a tendency to appeal to forms of immediate insight into truth, like Edwards' Sense of the Heart, the intuition of self-evident principles in the Declaration of Independence, and Emerson's Reason. Our understanding of this tendency is much improved by examining Locke's philosophy of science because Locke dealt with a variety of mental activities that might be loosely designated by the word "insight", trying his best to distinguish between those that he regarded as acceptable ways of reaching truth and those that he decried. Locke constructed a vocabulary which successive American philosophers used as they came upon the scene. Lockeian expressions like "innate principles", "self-evident principles", "intuition", "revelation", "the light of reason", "intuitive reason", and "enthusiasm" all play their parts in the literature of early American philosophy; and one of the most useful ways of coming to understand them is by examining the use made of them by Locke, who taught American philosophers how to talk, if not always how to think.[4]

Innate Principles, Intuition, and Natural Law

In the first book of his *Essay Concerning Human Understanding* (1690), Locke launched his historic attack on innate principles and innate ideas—which some say nobody ever believed in as defined by him.[5] Locke explained the word "innate" by the use of a metaphor. He said that the advocates of innate ideas like that expressed by the word "impossible" held that they were inscribed by God upon all human minds from birth, much as words are chiseled into tombstones. Locke also attributed to his opponents the view that a principle or general truth which is composed of the idea expressed by the word "impossible" and other ideas—e.g. "It is impossible for the same thing to be and not to be"—is inscribed upon the mind from birth. Locke denied both of these contentions because he thought that the mind is at birth a *tabula rasa,* which comes to have ideas only through experience, and experience may take the form of sensation—by which he meant the normal five ways of seeing, hearing, touching, tasting, and smelling—or reflection, by which he meant what we today call introspection or looking inward at the activities of the mind.

Locke vehemently denied the existence of innate principles. This denial was the consequence of his empiricism, or doctrine that all our ideas originate in experience; for if the mind at birth has no ideas like *impossible* inscribed on it, then *a fortiori* it has no principles like "It is impossible for the same thing to be and not to be" inscribed on it. However —and this is of the greatest importance—Locke did not deny the existence of what he called "self-evident principles". Indeed, he held that the principle "It is impossible for the same thing to be and not to be" is self-evident though not innate. A self-evident principle he identifies as one which we accept as true as soon as we understand the meanings of the words which compose it, and Locke certainly did not think that his empiricism was incompatible with belief in self-evident principles so conceived. An empiricism according to which no ideas and no principles are inscribed from birth on the mind, was empiricism enough for him. Locke held that although all ideas arise from experience, once we have them we can see immediately by looking at the ideas themselves whether they "agree" or "disagree"—to use Locke's terminology—and this is the way in which we arrive at knowledge in the strict sense. We learn the ideas of black and white through sensation, but having learned them we can see immediately that no black thing is white by seeing that the idea of black and the idea of white disagree. Here we use our intuition in arriving at a self-evident truth; we do not have to go beyond an examination of the two ideas contained in the truth itself. We do not have to keep looking at black and white objects in an effort to increase the probability of the statement that no black thing is white, for that statement is seen to be true once we understand the words composing it; that is why it expresses certain knowledge rather than mere probable opinion. According to Locke, we have knowledge in the strictest sense only when it is evident to us that the ideas of S and P expressed in a proposition of the form "All S is P" agree, or that they disagree in the case of a proposition of the form "No S is P". Any opinion or judgment which falls short of the certainty that arises from perceiving such agreement or disagreement, falls short of being knowledge. Thus, a man who never took the trouble to go through the proof of the proposition that the three angles of a triangle add up to two right angles, but merely accepts it on the authority of a reputable mathematician, does not know that the proposition is true but merely judges or opines that it is with a degree of probability.[6] This example also makes clear that for Locke some known propositions are self-evident and others are deduced from those that are self-evident. The theorem that the angles of a triangle add up to two right angles is known to those who prove it, but is not self-evident. It is known only through being deduced from other propositions which are self-evident, like "The whole is greater than any one of its parts" and "Things equal to the same thing are equal to each other". The ideas expressed in the theorem are seen to agree, but not immediately. They are seen to agree only after we have gone through a chain of reasoning which begins with self-evident truths whose component ideas *are* seen immediately to agree.

From the point of view of American colonial thought—as we shall see presently—one of the most important things about Locke's philosophy of science was the fact that he held not only that there are self-evident principles in mathematics but also that ethics can be a science only insofar as it too contains such principles from which theorems can be deduced. Because he defined knowledge as narrowly as he did, thinking of it as certain and as expressing necessary truth, or truth which could not be otherwise, the only way in which he could imagine that ethics or moral philosophy could express knowledge was by imitating mathematics. Locke held that all scientific knowledge is recordable in a deductive system of propositions which begins with self-evident principles that are certain and known by intuition, and from which we deduce theorems which are also certain but not self-evident. His model was pure mathematics, as it was for many ancient, medieval, and modern philosophers who treated the same question. Locke said that from such self-evident, necessary principles as "The whole is greater than the part" and "Things equal to the same thing are equal to each other" we can deduce a proposition like "The sum of the angles of a triangle is equal to two right angles", which is not self-evident but nevertheless necessary. It is a necessary truth because it cannot be false, and in addition it necessarily follows from self-evident necessary truths.

Locke maintained two distinct things about a system of strict science or knowledge: firstly, that it is organized deductively so that theorems follow necessarily from axioms; and, secondly, that these axioms are necessary truths, or statements which could not possibly be false. His point may be understood by bearing in mind that we often deduce truths that are not necessarily true from others that are not necessarily true. For example, the conjunctive statement "This page is white and has words printed on it" is true but not necessarily true, because, as some philosophers would say, it is conceivable or logically possible for the page to have been colored yellow or for it to have been blank. Therefore the conjunction is called by them a contingent statement. Still, the conjunction is *true* even though contingent; it accords with the actual facts even though we can imagine the facts being otherwise. But though the conjunctive statement is contingent, certain statements necessarily follow from it, most obviously each of the statements which are its conjuncts. Obviously, we can deduce the truth "This page is white" from the truth "This page is white and this page has words printed on it". The truth of the conjunction, we may therefore say, logically necessitates the truth of its conjunct "This page is white". But—and this is extremely important—the fact that the truth of the conjunction "This page is white and this page has words printed on it" logically necessitates the truth of the conjunct "This page is white" is perfectly compatible with the contingency of both the conjunction and its conjunct. The conjunction necessitates the conjunct even though we can imagine the conjunction being false and either one of its conjuncts being false. The former may necessitate the latter even though the former as well as the latter are not necessarily true; and we may deduce the latter from the former even though neither of them is necessarily true.

On the other hand, we may also deduce statements that *are* necessarily true from others that are necessarily true; and this is what happens in a strict science as Locke conceived it. In such a science, instead of beginning with contingently true premises like "This page is white and has words printed on it", we begin with necessarily true premises like "The whole is greater than one of its parts" and "Things equal to the same thing are equal to each other". From such premises, Locke holds, we may deduce necessarily true statements like "The sum of the angles of a triangle is equal to two right angles". Since ancient times philosophers have held, as Locke did, that there are deductive systems in which we deduce necessary truths from other necessary truths; but many philosophers of empiricist bent have held that whereas deductive systems of pure mathematics and logic are of this kind, deductive systems of physics are not. In other words, they have maintained that axioms of physics, like "All bodies attract each other", are in an important respect like "This page is white and has words printed on it" because such physical axioms describe a world which could conceivably have been different from what it is. They have held that the axioms and theorems of physics, by contrast to those of pure mathematics and logic, are not necessarily true in the sense I have explained because they have thought that whereas it is *not* conceivable that things equal to the same thing should not be equal to each other, it *is* conceivable that all bodies should not attract each other. This view puts them in opposition to what is often called "rationalism", where rationalism is understood as the doctrine that the axioms of *all* sciences—whether pure or natural—are necessary and also self-evident. By contrast to such empirically minded philosophers, rationalists have held that even physics should begin with self-evident, necessary axioms from which necessary theorems may be deduced.]

How, then, shall we characterize Locke's philosophy of physics? Is it rationalistic or not? In order to answer this question we must distinguish between Locke's conception of the ideal of physical science and his view of the state and prospects of physical inquiry in his time. Since Locke held that a strict science is by definition a deductive system whose axioms are self-evident, he was bound to hold—and did—that if physics were ever to become a science it would have to be based on self-evident axioms. But since Locke was an atomist, he believed that the axioms of physics would have to deal with the behavior of the minute parts of gross bodies. Thus he says in a passage that combines his rationalism and his atomism: "I doubt not but if we could discover the figure, size, texture, and motion of the minute constituent parts of any two bodies, we should know without trial several of their operations one upon another; as we do now the properties of a square or a triangle".[7] He expresses his atomism when he implies that knowledge about the *minute parts* of ordinary bodies would allow us to know the operations of those bodies on one another. He reveals his rationalistic conception of the ideal of science when he says that if we could discover the figure, size, texture, and motion of the atoms in men, rhubarb, opium, and hemlock we should know *without trial* that rhubarb purges, that opium puts men to sleep, and that hemlock kills as we now know that the sum of the angles of a triangle is 180 degrees. From this we may infer that according to Locke physics in its ideal state would contain axioms corresponding to "The whole is greater than any of its parts" and theorems corresponding to "The sum of the angles of a triangle is 180 degrees". In Locke's view, therefore, physical axioms would be self-evident and necessary; and from them, physical theorems about macroscopic bodies would be deduced. Such theorems Locke would also regard as necessary truths.

It must be noted, however, that Locke appears to deny that we *can* have the knowledge about atoms that would, if we had it, allow us to deduce general truths about macroscopic bodies. He says: ". . . as to a *perfect science* of natural bodies, . . . we are, I think, so far from being capable of any such thing, that I conclude it lost labour to seek after it".[8] It would appear that Locke did not think it possible to attain the knowledge of atoms he deemed requisite, though there are some passages which suggest the weaker conclusion that it would be exceedingly difficult to attain such knowledge. It is worth observing, however, that if Locke says that we *cannot* have that knowledge, he says so on grounds like those that lead him to say that we cannot have knowledge about plants and animals on distant planets. Such things, he says, are so far away that we do not receive ideas about them; and lacking such ideas, we cannot have knowledge about them. He adds: "If a great, nay, far the greatest part of the several ranks of bodies in the universe escape our notice by their remoteness, there are others that are no less concealed from us by their minuteness".[9] He then goes on to say that "an incurable ignorance" of the figure, size, texture, and motion of the minute parts of rhubarb and of the human organism is what prevents us from knowing *without trial* the truth that rhubarb will purge a man, as we now know the properties of a square. A present-day philosopher might at this point ask whether Locke regarded our ignorance of the properties of atoms as physically or logically incurable; and I am inclined to say that if Locke had been willing to make this distinction, he would have replied that the incurableness of this ignorance was at best physical, like the incurableness of our ignorance of the properties of bodies on distant planets. This would allow for the logical possibility that we might be able to establish physical principles about atoms, from which we could deduce the truth that rhubarb purges and the truth that hemlock kills.

However, as axioms of a strict science, the principles supposedly governing the behavior of atoms would be self-evident for Locke; and so long as Locke regards them as self-evident, he reveals his attachment to rationalism in the philosophy of physics. It must also be emphasized that Locke never says, as a Humeian or a logical positivist might, that even if we could discover the figure, size, texture, and motion of atoms, we could not formulate self-evident principles about them. Locke never suggests, as a forthright opponent of rationalism might, that principles which would govern the behavior of atoms would be fundamentally different in status from principles like "Things equal to the same thing are equal to each other" since the former could not be logically necessary or self-evident. Nor does Locke say, as an anti-rationalist might, that deduction of a generalization like "Rhubarb purges men" from laws about minute particles could not turn such a truth into a logically necessary truth. An anti-rationalist would deny that when Boyle's Law was derived from the kinetic theory of gases it assumed the same logical status as the law that the sum of the angles of every triangle is 180 degrees. He would regard the kinetic theory as logically contingent and as not self-evident; and he would regard Boyle's Law as logically contingent even after it was deduced from the kinetic theory. By contrast, Locke's attachment to the rationalist ideal might well have led him to regard the kinetic theory as logically necessary and self-evident, and Boyle's Law as logically necessary though not self-evident. The main point I wish to stress is that Locke's skepticism about our ability to learn the axiomatic principles of atomic physics exists alongside his rationalistic view that those principles would have to be self-evident in order for physics to become a science. The fact that he despaired of making physics a science makes him no less rationalistic as a philosophical analyst of the ideal of natural science.

Locke's rationalism concerning physics was in some respects similar to his rationalism concerning ethics, but in other respects different from it. In both cases he sketched the ideal discipline in the same way. Just as the ideal of physics was to become a demonstrative science, so, he held, was the ideal of ethics. And just as he maintained that the physics of his time was not a strict science, so he granted that ethics of his time was not. But whereas he was led to a sense of hopelessness about the likelihood of ever attaining a demonstrative science of physics, he was more sanguine about the likelihood of turning ethics into a demonstrative science. Moreover, the effect of his skepticism about attaining the high ideals he set for physics led him to stress the importance of settling for less in physics. He was given to saying that since we see how difficult or perhaps impossible it is to achieve a really scientific physics, replete with self-evident, necessary axioms and necessary theorems, we had better be satisfied with probability in experimental physics. And although there is a place in his correspondence where he revealed a willingness to settle for less than a demonstrative science of ethics by relying on the morality taught in the Gospel, Locke did not usually argue that self-evident moral principles are impossible or even difficult to find. I say "did not usually" because I think there are passages—which I shall cite presently—in which he diverged from his normal tendency to think that ethics contains self-evident principles from which other ethical truths may be deduced.

Locke said very boldly in his *Essay* that "morality is capable of demonstration, as well as mathematics"; [10] and in his *Second Treatise of Government* (1690), he declared that there is "nothing more evident than that creatures of the same species and rank, promiscuously born to all the same advantages of nature and the use of the same faculties, should also be equal one amongst another without subordination or subjection; unless the lord and master of them all should, by any manifest declaration of his will, set one above another, and confer on him by an evident and clear appointment an undoubted right to dominion and sovereignty".[11] He also said approvingly that this equality of men by nature was regarded by Richard Hooker in *The Laws of Ecclesiastical Polity* "as so evident in itself and beyond all question that he makes it the foundation of that obligation to mutual love amongst men on which he builds the duties we owe one another, and from whence he derives the great maxims of justice and charity".[12] It is clear that in the *Second Treatise* Locke thinks we can begin with self-evident, certain moral axioms like Hooker's principle of equality, and from them derive by purely logical means other principles like the maxims of justice and charity. This is consonant with what he says in the *Essay* when he places *"morality* amongst the *sciences capable of demonstration"* and claims that "from self-evident propositions, by necessary consequences, as incontestible as those in mathematics, the measures of right and wrong might be made out, to any one that will apply himself with the same indifference and attention to the one as he does to the other of these sciences".[13]

From Book I, Chapter I, of the *Essay* and from the *Second Treatise,* therefore, one might arrive at the following picture of Locke's thought on these matters: There are no innate principles but there *are* self-evident principles which may be logical, mathematical, or moral. Thus, Hooker's principle of equality is a moral proposition which is self-evident. Unfortunately, however, Locke says something in Book I, Chapter II, of the *Essay* which seems to upset this picture. In Book I, Chapter II, he says quite flatly that there are *no* self-evident moral or practical principles, and hence undermines his idea that morality is capable of demonstration. Early in his argument for the view that there are no innate practical or moral principles, he says that there are no *innate* practical principles simply because there are no *self-evident* practical principles, his point being that an innate principle should be *at least* self-evident, so that if it is not self-evident it cannot be innate. He first says: "I think it will be hard to instance any one moral rule which can pretend to so general and ready an assent as, 'What is, is'; or to be so manifest a truth as this, that 'It is impossible for the same thing to be and not to be.' Whereby it is evident that they [moral rules or principles] are further removed from a title to be innate; and the doubt of their being native impressions on the mind is stronger against those moral principles than the other [speculative principles]". His more crucial words immediately follow: "Not that it brings their truth at all in question. They are equally true, though not equally evident. Those speculative maxims carry their own evidence with them: but moral principles require reasoning and discourse, and some exercise of the mind, to discover the certainty of their truth. . . . But this is no derogation to their truth and certainty; no more than it is to the truth or certainty of the three angles of a triangle being equal to two right ones: because it is not so evident as 'the whole is bigger than a part,' nor so apt to be assented to at first hearing. It may suffice that these moral rules are capable of demonstration: and therefore it is our own faults if we come not to a certain knowledge of them".[14] It would seem, therefore, that the "judicious Hooker's" principle of equality cannot be regarded by the Locke of Book I, Chapter II, of the *Essay* as self-evident, because it is a moral or practical principle—it says among other things that men *should be* equal one amongst the other, without subordination or subjection.[15] But if it is not self-evident, how can we use it as an axiom in the theory of Natural Law?

Since our main concern is not with Locke but with his impact on American thought, we cannot tarry any longer over the difficulties in his philosophy. It must suffice to say here that although some Americans revised Locke's conception of reason, as we shall see in the next chapter, so far as I know, not one of them ever raised the question about Locke's con-

sistency which I have just raised about his ethics. They were
attracted by the *Two Treatises of Government,* where Locke
unquestionably treats moral principles of Natural Law as
self-evident, and they were attracted by ideas like those which
appear in the following passage in the *Essay:* "I would not
here be mistaken, as if, because I deny an innate law, I
thought there were none but positive laws", positive laws
being those enacted by an earthly sovereign or legislature.
Locke then goes on to say, "There is a great deal of difference
between an innate law, and a law of nature", his chief point
being that a law of nature is a moral principle that we can
come to know by the use and due application of our natural
faculties, whereas this is not true of innate principles as described by their advocates.[16] Now it is important to observe
that for Locke, whether a principle be self-evident and hence
seen to be true by intuition—or by what is also called in accordance with a long tradition "Intuitive Reason"—or
whether it be deduced from a self-evident principle by the use
of what is called "Discursive Reason"—or reason*ing*—it is to
be distinguished from the rejected innate principle by virtue
of the fact that *both* intuitive reason and discursive reason are
natural faculties of men. God has not implanted innate
knowledge in men, but he has given them the naturál faculties of intuitive reason and discursive reason which together
allow them to know axioms and theorems. Intuitive knowledge, Locke said, "is certain, beyond all doubt, and needs no
probation, nor can have any; this being the highest of all
human certainty. In this consists the evidence of all those
maxims which nobody has any doubt about, but every man
(does not, as is said, only assent to, but) *knows* to be true, as
soon as ever they are proposed to his understanding. In the
discovery of and assent to these truths, there is no use of the
discursive faculty, *no need of reasoning,* but they are known
by a superior and higher degree of evidence".[17] In spite of invidiously distinguishing between self-evident principles as

knowable by non-discursive reason and derived principles as knowable by discursive reasoning, Locke regarded both of them as demanding the use of our natural intellectual faculties in a way that innate principles do not. And it was precisely because innate principles do not—according to those who supposed that there are such things—demand the use of our rational powers, whether discursive or not, that Locke thought they were often said to exist by political reactionaries. Once it was admitted that there are such things as *innate* principles, men would be discouraged, he said, "from the use of their own reason and judgment". They would be led to believe and take upon trust without further examination such principles, "in which posture of blind credulity, they might be more easily governed by, and made useful to some sort of men, who had the skill and office to principle and guide them. Nor", he warned, "is it a small power it gives one man over another, to have the authority to be the dictator of principles, and teacher of unquestionable truths; and to make a man swallow that for an innate principle which may serve to his purpose who teacheth them".[18]

Here we can see how Locke's attack on innate principles and his defense of the existence of principles of Natural Law —whether self-evident or derived—were related to his defense of the Revolution of 1688, for it was that democratic revolution which he sought to justify by appeal to the self-evident principles enunciated in his *Second Treatise of Government,* principles that could be known by all men of rational mind. Here we can also see one of the reasons why some American revolutionary philosophers admired Locke's attack on innate principles. It gave them a philosophical device which they could use against those who would dictate political morality. Moreover, if they heeded the message in Locke's *Second Treatise of Government,* they could replace the dictators' *innate* principles by the self-evident moral principles which Locke, in his more consistent moods, *had* to postulate if he were to remain faithful to his idea that morality is capable of demonstration. And that idea, as we have seen, was the consequence of his notion that all knowledge in the strict sense, whether mathematical, physical, or moral, was of certain and necessary truth; and hence had to be expressed in propositions seen to be true by intuition or deduced from such by men of rational mind. Rarely has a philosophy of science had such direct effect on political theory and action.

Reason, Revelation, and Enthusiasm

It was one of the ironies of Locke's *Essay* that he was so rationalistic in a book which he wrote with the intention of sweeping scholastic rubbish from the way of great scientists like Boyle, Sydenham, Huyghens, and the "incomparable Mr. Newton", and with the intention of showing that all of our ideas originate in experience. Yet he was not only rationalistic in his philosophy of physics and of morality but also as rationalistic as a scholastic in his philosophy of religion. He believed that he could proceed from intuitively known self-evident propositions by deductive steps to the conclusion that God exists. He began with the allegedly self-evident proposition that he himself existed but that he did not always exist. Then he asserted a version of the principle of causation, which he also took to be self-evident, namely, that whatever begins to exist has been produced by something. On the basis of these premises, he thought he was entitled to conclude that "from eternity there has been something", and that this permanently enduring something is God. Locke's proof is less than convincing. It is true, of course, that if Locke had a beginning and whatever has a beginning was produced by something, then Locke was produced by something. And if his producer had a beginning, it too had a beginning, and so on indefinitely back in time. There will always be a beginner, so to speak, of things which begin. But we cannot infer from this, as Locke seems to, that one and the same thing exists from eternity as *the* beginner of everything.[19]

No matter what we may think of the cogency of this argument, it is important to remark that Locke's rationalism in religion held great significance for evangelical American religious thinkers of the eighteenth century, notably for Jonathan Edwards, as we shall see. It is true that Locke admits the possibility of establishing religious propositions by faith and revelation, but when one reads what he was to say about that process, one can see why thinkers of a mystical bent might find his views on revelation wanting. Locke says, *"Faith . . . is the assent to any proposition, not . . .* made out by the deductions of reason, but upon the credit of the proposer, as coming from God, in some extraordinary way of communication. This way of discovering [in modern language, uncovering] truths to men, we call *revelation".*[20] But having granted the possibility of uncovering religious truths to men by this method, Locke proceeds to limit it. For one thing, Locke says that no man inspired by God can communicate to other people what Locke calls a new simple idea. By "simple ideas" Locke meant such ideas as sweetness, hardness, and yellowness, which come to a passive mind through the sensations as a result of external objects impinging on the mind, or such ideas as those of thinking or willing, which come to man as a result of his reflecting on what goes on in his mind. Locke asserted that even St. Paul, who, "when he was rapt up into the third heaven", may have had some extraordinary simple ideas, could say no more to ordinary men than that there are such things "as eye hath not seen, nor ear heard, nor hath it entered into the heart of man to conceive".[21] Although Paul may have had unusual simple ideas, which came to him by what Locke calls *original* revelation or by God's own immediate impression on his mind, Paul could not communicate them to ordinary men by what Locke calls *traditional* revelation, simply because ordinary men, lacking those simple ideas,

just as a man blind from birth lacks the simple idea of yellowness, could not understand Paul. Locke also says in the same
spirit of limiting traditional revelation that when it instructs
us in truths which we can know by reason, knowing them
through the use of reason yields greater certainty. If a mathematical truth is revealed to us, we can be only as certain of its
truth as we could be that the revelation was in fact from God,
which means only with probability; whereas if we demonstrate it, we know it with certainty.[22] Moreover, Locke holds
that if we are confronted with an allegedly revealed truth
which contradicts what we claim to know by intuition or demonstration, we should always accept the dictates of the latter.
In sum, Locke's message about the boundaries of revelation
and reason is that the former should not be followed when it
is flatly opposed to self-evident or demonstrated truth, but
that it may be followed when it concerns matters on which
reason has nothing to say, or when it is authenticated and
deals with matters concerning which our natural faculties
yield no more than a lesser probability.

What Locke absolutely proscribes, however, is a third mode
of assent called "Enthusiasm".[23] This, he holds, sets reason
aside and sets up revelation without it. Therefore, he says, it
abandons both reason and revelation and "substitutes in the
room of them the ungrounded fancies of a man's own brain".[24]
A man who accepts a revelation which is *not* vouched for by a
rational assessment of the proposer's credit "puts out the light
of both" reason and revelation, but an Enthusiast claims to
have revelations whose authenticity need not be vouched for.
Enthusiasts are "men in whom melancholy has mixed with
devotion, or whose conceit of themselves has raised them into
an opinion of a greater familiarity with God, and a nearer
admittance to his favour than is afforded to others", and
"[they] have often flattered themselves with a persuasion of
an immediate intercourse with the Deity, and frequent com-
munications from the Divine Spirit".[25] Enthusiasm arises,

said Locke in his most quoted phrase on the subject, "from
the conceits of a warmed or overweening brain".[26] Enthusiasts
believe propositions because they presume that God revealed
them, but they do not *know* that God revealed them and they
make no effort to show that he did. They rest only on their
own feeling that the proposition comes from God without
having, for example, *"outward signs"* of the kind that Moses
had.[27] He saw the bush burn without being consumed and
heard a voice in it, and this, Locke says, "was something besides finding an impulse upon his mind to go to Pharaoh, that
he might bring his brethren out of Egypt: and yet he thought
not this enough to authorize him to go with that message, till
God, by another miracle of his rod turned into a serpent, had
assured him of a power to testify his mission, by the same miracle repeated before them whom he was sent to".[28] Locke's
main point is that we cannot rely merely on "the strength of
our private persuasion within ourselves"; we must show that
God has enlightened our minds.[29]

A Preview of "Insights" To Come

This concludes our discussion of the Lockeian views that had
special significance for the American philosophers we are to
consider. In summary, we should point out that Locke rejected innate principles and ideas but based his philosophy of
science on the notion of self-evident principles; he thought
that such principles could be perceived by intuition or intuitive reason; he thought that the principles of morality are immutable and necessary but used little discursive reason in or-
ganizing them deductively; he presented a poorly argued and
unoriginal demonstration of the existence of God; he allowed
for knowledge by revelation but he drew the line at religious
Enthusiasm and would have none of it.

I cannot resist the speculation that Locke was harsh with
Enthusiasts who appealed to an inner light partly because this

appeal was uncomfortably close to his own language about self-evident propositions. Knowledge of the truth of self-evident principles is, he says, "irresistible, and, like bright sunshine, forces itself immediately to be perceived, as soon as ever the mind turns its view that way; and leaves no room for hesitation, doubt, or examination, but the mind is presently filled with the clear light of it".[30] Yet when Locke speaks of the devotees of Enthusiasm, he says mockingly that they "see the light infused into their understandings, and cannot be mistaken; it is clear and visible there, like the light of bright sunshine. . . . This light from heaven is strong, clear, and pure; carries its own demonstration with it: and we may as naturally take a glow-worm to assist us to discover the sun, as to examine the celestial ray by our dim candle, reason".[31] But how could Locke distinguish between the two lights? Those who knew the truths of mathematics, he said, felt a light flooding their mind, and so did the Enthusiasts. Does Locke give us any way of deciding when the light is of the good kind? He tries to answer in the following passage: "Light, true light, in the mind is, or can be, nothing else but the evidence of the truth of any proposition; and if it be not a self-evident proposition, all the light it has, or can have, is from the clearness and validity of those proofs upon which it is received. To talk of any other light in the understanding is to put ourselves in the dark, or in the power of the Prince of Darkness, and, by our own consent, to give ourselves up to delusion to believe a lie. For, if strength of persuasion be the light which must guide us; I ask how shall any one distinguish between the delusions of Satan, and the inspirations of the Holy Ghost? He can transform himself into an angel of light. And they who are led by this Son of the Morning are as fully satisfied of the illumination, i.e. are as strongly persuaded that they are enlightened by the Spirit of God as any one who is so: they acquiesce and rejoice in it, are actuated by it: and nobody can be more sure, nor more in the right (if their own strong belief may be judge) than they".[32]

Now that we have finished our discussion of Locke's views on the nature and scope of science, I should say in anticipation of what follows that although his views commanded a great deal of admiration in America for many generations after Jonathan Edwards first read the *Essay Concerning Human Understanding*, they also formed a philosophy against which Americans reacted critically. In the early part of the eighteenth century, Jonathan Edwards departed from Locke's empiricism by adding a sixth sense to the normal five in order to gain access to religious truth; in the latter part of the century certain revolutionary theorists reacted against Locke's rationalism by giving passion or sentiment a fundamental role in the detection of moral truth; in the early part of the nineteenth century the Transcendentalists combined both of these departures from Locke in a full-scale effort to revive the fires of Enthusiasm that he had hoped so devoutly to douse; and in the later part of the nineteenth century William James deliberately flouted Locke's warning that "whatsoever credit or authority we give to any proposition more than it receives from the principles and proofs it supports itself upon, is owing to our inclinations that way, and is so far a derogation from the love of truth as such: which, as it can receive no evidence from our passions or interests, so it should receive no tincture from them".[33]

2 · Jonathan Edwards: The Doctrine of Necessity and the Sense of the Heart

In accordance with my decision to keep my intellectual sights as high as possible, I shall begin the American part of my story with Jonathan Edwards. In 1821 the learned Scottish philosopher Dugald Stewart said of Edwards that he was the "*one* metaphysician of whom America has to boast, who, in logical acuteness and subtility, does not yield to any disputant bred in the universities of Europe".[1] Edwards was born in East Windsor, Connecticut, in 1703, entered Yale in 1716, was graduated in 1720, and in 1722 became a pastor in a Presbyterian church in New York City. He spent about a year in that city, where—interestingly enough for the student of American attitudes toward urban life—his sense of divine things increased. After his New York stay he taught for a couple of years at Yale until he went to Northampton, Massachusetts, in 1726 to begin a ministerial career that ended when his parishioners dismissed him after twenty-five years of devoted service. During that period he became the leading historian and theorist of the Great Awakening, one of those intensely evangelical revivals that have periodically swept America. In 1741, Edwards had occasion to deliver a sermon in neighboring Enfield, Connecticut, called "Sinners in the Hands of an Angry God", which led future historians to cast him in the role of a fire and brimstone Calvinist—not surprisingly in the light of declarations like the following: "How awful are those words, Isa. lxiii. 3, which are the words of the great God. 'I will tread them in mine anger, and will trample them in my fury, and their blood shall be sprinkled upon my garments, and I will stain all my raiment.' It is perhaps impossible to conceive of words that carry in them greater manifestations of these three things, *viz.* contempt, and hatred, and fierceness of indignation. If you cry to God to pity you, he will be so far from pitying you in your doleful case, or showing you the least regard or favour, that instead of that, he will only tread you under foot. And though he will know that you cannot bear the weight of omnipotence treading upon you, yet he will not regard that, but he will crush you under his feet without mercy; he will crush out your blood, and make it fly, and it shall be sprinkled on his garments, so as to stain all his raiment. He will not only hate you, but he will have you, in the utmost contempt: no place shall be thought fit for you, but under his feet to be trodden down as the mire of the streets".[2]

Unreasonable as this may sound to contemporary ears, it appeared in a sermon which also revealed Edwards' power of reasoning and his tendency to use mechanical metaphors. The text for the sermon was a passage from *Deuteronomy,* "Their foot shall slide in due time"; and Edwards expatiated metaphorically on the fact that the wicked unbelieving Israelites were always exposed to destruction because they walked in slippery places. Those were places in which friction was at a minimum; and, to make his point more forcibly, Edwards portrayed the poor sinners on an inclined plane that sloped toward a fiery pit, a "lake of burning brimstone".[3] Such sinners were always liable to fall into destruction; and, more importantly, they were "liable to fall *of themselves,* without being thrown down by the hand of another; as he that stands or walks on slippery ground needs nothing but his own weight to throw him down".[4] One can imagine Edwards diagramming the situation of the sinners as he might diagram a problem in physics. One force pulled them down the plane because of their weight (interestingly enough he does not exploit all the possibilities of the metaphor and hence does not have steeper planes increasing danger). Since the coefficient of friction between the plane and their feet was small, the frictional force up the plane was also small; and therefore the net acceleration was presumably down the plane. Why, then, did they not fall into the fiery pit? Because, Edwards answers, there is a force pulling them up the plane which is exerted by God himself. Therefore, when the "due time" referred to in *Deuteronomy* comes, *"their foot shall slide.* Then they shall be left to fall, as they are inclined by their own weight. God will not hold them up in these slippery places any longer, but will let them go; and then, at that very instant, they shall fall into destruction; as he that stands on such slippery declining ground, on the edge of a pit, he cannot stand alone, when he is let go he immediately falls and is lost".[5]

This combination of fiery emotion and cool argument was typical of Edwards, the Lockeian philosopher of evangelical Calvinism when it was the religion of theocratic New England; and it was this combination that put him squarely in what I have called the middle band of the philosophical spectrum, ministering to the logical demands of metaphysics and the religious needs of his parishioners. As a Calvinist he held that natural man is always walking in slippery places because he is totally depraved and corrupt, that his heart is totally under the power of sin, and that he is utterly unable to love God or to do anything that is good or acceptable in God's sight without the intervention of sovereign grace. Accordingly Edwards' philosophical work consisted of two main parts, one in which he served as a logical but lawyer-like apologist for the doctrine that sinners may be judged morally even though they sin necessarily, and the other in which he describes and analyzes the state into which saints are lifted by God's grace. In discussing the necessity of sin he exhibits extraordinary ingenuity and says many things that are interesting and valuable in defense of an unbelievable theology; in describing the hearts of saints he reveals another side of himself and illustrates, as Plato and St. Augustine had before him, that a man may be both a logical thinker and a mystic. His discussion of free will constituted his main contribution to technical philosophy, whereas his reflections on sainthood made him an exceedingly relevant thinker in eighteenth-century New England.

Edwards' major philosophical concern was with the will, or the heart as he also calls it, rather than with the understanding. Whereas the understanding was for Edwards the faculty of perception and speculation, the will was the faculty by which the mind chooses, the faculty "by which the soul does not behold things, as an indifferent unaffected spectator, but either as liking or disliking, pleased or displeased, approving or rejecting".[6] The will, Edwards held, is the primary concern of the student of religion because "all virtue and religion have their seat more immediately in the will, consisting more especially in right acts and habits of this faculty".[7] Therefore he concentrated on it not only in his more mystical work, the *Treatise Concerning Religious Affections* (1746), but also in his more analytical *Freedom of the Will* (1754), more exactly entitled *A Careful and Strict Enquiry into the Modern Prevailing Notions of that Freedom of Will which is Supposed to be Essential to Moral Agency, Vertue and Vice, Reward and Punishment, Praise and Blame.*

It has been said by a close student of Edwards' reading that "the two authors whom Edwards most venerated were Isaac Newton and John Locke, and nothing they published escaped his notice".[8] Yet Edwards did not imitate Locke by producing a full-scale treatise on the mind, nor did he imitate Newton by producing anything like a mature work in natural science. Edwards did, however, write two sets of very precocious notes —entitled by the editor who discovered them "The Mind" and "Notes on Natural Science"—in which the influence of Locke and Newton is quite evident.[9] Indeed, so knowledgeably did the young Edwards discuss certain aspects of Newton's optical theory that scholars have argued about whether Edwards showed in his "Notes on Natural Science" a great undeveloped talent for physics. However, we need not consider Edwards' latent powers in science.[10] For our purposes the main question about the impact on Edwards of Newton the scientist, or of Locke, the philosopher who sought to remove philosophical rubbish from Newton's scientific path, is whether they influenced Edwards in his main philosophical enterprise, his theory of the will. And so far as I can see, they probably did, at least to the extent of encouraging him to apply the principle of universal causation to the will, that is to say, to treat all choices as having causes and hence to put them in the same category as Lockeian ideas and Newtonian accelerations.

On the other hand, in his *Religious Affections* Edwards abandoned what may be called the scientific outlook—as Newton and Locke themselves did when it suited them. Although Edwards in his scientific mood believed that all human choices have causes, in his mystical mood he held with St. Paul that one who is saved by God's grace has a super-empirical, spiritual knowledge of divine things. For Edwards, the natural man's choices and passions are under the sway of the great assumption of Newtonian science, the principle of causality, even though he insisted that the religious saint can, in moments of passion, see things beyond the reach of Newtonian science. By examining both aspects of Edwards' thinking we shall see how he tried to satisfy both his logico-scientific standards and his religious impulses. From a philosophical point of view the Edwards who applied those standards in his *Freedom of the Will* was the greater Edwards, but the rigorous method of analysis employed in that book disappeared from the center stage of American philosophy when Transcendentalism emerged as the dominant movement in the early nineteenth century. It was then that the "heart religion" of Edwards' *Religious Affections* was especially admired by romantic apostles of what came to be called "the newness" by literary philosophers who could neither follow nor appreciate what they regarded as Edwards' logic-chopping in his *Freedom of the Will.*

These same devotees of the newness despised Locke, whose *Essay* Edwards read at the age of fourteen with more pleasure "than the most greedy miser finds, when gathering up handfuls of silver and gold, from some newly discovered treasure". Locke's great *Essay* exerted an enormous influence on Edwards' thought by providing the general framework within which he worked. As we have seen, it contained an attack on religious Enthusiasm which forced Edwards to think hard about how to present a rationale for "heart religion" and the Great Awakening; and it formulated the problem of free will in the form in which Edwards wrestled with it. Having said something about Locke on Enthusiasm in the previous chapter, we may now say something about Locke on free will.

Like Edwards after him and like many thinkers before him, Locke distinguished as follows between the Understanding and the Will. By the Understanding he meant what he calls the power of perception. He construed this power very broadly as covering, for example, the perception of something like yellowness, the understanding of the word "yellow", and also our knowledge of the fact that no yellow thing is blue, which knowledge, as we have seen, he speaks of as based on our perceiving the "disagreement" between the ideas of yellowness and blueness. Locke says that "in bare naked perception, the mind is, for the most part, only passive; and what it perceives, it cannot avoid perceiving".[11] If I open my eyes and a red patch comes before them, I am not able to choose whether to see the patch. I see it whether I want to or not. In the same way, if I attend to the ideas of yellow and blue, their disagreement forces itself upon me and it is something which I cannot, so to speak, think away. By contrast, in exercising my will I choose or refuse to perform certain bodily actions, like lifting my arm or walking. In keeping with a long tradition before him, Locke maintained in some parts of the *Essay* that an action is free if and only if it is done in accordance with the choice, or what he also calls the volition, of the agent. I am free to lift my arm just in case it is true that I will lift it if I choose to lift it and not lift it if I do not. Therefore the question as to whether my *choosing* is determined never arises when I am simply asking whether my action is free. However, in the course of a long and rambling discussion of these topics in later editions of the *Essay,* Locke tried to deal with critics who said that the choice must be free if the action is to be called free, and there Locke virtually retracted the fundamental thesis of the earlier editions.[12] Since Edwards also deals with such an objection in a manner that is of greater interest to us, we shall save a discussion of this problem for a later part of this chapter.

Now that Locke's ideas on free will and Enthusiasm have been described briefly, we may turn to Edwards' treatment of free will and then to Edwards on the religious affections. Although the second Edwards became, as I have said, the darling of the Transcendentalists, the first Edwards was closer to the analytical strain in Locke. Edwards the logician and philosopher of science showed his talent mainly in his attack on his so-called Arminian opponents and in his discussion of the relationship between necessity and free will. He thought that the Arminians espoused absurd definitions of freedom and showed this rather easily. But his more interesting, even though less successful, attempt was to show that although natural men sin necessarily because they are born in original sin, the necessity of their sinning does not excuse them from moral judgment. Let us begin with Edwards' campaign against the Arminians, who were so named because of their connection with the Dutch theologian Jacobus Arminius (1560–1609).[13]

Edwards Against the Arminians

Edwards agreed with his Arminian opponents that only on certain occasions are persons "properly the subject of command or counsel, praise or blame, promises or threatenings, rewards or punishments".[14] Using classical illustrations, we may say that Brutus is properly the subject of moral judgment for having stabbed Caesar, but deny that a man who is bound in unbreakable chains is properly the subject of moral judgment for failing to save a drowning man. Since Edwards held, in company with the Arminians, that actions on which we properly pass moral judgment must be free or voluntary, like the Arminians he had to face the question: "What is a free or voluntary action?". To this question Edwards advanced a simple and unoriginal answer. He held that a man acted freely if and only if he did as he chose to do, *period*. His Arminian opponents protested against this analysis on the ground that it was incomplete. They insisted that we must not put a period after "he did as he chose to do" but rather must say more. They claimed that a man's past action was free if and only if *two* conditions were satisfied: firstly, that he did as he chose to do; and, secondly, that his *choice* was free in a sense which, according to Edwards, varied from one Arminian text to another. For some Arminians a free choice was one determined by the chooser's own will; for others it was uncaused or contingent; and for still others it was made while the chooser's mind was in a state of indifference. After analyzing these three senses, Edwards concluded that the class of voluntary actions as defined in any one of these senses was necessarily empty, like the class of round squares. No action could be brought about by choice as characterized by the Arminians in their second condition, he said, for there couldn't be such choices. Let us turn to the details of Edwards' attempt to demolish the various versions of the Arminians' analysis of free choice.

Self-determination. According to the Arminian doctrine of self-determination, my walking to the door—an external action—is free if and only if, firstly, it was brought about by my choosing to walk; and, secondly, my choosing to walk was in turn brought about by another choice of mine. This is Edwards' interpretation of the Arminian notion of liberty of will since he construes the requirement that the choice to walk be made *by the will* as meaning that it is brought about by another choice rather than by the abstract power or faculty called the will. Here he follows Locke in scouting the absurdity of speaking of *the will* willing—rather than of the soul or the man willing [15]—and thinks he shows a certain polemical generosity toward his opponents in interpreting them in this way. Edwards' generosity keeps the Arminians out of the frying pan of the "grossest and plainest absurdity" [16] only to lead them, as may already be evident, into the fire of an absurdity which is just as devastating. For now Edwards propounds a dilemma for his opponents. They say that his walking is voluntary if and only if it has been brought about by his choosing to walk which is itself voluntary. But if his *choosing* to walk is voluntary, it must be brought about by his choosing to choose to walk. Therefore Edwards asks: How about this choosing to choose to walk? It too must be voluntary, must it not? But if *it* is voluntary, it must be brought about by a choosing to choose to choose to walk. So it is evident that we are launched on a never-ending regress. For my walking to be voluntary, it must be at the tail-end of a train of choices that is infinite in length and hence impossible. But what if the other horn of the dilemma be adopted by the Arminian and he says that there is a first choice which is *not* determined by a prior choice, in other words, not determined by the will—as Edwards would force the Arminian to say on *his* interpretation of the phrase "determined by the will"? In that case, Edwards says, the external action, the walking, cannot be voluntary, because it does not originate in the will if the choice which brings it about does not. Suppose one says that Jonathan's walking is brought about by his choosing to walk and that this in turn is said to be the absolutely first choice in the series. Then his walking cannot be voluntary since the fact that the first choice is not itself determined by a choice, i.e. not voluntary, makes every succeeding action or choice non-voluntary. Because both horns of the dilemma lead to absurdity, there is an inconsistency, says Edwards, in the Arminian notion that a free act is one that is brought about by a choice which is brought about by the will. "This Arminian notion of liberty of the will," Edwards concludes, "consisting in the will's self-determination, is repugnant to itself, and shuts itself wholly out of the world." [17] In other words, it has the same logical status as the notion of a round square. There could not be a free act of the kind identified by Arminians in this way.

Contingency. It should be remembered that the great difference between Edwards and the Arminian consists in the fact that whereas Edwards is content to call an external act free if and only if it is brought about by a choice or volition, the Arminian thinks that such an act is free if and only if it is brought about by a volition *of a certain kind*. We have just seen why Edwards rejects the Arminian characterization of that kind of volition as one "determined by the will"; but when Edwards goes on to consider what he calls evasions of his argument, he formulates another Arminian characterization of the volition, namely, that the volition is uncaused. Edwards now points out that although the Arminian keeps saying that the "will determines itself" and thereby implies that *something* determines choices or volitions, when the Arminian's evasions are examined closely it becomes evident that for the Arminian "nothing at all determines the will".[18] Therefore, "there is a great noise made about self-determining power, as the source of all free acts of the will: but when the matter comes to be explained, the meaning is, that no power at all is the source of these acts, neither self-determining power, nor any other, but they arise from nothing; no cause, no power, no influence, being at all concerned in the matter". And even though this is "very inconsistent with many other things in their scheme, and repugnant to some things implied in their notion of liberty", Arminians seem to be committed to it when they say that free acts of the will are causeless.[19]

Edwards, however, does not limit himself to pointing out this inconsistency within the body of Arminian doctrine. The supposition that acts of the will are causeless, he argues, is incompatible with the principle that "whatsoever begins to be, which before was not, must have a cause why it then begins to exist". This principle, he continues, "seems to be the first dictate of the common and natural sense which God hath implanted in the minds of all mankind, and the main foundation of all our reasonings about the existence of things, past, present, or to come".[20] In other words, Edwards thinks that surrendering the principle of universal causation would leave us without a proof of the existence of God, of external physical objects, and of the past, since he believes that the proof of the existence of all those things depends on the assumption that every event has a cause. He holds that the inference from the existence of creatures to the existence of a creator depends on our being able to say that the creatures must have been brought into existence by something, and that the inference from our "own immediately present ideas" to external objects both contemporary and past is grounded on the principle that our immediately present ideas have causes which are those objects. Therefore to surrender the principle of universal causation would be to leave ourselves in an absurd and intellectually desperate situation.

It should be observed that at one point Edwards tries to deal with the view that the principle of universal causation should be revised to read somewhat as follows: "All things that come to be, *except acts of will,* have causes". Adopting such a revised principle would allow for the validity of the proofs that Edwards is concerned about because neither the proof of God's existence nor of the existence of external objects requires that *choices* have causes. What, then, does Edwards say about such a scaling down of universal causation? Not something that does him great philosophical credit. He begins by asserting that if acts of will are said to be events which have no causes, there must be an explanation for their being different in this way from other events. But if there is such an explanation, he argues, then these acts of will are *not* causeless. His words are: "If any should imagine, there is something in the sort of event that renders it possible for it to come into existence without a cause; and should say, that the free acts of the will are existences of an exceeding different nature from other things; by reason of which they may come into existence without any previous ground or reason of it, though other things cannot; if they make this objection in good earnest, it would be an evidence of their strangely forgetting themselves: for they would be giving an account of some ground of the existence of a thing, when at the same time they would maintain there is no ground of its existence".[21] But let us look at this closely. Let us suppose that the first "thing" or event of which Edwards speaks is my choosing to walk; and let us suppose further that my choosing to walk is uncaused, and that there is also such a thing as the causelessness of my choosing to walk. Presumably, this cause-

lessness of my choosing to walk is different from my choosing
to walk; and therefore if one asserts that there is a cause of the
causelessness of my choosing, one is not driven by that into asserting that there is a cause of my choosing. There may be an
explanation of the causelessness of a choice without it following that there is a cause of the choice itself. In all fairness to
his opponents, it must be said that Edwards does not score
heavily against them here. He does not convincingly refute
the view that the principle of universal causation may be
scaled down to the statement "all things that come to be, except acts of will, have causes". And if he cannot refute this
view he still leaves open an Arminian avenue of escape.

Indifference. As we have seen, Edwards also attacked the Arminian view that a free act is one which is brought about by a
choice made while the mind is "indifferent". In saying this,
some Arminians meant that free actions are determined or
caused by choices which are made while the mind is not acted
on by any "motive" or "ground of preference".[22] By contrast,
Edwards maintained that if "the mind prefers something,
then the idea of that thing preferred, does at that time pre-
ponderate, or prevail in the mind; or, which is the same
thing, the idea of it has a prevailing influence on the will".[23]
According to Edwards, the statement "Jonathan chose to walk
to the door" means the same as "The motive for Jonathan's
choosing to walk to the door was stronger than his motive for
choosing not to walk to the door". Therefore, Edwards held,
it is self-contradictory to say that Jonathan made a choice at a
time when no idea was "preponderating" or "prevailing" in his
mind, or when no motive was prevailing in it, that is to say,
when it was indifferent.

Unfortunately for Edwards, the analysis of choice which he
offers while attacking the Arminian doctrine of indifference,
created a serious difficulty for him, since in addition to offering an analysis of what choice is, he also held to a psychologi-

cal theory of the cause of choice. He maintained in the latter that "the will is always determined by the strongest motive". Yet if choice is analyzed as he analyzes it, then his psychological theory turns out to be a truism, as should be evident already.

The doctrine that the will is always determined by the strongest motive, he says in the earliest pages of his *Enquiry,* is "the thing of chief importance to the purpose of the ensuing discourse".[24] Therefore, it is essential to see how it figures in his system before turning to the difficulty I have mentioned. Were Edwards interested only in analyzing what it is to be a free or voluntary action, he need not have advanced any doctrine as to what causes or determines choice. He makes this clear in the following passage: "One thing more I would observe concerning what is vulgarly called liberty; namely, that power and opportunity for one to do and conduct as he will, or according to his choice, is all that is meant by it; without taking into the meaning of the word, anything of the cause or original of that choice; or at all considering how the person came to have such a volition; whether it was caused by some external motive, or internal habitual bias; whether it was determined by some internal antecedent volition, or whether it happened without a cause; whether it was necessarily connected with something foregoing, or not connected. Let the person come by his volition or choice how he will, yet, if he is able, and there is nothing in the way to hinder his pursuing and executing his will, the man is fully and perfectly free, according to the primary and common notion of freedom".[25] In addition to having said this, however, Edwards also advanced his thesis that a volition is determined or caused by what he called the strongest motive. He did not advance this extra thesis because he wanted to replace the Arminian's second requirement for being a voluntary action by another one of his own. In other words, Edwards did not analyze the statement that a man performed an act freely as equivalent to the conjunctive statement that his action was determined by his choice *and* that his choice was determined by his strongest motive. Edwards upheld the doctrine that choice is determined by the strongest motive simply because he believed that choices had causes of a certain kind and he wanted to specify that kind. On Edwards' view, a minister who induces one of his parishioners to perform an action causes the parishioner to choose to perform that action, but *how* does the minister cause the parishioner to choose to perform that action? The answer to this question, Edwards thought, depends on a general theory of what causally determines choice and Edwards' theory was that choice is causally determined by the strongest motive.

The important point to observe, however, is that Edwards cannot defend such a theory of what causally determines choice if only because Edwards says elsewhere that fact *A* cannot determine fact *B* if facts *A* and *B* are identical. For example, the fact that John was begotten by James cannot be causally explained by the fact that James begat John, simply because the fact of James' begetting John is identical with the fact of John's being begotten by James. Edwards held that whenever we say that Jonathan chose to walk we *mean* that his motive for choosing to walk was stronger than his motive for not choosing to walk, and therefore the fact of Jonathan's choosing to walk is identical with the fact of Jonathan's having a stronger motive for walking than for not walking. But in that case Edwards cannot say that Jonathan's choosing to walk is causally explained or determined by his having a stronger motive for walking than for not walking. That would be like saying that James' begetting of John causally explains or determines John's being begotten by James, and hence absurd. Another way of stating the point is that the conditional statement, "If Jonathan's motive for choosing to walk is stronger than his motive for not choosing to walk, then Jonathan chooses to walk" must, in Edwards' own view, be a truism and also not a truism. Edwards cannot consistently subscribe to the doctrine that "Jonathan chose to walk" means the same as "Jonathan's motive for choosing to walk is stronger than his motive for not choosing to walk", *and* to the doctrine that the will is *causally determined* by the strongest motive. That would be like saying that the candidate's losing the election was *caused by* the fact that he got a minority of the votes and also that "losing the election" *is synonymous with* "getting a minority of the votes".[26]

Necessity and Free Will

So far we have confined ourselves to Edwards' attack on Arminian analyses of what it means to say that a man performed a free action or a voluntary action, and to difficulties into which Edwards falls when he combines that attack with a certain analysis of choice and a certain theory of what causes choice. Now we may turn to Edwards' historically more important effort to show that a man who necessarily makes choices that are wrong is nevertheless morally judgeable. Such a problem was of great concern to Edwards because he held that men are born in original sin and therefore possessed of a disposition which necessitated their making wrong choices. How, if Brutus' decision to stab Caesar is necessitated, can we morally judge his decision to do so? Edwards' answer is that Calvinists who judge choices that are admitted by them to be necessary employ the word "necessary" here as a term of art; the choices are for them only "philosophically necessary". When they say that a sinful choice is necessary, they do not mean by "necessary" what we mean by it in ordinary language when we say it was necessary that a man who was overwhelmed by a wave did not succeed in saving a drowning woman. The latter, or ordinary, use of "necessary" is an exculpating use, according to Edwards, but the Calvinist's is not. To say in ordinary language that it was necessary that this

man did not save the woman is to say that he did not save her
even though he chose to save her. By contrast, a Calvinist who
uses the word "necessary" as a term of art may agree that Brutus' decision to stab Caesar was made necessary by Brutus'
being born in original sin, and yet not excuse or exculpate
Brutus on that score. The question to ask now is why Edwards holds that the Calvinist's sense of "necessary" is not exculpating. In order to answer, we must turn to some of Edwards' more general reflections on the word "necessary".[27]

Edwards says that "necessary" as used in common speech is
a relative term. For example, if we say that it was necessary
that a very heavy object, o, should have fallen to the ground,
what we mean is that o fell in spite of our efforts to keep it
from falling. We mean, Edwards says in slightly awkward terminology, that this state of affairs was necessary to *us*. Therefore, the statement "Necessarily, o fell to the ground" may be
transformed into the statement "o fell to the ground in spite
of my [the speaker's] effort to keep o from falling to the
ground". The general form into which such a statement is
transformed is: "p is the case even though I [the speaker]
willed that not-p be the case". Using this idea in defense of
Calvinism, Edwards goes on to say that a sentence of the form
"p is the case even though I willed that not-p be the case"
must, to be meaningful, refer in its second clause to what he
calls a *supposable* willing, or volition, or choice, or effort.
The point of this stipulation may be seen when we try to use
Edwards' recipe to transform a statement like "It was necessary that I made choice c at 9 a.m.". Edwards' formula requires us to expand this into something that begins, "I made
choice c at 9 a.m. even though . . .", but how shall we complete the sentence? Edwards' answer is that we can never complete it according to the above recipe without lapsing into
nonsense. His point is that the sentence about a choice that I
put after "even though" cannot refer to a supposable choice
for it will always express something incompatible with the

statement "I made choice *c* at 9 a.m.". In other words, the sort of complex sentence I construct in accordance with the recipe, namely, "I made choice *c* at 9 a.m. even though I chose at 9 a.m. not to make choice *c* at 9 a.m.", will be absurd. If we suppose that I made the choice at 9 a.m., we cannot meaningfully suppose that at 9 a.m. I made a choice *not* to make choice *c* at 9 a.m. By contrast, if we attribute necessity to the object's falling, we *can* meaningfully suppose that we were exerting our wills in opposition to its falling *while it was falling*. In other words, implicit in his recipe for transforming "Necessarily, *p*" there seems to be the idea that the event recorded in "*p*" is simultaneous with our willing that it not occur. This is crucial to his contention that his recipe cannot be successfully used in order to attribute necessity to my choice *c* at 9 a.m. for, he says, I cannot be supposed to have made an opposing choice *at the time* at which I made the choice I did make. That is why, Edwards argued, we cannot meaningfully affirm that our choices are necessary in the ordinary sense of "necessary".[28] Our choices are caused and therefore what he called "philosophically necessary" but that, he held, does not make them unjudgeable.

The importance of this step cannot be overestimated. Edwards maintains that the only way to show that any event is not to be judged morally is by showing that it is necessary in the ordinary sense. The falling of the object is removable from the realm of moral judgeability but Brutus' *choosing* to stab Caesar cannot be removed from it. The reason is that we cannot meaningfully report our ground for removing it in an ordinary statement of necessity. The fact that we cannot *meaningfully affirm* the necessity of a choice like Brutus' in the ordinary sense of "necessary" is what Edwards exploits to the hilt when he tries to answer Arminians who attack Calvinists for passing moral judgment on necessary choices. He tries to seal the lips of the Arminians by arguing that they cannot meaningfully make the only sort of statement about the choice that would remove the choice from the realm of moral judgment, namely, that the choice is necessary in the ordinary sense. But what Edwards apparently forgets is that *he* cannot meaningfully support the contention that a choice *is* subject to moral judgment, for he cannot meaningfully affirm that a choice is *not* necessary in the ordinary sense. Presumably, in Edwards' view it is meaningless to affirm the necessity or the non-necessity of choices in the ordinary sense. Therefore, since it is only by affirming that a choice is not necessary in the ordinary sense that Edwards can show it to be subject to moral judgment, Edwards has said too much for his purposes. True, he has prevented the Arminian from meaningfully *excusing* a choice on the score of its ordinary necessity, but by the same token he has prevented the Calvinist from showing that it *is subject to* moral judgment. Edwards' view seems to be that a choice is morally judgeable unless proven not so, but that it can never be proven not so. Yet one who holds that the judgeability of each choice must be positively established would say that Edwards cannot *establish* the judgeability of any choice. And if Edwards cannot establish the judgeability of a choice like Brutus' to stab Caesar, he cannot establish the judgeability of Brutus' action in stabbing Caesar. Thus Edwards ironically cuts the ground from under all moralists.

It may be said in concluding this section that Edwards is at his most effective on free will when dealing with the Arminian doctrine of self-determination. However, in spite of the deficiencies in other parts of his *Freedom of the Will,* that work is a thorough and subtle treatment of its subject. No other American philosopher, whether religious or not, has produced a more careful discussion of free will. It is true that Edwards' argument is always guided by his religious faith, but within the confines of his orthodoxy Edwards moved with great intellectual power and skill. He often used techniques of argument and analysis that were not original with him, but his writings on free will certainly justify Dugald Stewart's description of him as an American metaphysician who, in logical acuteness and subtlety, did not yield to any disputant bred in the universities of Europe.

The Sense of the Heart

It would be difficult to accept this judgment if Edwards had left us only his *Treatise Concerning Religious Affections,* for even though that work exhibits his skill at making fine distinctions, it is a very obscure work and hardly a model of the kind of logical analysis exhibited in *Freedom of the Will.* In his *Religious Affections* Edwards is concerned to delineate what it is to be a truly religious person, and this leads him very quickly to his favorite subject, the will. As we have seen, he believed that the human soul has two faculties: the understanding, which perceives and speculates, and the will, which is exercised when a man approves or disapproves. A person through the exercise of his understanding perceives or has ideas, and those ideas cause him to have affections or emotions through the exercise of his will. For Edwards, being religious consists for the most part in having *holy* affections, and so his problem was to distinguish holy affections from others. This he did by arguing that such affections are caused by a certain kind of idea in the understanding. What kind of an idea? Edwards said that it was the idea of God's loveliness or excellency, which could not come through the normal five senses and therefore had to come through what he called the Sense of the Heart. Once the saint or truly religious person comes through grace to have this extra sense, he can have the idea that allows him to know that God is lovely, just as a man previously blind can know that the sky is blue when he comes to see and hence comes to have the ideas which are components of the proposition that the sky is blue.

In order to understand Edwards we must recall Locke's

view that there are in the understanding what he called simple ideas of sensation—ideas like whiteness, which come to us
through sight; ideas like hardness, which come to us through
touch; ideas like sweetness, which come to us through tasting;
and others which come to us through hearing and smelling.
However, Locke added that he did not "believe it impossible
to God to make a creature with other organs, and more ways
to convey into the understanding the notice of corporeal
things than those five", and, Locke continued, "he that will
not set himself proudly at the top of all things, but will consider the immensity of this fabric, and the great variety that is
to be found in this little and inconsiderable part of it which
he has to do with, may be apt to think that, in other mansions
of it, there may be other and different intelligent beings, of
whose faculties he has as little knowledge or apprehension as
a worm shut up in one drawer of a cabinet hath of the senses
or understanding of a man; such variety and excellency being
suitable to the wisdom and power of the Maker".[29] The possibility here admitted by Locke lay at the basis of several important developments in eighteenth-century thought. The
most famous occurred in ethics, where the so-called Moral
Sense theorists—notably Shaftesbury and Hutcheson—argued
that moral ideas do not arise from reason but rather from a
sense other than the conventional five upon which Locke concentrated in his *Essay.* Edwards subscribed to that doctrine in
ethics—notably in his posthumous *Nature of True Virtue*—
and also to a variant of it in the view of religion that he defended in his *Religious Affections.*[30] There he argued that
through the saving influences of the Spirit of God, those who
are sanctified come to have the extraordinary sense which admits into their understandings the simple idea of God's excellency or loveliness.[31]

A complication in Edwards' theory is that so-called natural
men who are not saints and do not have a Sense of the Heart
can also have what some might call knowledge of God's loveli-

ness, but this, he says in a Pauline spirit, is "but the shadow of knowledge, or the form of knowledge, as the Apostle calls it".[32] Edwards declares in his sermon "A Divine and Supernatural Light" that a man may have knowledge by hearsay that a person is beautiful, but such knowledge is quite distinct from that which is had by someone who sees the beautiful person's countenance. "The former rests only in the head, speculation only is concerned in it; but the heart is concerned in the latter. When the heart is sensible of the beauty and the amiableness of a thing, it necessarily feels pleasure in the apprehension. It is implied in a person's being heartily sensible of the loveliness of a thing, that the idea of it is sweet and pleasant to his soul; which is a far different thing from having a rational opinion that it is excellent." [33] This observation Edwards transfers to the case of the saint's perception of God's loveliness. The saint does not know it as he would if he had learned of it merely by hearsay. He knows it by virtue of having a Sense of the Heart which allows him to "see" the loveliness of God as natural men who are not blind see the blueness of the sky.

Because of his strong logical and scientific predilections, Edwards was very anxious not to be accused of being what Locke called an Enthusiast, or someone who did not give understanding its due in religion. He was very eager to steer a course between the lunacy of extreme evangelical religion and what he called formalism, yet it is clear that once Edwards expanded the understanding to the point where it had a sixth sense or "inlet"—to use Locke's word—it was a *very different* understanding, and the spiritual knowledge that Edwards regarded as the foundation of true religion was a very special kind of knowledge. It was not like mathematical knowledge nor was it knowledge based on what Edwards called doctrinal explication of the mystical meaning of the Scripture, as is evident from the following passage: "He that explains what is meant by the stony ground, and the seed's springing up sud-

denly, and quickly withering away, only explains what propositions or doctrines are taught in it. So he that explains what
is typified by Jacob's ladder, and the angels of God ascending
and descending on it, or what was typified by Joshua's leading
Israel through Jordan, only shows what propositions are hid
in these passages. And many men can explain these types, who
have no spiritual knowledge. 'Tis possible that a man might
know how to interpret all the types, parables, enigmas, and allegories in the Bible, and not have one beam of spiritual light
in his mind; because he mayn't have the least degree of that
spiritual sense of the holy beauty of divine things which has
been spoken of, and may see nothing of this kind of glory in
anything contained in any of these mysteries, or any other
part of the Scripture".[34] Thus we see that according to Edwards an unsanctified exegete can tell us what mystical propositions are hidden in biblical language without sensing the
beauty of God's holiness and therefore without having spiritual knowledge or heart religion.

Not only did Edwards deny that the saint's knowledge is
mathematical or exegetical but also he denied that it is historical knowledge, as we can see from the following passage:
"Unless men may come to a reasonable solid persuasion and
conviction of the truth of the gospel, by the internal evidences of it, in the way that has been spoken, viz. by a sight of
its glory; 'tis impossible that those who are illiterate, and unacquainted with history, should have any thorough and effec-
tual conviction of it at all. They may without this, see a great
deal of probability of it; it may be reasonable for them to give
much credit to what learned men, and historians tell 'em; and
they may tell them so much, that it may look very probable
and rational to them, that the Christian religion is true; and
so much that they would be very unreasonable not to enter-
tain this opinion. But to have a conviction, so clear, and evident, and assuring, as to be sufficient to induce them, with
boldness, to sell all, confidently and fearlessly to run the ven-

ture of the loss of all things, and of enduring the most exqui-
site and long-continued torments, and to trample the world
under foot, and count all things but dung, for Christ; the evidence they can have from history, cannot be sufficient".[35] According to Edwards, not even the fundamental philosophical
thesis of the *Religious Affections,* namely, that a truly religious man must have gracious affections, can be known in the
appropriate way by a natural man, since it is only through the
Sense of the Heart that "the truth of all those things which
the Scripture says about experimental religion, is hereby
known; for they are now experienced".[36] This means, of
course, that when and only when we come to have a Sense of
the Heart will we know and see that having a Sense of the
Heart is absolutely essential to being truly religious.

The truths which Edwards' saint perceives, and upon which
his religious affection is founded, are very different from
those that Locke dealt with when he described the normal operations of the understanding. They were not ordinary sensory propositions, like "This is red", because the truths perceived by Edwards' saint refer to ideas of a *supernatural* sense.
Moreover, it should be stressed as we approach the
Transcendentalists, the truths perceived by Edwards' saint
were not like Locke's self-evident truths, which are also perceived by Locke's understanding. Edwards' saint, it must be
repeated, was able to perceive the truth of propositions that
were far more mysterious than "This is red" or "Whatever is,
is", and that is why the saint's thought processes were very different from those to which Edwards appealed in his *Freedom
of the Will.* Whereas it took a saint to know in the full Pauline, Edwardsean sense the truth of the doctrine of original
sin, it supposedly took no more than a clear-headed man to
see that a man who sinned necessarily in the philosophical
sense could be judged morally. In his *Freedom of the Will*
Edwards insists that he is engaged in metaphysics, and that he
is willing that his "arguments should be brought to the test of

the strictest and justest reason, and that a clear, distinct and determinate meaning of the terms [he uses] should be insisted on". His reasoning there, he claims, "depends on no abstruse definitions or distinctions, or terms without a meaning, or of very ambiguous and undetermined signification, or any points of such abstraction and subtlety, as tend to involve the attentive understanding in clouds and darkness".[37] But the situation is very different in the *Religious Affections*. According to Edwards, the saint senses God as St. Paul sensed him when, as Locke says, Paul was "rapt up into the third heaven". It will be recalled that, according to Locke, "whatever new ideas his [Paul's] mind there received, all the description he can make to others of that place, is only this, That there are such things, 'as eye hath not seen, nor ear heard, nor hath it entered into the heart of man to conceive'".[38] These dark words of Paul meant much not only to Edwards but also to the Transcendentalists, who tried to meet the challenge of Locke's empiricism by postulating a device not unlike Edwards' Sense of the Heart. But before turning to them, we must examine an earlier chapter in the history of American avenues to fundamental truth.

3 · "We Hold These Truths To Be Self-Evident"

Whereas American philosophy in the first half of the eighteenth century reached its high point in Edwards' writings on the foundations of religion, the most important philosophical ideas of the latter part of the century appear in the writings of revolutionary colonists interested in the foundations of law and politics. Like Edwards, colonial political and legal theorists were influenced by Locke's conception of science as a deductively ordered body of propositions headed by self-evident truths, but like Edwards they too made fundamental revisions in Locke's philosophy. Whereas the most notable of Edwards' departures from Locke's doctrine was Edwards' belief in a sixth sense which gave saints insight into the loveliness and excellency of God, revolutionary lawyers were apt to be less evangelical and less mystical in their concerns. They were primarily occupied with finding a way to justify a revolution, and the most notable element in their divergence from Locke was their revision of his doctrine of Natural Law.

Before turning to the details of that revision it is well to remind ourselves of the conspicuous link between Locke and the revolutionaries that was revealed in their use of the word

"self-evident" in the Declaration of Independence: "We hold
these truths, to be self-evident, that all men are created equal,
that they are endowed by their Creator with certain unalienable Rights, that among them are Life, Liberty and the pursuit
of Happiness.—That to secure these rights, Governments are
instituted among Men, deriving their just powers from the
consent of the governed,—That whenever any Form of Government becomes destructive of these ends, it is the Right of
the People to alter or abolish it, and to institute a new Government, laying its foundation on such principles and organiz-
ing its powers in such form, as to them shall seem most likely
to effect their Safety and Happiness". If we read these words
after reading Locke, we might be led to think that all the revolutionaries adopted (*1*) his idea that self-evident moral principles are seen to be true by the use of intuitive reason and
(*2*) his idea that many other moral principles could be deduced from them by the use of discursive reason. But the fact
is that the Declaration of Independence does *not* go on to deduce several moral principles from the allegedly self-evident
ones; and when we examine the writings of some of the more
philosophical revolutionaries we find that they did not hold
that so-called self-evident moral principles are seen to be true
by intuitive reason. We find some colonists denying that the
moral doctrine of Natural Law can be turned into a demonstrative science like mathematics; and we find some asserting
that self-evident moral principles are accepted on the basis of
sentiment rather than intuitive reason. Furthermore, we discover that this double departure from Locke's doctrine was
linked with the democratically oriented idea that moral judgment does not require the kind of advanced intellectual
power required either for deduction in mathematics or for
the perception of the truth of mathematical axioms. One of
the more fundamental revolutionary ideas was that perception of the truth of moral principles requires only the sentiments possessed by all men, no matter how unlearned or un-

philosophical they may be. When we recall that Locke himself looked upon his theory of Natural Law as a step away from the anti-democratic doctrine of innate principles, we realize that some revolutionaries may well have thought that their philosophy was even more democratic than Locke's. I shall begin with a discussion of certain revolutionaries' divergence from Locke's idea that morality is a demonstrative science in which many moral principles may be deduced by discursive reason, and then turn to the divergence from his view that moral axioms are seen to be true by the use of intuitive reason. It should be borne in mind that divergence from the view that morality is a demonstrative science is compatible with maintaining that some moral principles are seen to be true by intuitive reason. In fact, some philosophers who have held that intuitive reason perceives the truth of self-evident moral principles have gone on to deny that morality is a demonstrative science—for example, Thomas Reid, as we shall see below. On the other hand, we shall also see that the American legal philosopher, James Wilson, went further than his master Reid and held not only that morality is not a demonstrative science because very few theorems can be deduced in it, but also that the axioms of morality are supported by appealing to sentiment rather than reason.

Reid's Criticism of Locke

Anyone not sympathetic to Locke's view that morality is a demonstrative science might have scored against him by pointing out that he himself failed to construct such a science when asked to do so. One of the more candid passages in Locke's very candid writings is his reply to Molyneux, who, prompted by Locke's statement that morality is capable of demonstration, asked him to deliver the goods, so to speak. Molyneux wrote: "One thing I must needs insist on to you, which is, that you would think of obliging the world with a

Treatise on Morals, drawn up according to the hints you frequently give in your *Essay* of their being demonstrable according to mathematical method. This is most certainly true; but then the task must be undertaken only by so clear and distinct a thinker as you are, and there is nothing I should more ardently wish for than to see it". To this Locke replied: "Though by the view I had of moral ideas, when I was considering that subject, I thought I saw that morality might be *demonstratively* made out, yet whether I am able so to make it out is another question. Every one could not have demonstrated what Mr. Newton's book hath shown to be demonstrable". After Molyneux continued to urge him to undertake the difficult task, Locke ended the exchange by writing: "The Gospel contains so perfect a body of Ethics that reason may be excused from that inquiry, since she may find man's duty clearer and easier in revelation than in herself. This is the excuse of a man who, having a sufficient rule of his actions, is content therewith, and thinks he may employ the little time and strength he has in other researches wherein he is more in the dark".[1]

This admission did not refute Locke's view that morality is *capable* of demonstration, but some of his critics did not rest their case merely on his failure to construct a system of moral axioms and theorems. They went on to question the very possibility of such a system. One of Locke's most distinguished critics was Thomas Reid, the Scottish philosopher of Common Sense. Reid explicitly disassociated himself from Locke's view that morality is capable of demonstration even though Reid held that there are self-evident moral principles. By focusing on his views, we shall see why Locke's idea that morality is capable of becoming a demonstrative science came under fire even from those who believed that some moral principles are self-evident.

The similarity between Reid's views and those of Locke on self-evident truths becomes obvious when we find Reid saying that there are "propositions which are no sooner understood than they are believed".[2] As soon as these propositions are entertained by the mind, Reid says, the mind must affirm them to be true. "There is no searching for evidence, no weighing of arguments; the proposition is not deduced or inferred from another; it has the light of truth in itself, and has no occasion to borrow it from another. Propositions of [this] kind, when they are used in matters of science, have commonly been called *axioms;* and on whatever occasion they are used, are called *first principles, principles of common sense, common notions, self-evident truths.*"[3] Continuing in a Lockeian spirit, Reid held that it is demonstrable that all knowledge acquired by reasoning must be built upon first principles. He emphasized the democratic character of a philosophy which stressed the importance of self-evident principles of Common Sense. Reid maintained that in controversies over whether a principle is self-evident, "every man is a competent judge; and therefore it is difficult to impose upon mankind. To judge of first principles, requires no more than a sound mind free from prejudice, and a distinct conception of the question. The learned and the unlearned, the Philosopher and the day-labourer, are upon a level, and will pass the same judgment, when they are not misled by some bias, or taught to renounce their understanding from some mistaken religious principles. In matters beyond the reach of common understanding, the many are led by the few, and willingly yield to their authority. But, in matters of common sense, the few must yield to the many, when local and temporary prejudices are removed".[4]

In spite of agreeing with Locke that there are self-evident moral principles, Reid went on to disagree with him about the possibility of constructing a demonstrative moral science. Reid began his argument by considering a feeble effort on Locke's part to satisfy the kind of request that Molyneux had made of him. Locke had cited what he regarded as two moral statements which are deducible theorems, namely: "Where there is no property there is no injustice", and "No government allows absolute liberty". Locke had said of the first that it is "a proposition as certain as any demonstration in Euclid",[5] and therefore deduced from axioms. Reid made several observations in response. First, he pointed out that Locke's two illustrative truths are intuitively known rather than demonstrated, since the first follows from the definition of injustice and the second from the definition of government.[6] What he had in mind might be more clearly expressed by using another illustration. If one defines a square as a rectangle with equal sides, then the statement "Every square is a rectangle with equal sides" is derived by putting the defining expression (*definiens*) in place of the defined expression (*definiendum*) in a substitution-instance of the principle of identity, namely, "Every square is a square". Now the latter is a special case of a self-evident principle of logic and is intuitively known; therefore, according to Reid, any statement derived from it merely by putting *definiens* for *definiendum* is also intuitively known. His point was that such derivation is not demonstration. Hume had made the same point much earlier when he said in *An Enquiry Concerning Human Understanding*: "That *the square of the hypothenuse is equal to the squares of the other two sides,* cannot be known, let the terms be ever so exactly defined, without a train of reasoning and enquiry. But to convince us of this proposition, *that where there is no property, there can be no injustice,* it is only necessary to define the terms, and explain injustice to be a violation of property".[7]

Reid held that a proposition like "Where there is no property there is no injustice" is not a moral proposition simply because it was (as Hume had said) an imperfect definition, and definitions do not state moral principles. Reid went further and said that the proposition "Where there is no property there is no injustice" may be seen to be true merely by

examining abstract entities like property and injustice, and
seeing what their relations are. By contrast, he held, a moral
principle like "Every man should be faithful to his engagements" cannot be established merely by examining abstract
entities *even though it too is self-evident.* The fact that Reid
distinguished between two kinds of self-evident propositions
—those that may be established merely by examining the relations between entities like property and injustice and those
that may not be—makes it easier to understand why he did
not regard morality as a demonstrative science, whereas he
did regard mathematics and metaphysics as demonstrative sciences.

Reid thought that metaphysical and mathematical statements are about abstract ideas whereas moral principles are
not; and he held that we can derive many theorems from
self-evident propositions in mathematics. He believed that
in morals we can deduce almost no theorems, in metaphysics
very few, and in mathematics very many. Reid declared: "The
field of demonstrative reasoning . . . is the various relations
of things abstract, that is, of things which we conceive, without regard to their existence. Of these, as they are conceived
by the mind, and are nothing but what they are conceived to
be, we may have a clear and adequate comprehension. Their
relations and attributes are necessary and immutable. They
are the things to which the Pythagoreans and Platonists gave
the name of ideas. I would beg leave to borrow this meaning of the word *idea* from those ancient Philosophers, and
then I must agree with them, that ideas are the only objects
about which we can reason demonstratively". The question
then arises for Reid: In what fields *can* we create demonstrative sciences if we cannot do so in ethics? And Reid says in
reply: Mainly in mathematics. He goes on to explain that in
metaphysics we cannot go very far because "there are many
even of our ideas about which we can carry on no considerable train of reasoning. Though they be ever so well defined

and perfectly comprehended, yet their agreements and disagreements are few, and these are discerned at once. We may go a step or two in forming a conclusion with regard to such objects, but can go no farther". By contrast, Reid says, "it is otherwise in mathematical reasoning. Here the field has no limits. One proposition leads on to another, that to a third, and so on without end".[8]

James Wilson, Revolutionary Legal Philosopher

I have devoted so much space to Reid mainly because he exerted considerable influence on James Wilson, probably the most distinguished colonial philosopher of law. Examining this influence provides us with some idea of the early impact on American thought of the Scottish philosophy of Common Sense, which made so much of self-evident principles in all fields of inquiry. But, as we shall soon see, Wilson's conception of a self-evident principle of morality owed more to the writings of David Hume than it did to those of Reid—a fact which is too little noticed by those who concentrate on Wilson's disapproval of Hume's theory of perception and on the revolutionaries' disapproval of Hume's politics. Wilson accepted Reid's (and Hume's) idea that morality could not be a demonstrative science but adopted a view of moral principles more like Hume's than like Reid's.

James Wilson was born in Scotland in 1742, had university training there, came to this country in 1765, and died in 1798 after an impressive career as lawyer, revolutionary pamphleteer, judge, and law professor. It has been said that "he was one of six men who signed both the Declaration of Independence and the Constitution; and his contribution to the deliberations of the Federal Convention was second only to Madison's. He was the principal figure in the struggle to secure ratification of the Constitution in Pennsylvania, the approval of that state being indispensable to the success of the whole constitutional movement. The important Pennsylvania state constitution of 1790 was very largely his work. He was one of the original justices of the Supreme Court of the United States and was commonly accepted in a nation already much dominated by lawyers as the most learned and profound legal scholar of his generation".[9] Wilson is well-known among students of American revolutionary thought for his 1774 pamphlet, *Consideration On The Nature And Extent Of The British Parliament,* in which the following words appeared before the Declaration of Independence was written: "All men are, by nature, equal and free: no one has a right to any authority over another without his consent: all lawful government is founded on the consent of those who are subject to it: such consent was given with a view to ensure and to increase the happiness of the governed, above what they could enjoy in an independent and unconnected state of nature. The consequence is, that the happiness of the society is the *first* law of every government". Wilson then goes on to say that "this rule is founded on the law of nature: it must control every political maxim: it must regulate the legislature itself", to which he appends the footnote: "The law of nature is superiour in obligation to any other".[10] This pamphlet, however, was not the occasion for extended reflections on the nature of Natural Law. Wilson exhibited his concern with that difficult question in his *Lectures on Law,* which were delivered in 1790–91 at the College of Philadelphia (later called the University of Pennsylvania). In those lectures he showed that he was not only versed in the technique of his profession but also a student of moral philosophy. He not only knew his Bracton, Coke, and Blackstone but also relied heavily on Reid and Hume in his discussions of morals and Natural Law.

To see how closely Wilson followed Reid, we may quote two passages, one from each. Reid argued: "Moral truths . . . may be divided into two classes, to wit, such as are self-evident to every man whose understanding and moral faculty are ripe, and such as are deduced by reasoning from those that are self-evident. If the first be not discerned without reasoning, the last never can be so by any reasoning. If any man could say with sincerity, that he is conscious of no obligation to consult his own present and future happiness; to be faithful to his engagements; to obey his Maker; to injure no man; I know not what reasoning, either probable or demonstrative, I could use to convince him of any moral duty. As you cannot reason in mathematics with a man who denies the axioms, as little can you reason with a man in morals who denies the first principles of morals. The man who does not, by the light of his own mind, perceive some things in conduct to be right, and others to be wrong, is as incapable of reasoning about morals as a blind man is about colours".[11] Without quoting Reid, Wilson asserted in almost the same language (though it should be pointed out in fairness that he asserted what follows in lectures that were published posthumously and hence did not have the benefit of notes that he may have wished to add): "Moral truths may be divided into two classes; such as are self-evident, and such as, from the self-evident ones, are deduced by reasoning. If the first be not discerned without reasoning, reasoning can never discern the last".[12] Furthermore, Wilson used some of the same illustrations as Reid used when Wilson identified the principles of Natural Law as moral maxims which are self-evident: "that no injury should be done" and "that a lawful engagement, voluntarily made, should be faithfully fulfilled".[13] It is also important to note that after Wilson divided moral truths into those that are self-evident and those that are deduced by reasoning, he said that "the cases that require reasoning are few, compared with those that require none".[14] Here he followed Reid.

Had Wilson said nothing more, he would have shown himself to be a critic only of Locke's idea that morality contains as many theorems as mathematics, a critic who might be prepared, however, to agree with Locke that the first principles of morality and Natural Law may be seen to be true by the use of intuitive reason. The fact is, however, that Wilson also took a second anti-Lockeian step and aligned himself with Moral Sense philosophers by asserting that the self-evident propositions of morality rest on sentiment rather than reason. He says at one point: "A man may be very honest and virtuous, who cannot reason, and who knows not what demonstration means. If the rules of virtue were left to be discovered by reasoning, even by demonstrative reasoning, unhappy would be the condition of the far greater part of men, who have not the means of cultivating the power of reasoning to any high degree".[15] In this passage Wilson showed that he believed that the rules of virtue are not discovered by any kind of reason—intuitive or discursive—and that he believed this to be lucky for "the far greater part of men". The first belief was connected with his adoption of the doctrines of the Moral Sense school and the second with his idea that such a doctrine had democratic implications. I turn now to Wilson's connection with the Moral Sense school.

When Wilson addressed himself to the question of how we know that the self-evident principles of morality are true, he did not say that we know that they are true because we see them to be true as soon as we understand their terms. On the contrary, Wilson spoke of "feeling" that certain fundamental moral principles are true, and expressed his views in the following dramatic way: "If I am asked—why do you obey the Will of God? I answer—because it is my duty so to do. If I am asked again—how do you know this to be your duty? I answer again—because I am told so by my moral sense or conscience. If I am asked a third time—how do you know that you ought to do that, of which your conscience enjoins the performance? I can only say, I *feel* that such is my duty. Here investigation must stop; reasoning can go no farther".[16] Wilson also wrote in the same vein: "The *ultimate* ends of human actions, can never, in any case, be accounted for by reason. They recommend themselves entirely to the sentiments and affections of men, without dependence on the intellectual faculties. Why do you take exercise? Because you desire health. Why do you desire health? Because sickness is painful. Why do you hate pain? No answer is heard. Can one be given? No. This is an ultimate end, and is not referred to any farther object".[17] This passage bears a striking resemblance to one from David Hume, though Wilson's *Lectures on Law* lack a citation or a quotation of the following statement by Hume: "It appears evident that the ultimate ends of human actions can never, in any case, be accounted for by *reason,* but recommend themselves entirely to the sentiments and affections of mankind, without any dependance on the intellectual faculties. Ask a man *why he uses exercise;* he will answer, *because he desires to keep his health.* If you then enquire, *why he desires health,* he will readily reply, *because sickness is painful.* If you push your enquiries farther, and desire a reason *why he hates pain,* it is impossible he can ever give any. This is an ultimate end, and is never referred to any other object".[18] In the same Humeian vein Wilson held that reason "conveys the knowledge of truth and falsehood" whereas the moral sense conveys "the sentiment of beauty and deformity, of vice and virtue", and that "without the moral sense, a man may be prudent, but he cannot be virtuous".[19]

All of this clearly shows that although Wilson followed Thomas Reid on many matters, he departed from him on the subject of the Moral Sense. The view defended by Wilson under the influence of Hume was not regarded favorably by Reid, even though Reid was willing to use the phrase "Moral Sense" as equivalent to "Common Sense" in the realm of ethics. Reid insisted that the Moral Sense *judges;* it arrives at propositions and does not merely serve as a power "by which we have sensations as ideas", i.e. as a Lockeian "inlet" through which we get ideas which we only later combine into judgments. And Reid held that insofar as statements about ultimate moral ends express judgments, they are *necessarily* true. That was his main reason for criticizing certain versions of the Moral Sense theory. He feared that they were too naturalistic and too relativistic, to use later philosophical parlance. They led to the view, he complained, that every moral principle implicitly asserts something of the form "I felt that so-and-so ought to be done under such-and-such circumstances", and this view, Reid thought, implies that a moral principle is not a necessary truth but records a merely contingent matter of fact, one that is contingent upon the constitution and feelings of the speaker.[20]

I return now to the idea that the doctrine of Moral Sense was a democratic one. We have seen that Wilson said that if the rules of virtue were left to be discovered by any kind of reason—intuitive or discursive—unhappy would be the condition of the greater part of men, who have not the means of cultivating the power of reason to any high degree. And this was very close to the view of Thomas Jefferson, who, although he did not write as systematically as Wilson did on the nature of moral knowledge, offered the following advice to a nephew in 1787: "Moral philosophy. I think it lost time to attend lectures in this branch. He who made us would have been a pitiful bungler if he had made the rules of our moral conduct a matter of science. For one man of science, there are thousands who are not. What would have become of them? Man was destined for society. His morality therefore was to be formed to this object. He was endowed with a sense of right and wrong merely relative to this. This sense is as much a part of his nature as the sense of hearing, seeing, feeling; it is the true foundation of morality. . . . The moral sense, or conscience, is as much a part of man as his leg or arm. It is given to all human beings in a stronger or weaker degree, as force of members is given them in a greater or less degree. It may be strengthened by exercise, as may any particular limb of the body. This sense is submitted indeed in some degree to the guidance of reason; but it is a small stock which is required for this: even a less one than what we call Common sense. State a moral case to a ploughman and a professor. The former will decide it as well, and often better than the latter, because he has not been led astray by artificial rules. In this branch therefore read good books because they will encourage as well as direct your feelings. The writings of Sterne particularly form the best course of morality that ever was written".[21]

The Argument of the Declaration of Independence

We have now seen that at least two very important signers of the Declaration of Independence did not accept Locke's view that the self-evident principles of morality are established as the axioms of mathematics are. Let us now observe that the argument of the Declaration did not proceed from axioms of morality to theorems of morality in the Lockeian manner.

As everyone knows, the framers first assert that a decent respect to the opinions of mankind requires a people who are dissolving their political bands with another to say why they do so. Then the framers begin their defense by saying that all men have certain moral rights which are formulated in self-evident truths, that there is another self-evident truth which says that governments are instituted among men to secure these rights, and that governments derive their just powers from the consent of the governed. Furthermore, it is a self-evident truth that when a government is destructive of the very ends for which it is instituted, the people have a right to abolish it and replace it by another that will seem more likely to them to "effect their safety and happiness". Then, with a bow in the direction of prudence—"governments long established should not be changed for light and transient causes"—the framers assert that a long train of abuses and usurpations not only shows that the government they were overthrowing did *not* accomplish the ends previously described, but even shows "a design to reduce them under absolute despotism". Therefore they conclude that it is their right—nay, their duty—to "throw off such government". After this the catalogue of abuses and usurpations is presented. In shorter form, the argument runs: (*a*) We have such and such rights (self-evident moral principle); (*b*) Governments should protect those rights (self-evident moral principle); (*c*) When a government does not protect those rights, the governed have a right (nay, a duty) to abolish those governments (and replace them with ones that they think likely to be superior in this respect) (self-evident moral principle); (*d*) The British government did not protect those rights; indeed, it tried to institute a despotism (non-self-evident statement of fact). Therefore, (*e*) We have a right (nay, a duty) to abolish this government. Compressed even further, the argument takes this form: (*1*) Whenever such and such is the case, a people have a right to act in this manner; (*2*) Such and such *is* the case; (*3*) Therefore, we have a right to act in this manner. The first statement is a self-evident moral premise; the second statement is a factual premise; the last is what is sometimes called a singular moral conclusion about a specific course of action.

Now, it may be asked: Is this not a case of demonstration of the kind that Locke had in mind? The answer is of course "no", because Locke meant by demonstration a chain of reasoning from self-evident necessary principles to a deduced necessary conclusion, whereas the Declaration's chain of reasoning contains one non-self-evident, non-necessary, factual premise, namely, the second, in which the grievances and usurpations are presented. Therefore, the Declaration's main argument was not one that moved from only self-evident premises to a conclusion demonstrated according to mathematical method. In spite of all of their hero Locke's talk about the possibility of demonstration in morals, the framers never used it in the most powerful piece of moral writing that Locke ever influenced.

In summary of this chapter we may say that certain very influential revolutionary theorists made two fundamental revisions of the doctrine of Natural Law as that had been defended by Locke. First of all, they abandoned the idea that morality can ever become a demonstrative science which contains lots of moral theorems deduced from moral axioms; and, secondly, they viewed the self-evident principles of morality as not "accounted for by reason" but rather by the sentiments and affections of mankind. These two deviations from Locke, along with Edwards' introduction of a Sense of the Heart into theology, reflected the powerful democratic animus in American religious, moral, and legal thought of the eighteenth century. Edwards had pled for the view that an ignorant man can see the loveliness of God more easily than a learned one; and Wilson had subscribed to (1) the idea that ordinary men are as fit to perceive the fundamental principles of morality as philosophers because sentiment and affection are mainly required for that task, and (2) the idea that because deduction plays virtually no part in the development of morality, a powerfully scientific or logical mind is not necessary for learning the truths that should guide our behavior in society. In the next chapter we shall see how denigration of Locke's version of Reason, elevation of the heart and the Moral Sense, a preference for the views of ploughmen over those of professors, and a great respect for literary men as moral seers became staples of the movement known as Transcendentalism.

4 · Transcendentalism: "Hallelujah to the Reason Forevermore"

Were I interested in surveying all American ideas which lay claim to being philosophical, I would not skip so quickly to Transcendentalism in this chapter and to Ralph Waldo Emerson in the next; but it is fair to say that after the philosophical ideas of Edwards and those associated with the Declaration of Independence, the ideas of the Transcendentalists and of Emerson were the most important to appear on the American scene.[1] The young Emerson was a member of the Transcendentalist movement, and the mature Emerson's tenure as America's nineteenth-century oracle was partly dependent on what he had learned in the days when he and his fellow-Transcendentalists were shedding the doctrines of John Locke for what they took to be the deeper and more exciting theories of German idealism.[2] So once again poor Locke was the target of American disapproval, this time by a group of young men, most of whom had begun their lives as Unitarian ministers.[3] Later we shall examine some of the reasons for their discontent with Locke, but before we do, it will be useful to say something about the Unitarianism to which they subscribed before they became Transcendentalists.

According to William Ellery Channing, one of the leading figures in the history of American Unitarianism, that doctrine contained on the one hand a set of principles about the method of interpreting the Scriptures and on the other a set of more substantive theological doctrines. Among the latter there was preeminently the doctrine implied by the use of the word "Unitarian": the belief in one God and opposition to Trinitarianism.[4] There was also the view that "Jesus Christ is a being distinct from and inferior to God",[5] the view that God is incapable of the cruelty which is implicitly attributed to him by certain Calvinists,[6] and the view that Jesus was sent by the Father to effect a moral or spiritual deliverance of mankind.[7] Jesus, Channing asserted, accomplished this sublime purpose by a number of methods: by giving moral instruction; by his promises of pardon; by his spotless moral example; by his sufferings and death; by the resurrection, "which powerfully bore witness to his divine mission"; by his continual intercession; "and by the power with which he is invested of raising the dead, judging the world, and conferring the everlasting rewards promised to the faithful".[8]

One of these more substantive theological doctrines, the one concerning the cruelty of the Calvinist's God, was full of philosophical implications, since it bore on the problem of free will. But not one of these doctrines had as much philosophical significance for Transcendentalists-to-be as Channing's views of the role of reason in religion. In explaining the Unitarian method of interpreting the Bible, Channing called upon man to "exercise [his] reason upon it perpetually, to compare, to infer, to look beyond the letter to the spirit, to seek in the nature of the subject and the aim of the writer his true meaning; and, in general, to make use of what is known for explaining what is difficult, and for discovering new truths".[9] Channing also deplored religious Enthusiasm. "We cannot," he said, "sacrifice our reason to the reputation of zeal. We owe it to truth and religion to maintain that fanaticism, partial insanity, sudden impressions, and ungovernable transports, are any thing rather than piety." [10] These Unitarian appeals to reason were clearly in accord with the thinking of Locke, who, Channing was proud to say, had been a Unitarian.[11] They were also appeals that the young Transcendentalists associated with the "pale negations" of "corpse-cold" Unitarianism, which, some of them held, was the religious ideology of State Street commercialism. Unitarianism, they declared, used priests and scholars to interpret ancient texts to discover truths that are obvious to all good and sincere men of feeling. Therefore many of the Unitarians-turned-Transcendentalists accepted the following words that were uttered by George Ripley, the most articulate representative of all of the strains within Transcendentalism—philosophical, religious, and political: "There is a class of persons, who desire a reform in the prevailing philosophy of the day. These are called the Transcendentalists—because they believe in an order of truths which transcends the sphere of the external senses. Their leading idea is the supremacy of mind over matter. Hence they maintain that the truth of religion does not depend on tradition, nor on historical facts, but has an unerring witness in the soul. There is a light, they believe, which enlighteneth every man that cometh into the world; there is a faculty in all, the most degraded, the most ignorant, the most obscure, to perceive spiritual truth when distinctly presented; and the ultimate appeal, on all moral questions, is not to a jury of scholars, a hierarchy of divines, or the prescriptions of a creed, but to the common sense of the human race".[12]

The deepest roots of this Transcendentalist revolt against Unitarianism and Lockeian empiricism are too deep and tangled to be traced here, but it is worth observing that the Transcendentalists diverged from Locke by using terminology somewhat different from that used by Edwards and Wilson. We have seen that Edwards revised Locke by adding a Sense of the Heart which would perceive religious truth, while Wilson appealed to the Moral Sense in his philosophy of law; but Emerson and his fellow-Transcendentalists were less given to speaking of a *sense* as the source of spiritual truth. Instead, they were more inclined to transform the traditional notion of Reason by emotionalizing it, so to speak, by treating Reason itself as if it were a faculty that might be exercised in *feeling*. This emotionalizing of Reason had a few proximate sources which may be profitably described before turning to the ideas of some of the American Transcendentalists. It will be useful to say something brief in this chapter about the influence of the German thinker, Friedrich Heinrich Jacobi, and, of course, about the indirect impact of Kant, who was known to Emerson mainly through his reading of Coleridge.

Jacobi advanced his mystical views in opposition to views which Kant had set forth in the *Critique of Pure Reason*, without knowing, as A. O. Lovejoy has observed, Kant's own doctrines in the *Critique of Practical Reason*. Jacobi insisted that we must go beyond the Reason described in the *Critique of Pure Reason* and recognize, as Lovejoy has pointed out, that "we have a power, however seldom exercised, not merely to imagine, postulate or believe in, but to *know,* with the most indubitable kind of knowledge, a realm of realities other than that of sense-experience, and not subject to the categories and laws which hold good of the sensible world. This knowledge is not the result of any process of inference, it is not mediated through general concepts; it is a direct 'intuiting' or 'perceiving' of 'the supersensible,' analogous, in its immediacy and indubitability, to physical vision, though differing from it utterly in the nature of that which it discloses".[13] This Jacobian power was identified with faith and feeling; and the first historian of Transcendentalism, Octavius Brooks Frothingham, announced that Jacobi had taken the first important step in the direction of pure Transcendentalism and that his "Faith or Feeling Philosophy" gave the movement an impulse toward mysticism.[14]

When Immanuel Kant was first confronted with Jacobi's distinction between the exalted Reason and the lowly Understanding, Kant declared with annoyance: "It is a consequence not only of the natural laziness but also of the vanity of men, that those who live on the income from property which they own—be it small or large—consider themselves more genteel than those who have to work for their living. . . . This tendency of human nature has of late reached such a pitch that a so-called philosophy is now advertised in which, in order to possess all philosophical wisdom, one has no need to work, but has only to listen to and enjoy the oracle that speaks within oneself. . . . The pretension to philosophize under the influence of a higher *feeling* is best of all adapted to produce this genteel tone. . . . And if I can make people believe that this feeling is not merely a subjective peculiarity of my own, but can be possessed by everybody, and that consequently it is something objective, a genuine piece of knowledge attained, not by reasoning from concepts, but by an intuition which grasps the object itself—then I enjoy a great advantage over all those who must first justify their statements before they are entitled to regard them as true. . . . So hurrah for the philosophy of feeling, which leads us directly to the reality itself! Down with ratiocination by means of concepts, which seeks truth only through the roundabout way of general notions . . .".[15]

Although Kant so scathingly disassociated himself from Jacobi's views, his own *Critique of Practical Reason* also provided the Transcendentalists with an admired avenue to a supersensible world. It is essential to recall that in the *Critique of Pure Reason* Kant tried to show that the Understanding or Pure Reason cannot lead us to any knowledge of what things are in themselves or what we are in ourselves, since it cannot penetrate beyond the realm of possible experience. Because objects in this realm are necessarily subject to the principle of causality, man as an empirical object also is. To escape this predicament, Kant appealed to the Practical Reason, or moral consciousness, which assured him by steps we need not recount here that there is a supersensible, noumenal world consisting of entities that are in neither space nor time, and hence not subject to causal influence. By showing that there is such another world, Kant "solved" the problem of free will in a manner that was admired by Transcendentalists. The human individual, he said, has an empirical *and* a noumenal ego; and whereas the former is subject to causality, the latter is not and is therefore free in just the sense in which it must be free if we are to be able to pass moral judgments on human actions. The mind as described in the *Critique of Pure Reason* could not supply assurance of the existence of the noumenal world of free egos, but the *Critique of Practical Reason* did supply such assurance to American Transcendentalists who could not subscribe to Edwards' deterministic views on the will even though they greatly admired his mysticism.

Jacobi's Reason and Kant's Practical Reason were often cited by Transcendentalists who wished to oust Locke's version of Reason from its position of preeminence in American thought; and often they relied on Coleridge for their understanding of these German philosophers. Perhaps the most poignant expression of the new dispensation is to be found in a letter of Emerson to his brother Edward in May of 1834, where he writes: "Let me ask you do you draw the distinction of Milton Coleridge & the Germans between Reason & Understanding. I think it a philosophy itself. & like all truth very practical". For us the most important part of the letter reads: "Reason is the highest faculty of the soul—what we mean often by the soul itself; it never *reasons,* never proves, it simply perceives; it is vision. The Understanding toils all the time, compares, contrives, adds, argues, near sighted but strong-sighted, dwelling in the present the expedient the customary. Beasts have some understanding but no Reason. Reason is potentially perfect in every man—Understanding in very different degrees of strength. The thoughts of youth, & 'first thoughts,' are the revelations of Reason. The love of the beautiful & of Goodness as the highest beauty the belief in the absolute & universal superiority of the Right & the True But understanding that wrinkled calculator the steward of our house to whom is committed the support of our animal life contradicts evermore these affirmations of Reason & points at Custom & Interest & persuades one man that the declarations of Reason are false & another that they are at least impracticable. Yet by & by after having denied our Master we come back to see at the end of years or of life that he was the Truth. . . . Religion Poetry Honor belong to the Reason; to the real the absolute. . . . The manifold applications of the distinction to Literature to the Church to Life will show how good a key it is. So hallelujah to the Reason forevermore".[16]

This letter may be taken as a text for this chapter, but in order to understand the "Reason" that Emerson hallelujahed, it will be useful to turn first to the writings of some of the contemporaries of his youth and then, in the next chapter, to the great man himself. In this way we shall be able to call on his less brilliant, less oracular friends of the Transcendentalist period to help illuminate the philosophical ideas he shared with them before examining the use he made of these ideas in dealing with his favorite concerns: religion, poetry, honor, literature, the Church, and life. Many participants in what Transcendentalists called "the newness" can help us unravel the main strands of that excited period in American thought. It is especially useful to turn to James Marsh, the Vermonter who introduced the Transcendentalists in 1829 to Coleridge's version of the contrast between Reason and Understanding;

to George Ripley, the founder of Brook Farm and one of the clearer-headed Transcendentalists; to James Walker and Orestes Brownson, who specialized in appeals to sentiment; and in the next chapter, to Theodore Parker, the learned popularizer of the leading American philosophical movement between the Revolution and the Civil War.[17]

Although Emerson speaks in his letter to his brother of the distinction between Reason and Understanding drawn by Coleridge and the Germans, it is well to keep in mind that Emerson had little knowledge of the Germans at the time. Therefore the really important reference is to Coleridge, with whom Emerson probably made his first acquaintance by way of an edition of the *Aids to Reflection* which was edited by James Marsh and published in Burlington, Vermont, in 1829. This contained a long "Preliminary Essay" by Marsh, then President of the University of Vermont, which clarifies the historical path from Edwards to Emerson by showing why the Transcendentalists deplored Edwards' determinism [18] but admired his mysticism. The Transcendentalists decisively abandoned that part of Edwards' thought which linked him most closely with Locke but clung to that part which linked him with Enthusiasm and evangelical Christianity. Marsh's "Preliminary Essay" helps explain why they broke with the more analytical side of Edwards, and presently we shall see, by referring to the writings of George Ripley, why they clung to the Edwards of the *Religious Affections*.

Transcendentalism Against Edwards' Determinism

Marsh argued that Edwards the determinist not only had not provided adequate metaphysical support for evangelical Christianity but also had subscribed to doctrines which stood in the way of providing that support. Marsh's essay was primarily an attack on doctrines in Edwards' *Freedom of the Will*, and Coleridge provided Marsh with much ammunition.[19] In a letter to Coleridge written in the year in which the American edition of the *Aids to Reflection* appeared, Marsh remarked: "There has lately risen some discussions among our most able orthodox divines, which seem to me likely to shake the authority of Edwards among them; and I trust your 'Aids to Reflection' is, with a few, exerting an influence that will help to place the lovers of truth and righteousness on better philosophical grounds".[20] The Transcendentalist James Freeman Clarke could see that Marsh was attacking Edwards along with Locke, for Clarke wrote in 1837 that those who condemn "the philosophy of Coleridge or Marsh, . . . show that they are followers of a Locke or Edwards".[21]

When we read Marsh's "Preliminary Essay", we can see what Marsh meant. Marsh insisted first of all that one must have a metaphysics superior to Locke's—and Edwards, he said, did not have one—in order to deal properly with "experimental religion", a favorite phrase of Edwards. "Let it be understood, . . ." Marsh declared, "that by the prevailing system of metaphysics, I mean the system, of which in modern times Locke is the reputed author, and the leading principles of which, with various modifications, more or less important, but not altering its essential character, have been almost universally received in this country." Then he showed his attitude toward Edwards by saying, "In the minds of our religious community especially some of its most important doctrines have become associated with names justly loved and revered among ourselves, and so connected with all our theoretical views of religion, that one can hardly hope to question their validity without hazarding his reputation, not only for orthodoxy, but even for common sense". Marsh goes on to say in a passage that makes it certain that he is here referring to Edwards, "To controvert . . . the prevailing doctrines with regard to the freedom of the will, the sources of our knowledge, the nature of the understanding as containing the controlling principles of our whole being, and the universality of the law of cause and effect . . . may even now be worse than in vain". So long as we hold the doctrines of Edwards, Marsh warned, we can make and defend "no essential distinction between that which is *natural,* and that which is *spiritual"*, and "we cannot even find rational grounds for the feeling of *moral obligation"*. According to Marsh, the chief source of difficulty in Edwards' system was the view that "the acts of the *free-will* are pre-determined by a cause *out of the will,* according to the same law of cause and effect, which controls the changes in the physical world". In an obvious allusion to Edwards, Marsh expressed his awareness that "much has been said and written to make out consistently with these *general* principles, a *distinction* between *natural* and *moral* causes, natural and moral ability, and inability, &c.". But this, Marsh claimed, was not enough to protect Edwards and his followers from a fatal difficulty: they put man on the same level with the brutes. Marsh concluded that so long as we refuse to admit that men have a power of rising above the causal law which connects a choice with its natural antecedents, we shall be involved in perplexities both in morals and religion.[22]

Transcendentalism and Edwards' Mysticism: Internal Evidence and Feeling the Truth

Although attacks like those of Marsh lowered the reputation of Edwards' determinism, Edwards' Sense of the Heart was clearly a native American antecedent of Emerson's Reason. Octavius Brooks Frothingham confidently asserted the continuity between Transcendentalism and the mystical Edwards. "The spiritual writings of Jonathan Edwards, the 'Treatise on the Religious Affections' especially," Frothingham said, "breathe the sweetest spirit of idealism. Indeed, whenever orthodoxy spread its wings and rose into the region of faith, it lost itself in the sphere where the human soul and the divine were in full concurrence. Transcendentalism simply claimed for all men what Protestant Christianity claimed for its own elect." [23] Edwards made room for the elected Protestant saint's mystical insight by adding another sense to the saint's otherwise Lockeian mind, but the Transcendentalists hoped to show that *all* men had a non-sensory power which allowed them to see divine things directly, the power called "Reason" by Transcendentalists. This theological link between Edwards and the Transcendentalists is evident in the writings of Emerson's friend and cousin, George Ripley, who favored the use of what was called "internal evidence" in establishing the divine origin of Christianity. Ripley therefore spent a good deal of his youth arguing against the Unitarian view that it could be established only by appealing to the external evidence of miracles, for he held with St. Paul that one could immediately see the glory of God in the face of Jesus Christ and that merely by examining the morality taught by Jesus, one could see that he was a divine messenger. (It is hard, I may say, to see why the inference from Jesus' morality or even his face, as viewed through the Gospel, should be regarded as so direct by comparison to the inference from his alleged miracles.) Reason, according to Ripley, was the faculty of directly seeing the divinity of Christianity, whereas the Understanding was the lesser tool used by the Unitarians in their search for indirect external evidence. It is not surprising, therefore, to find Ripley saying that Paul's meaning "cannot be better illustrated, than by the following admirable remarks from the most profound theologian, whom this country has produced" —namely, Edwards—and to find Ripley quoting Edwards' statement that one may receive assurance of Christ's divinity upon sensing his spiritual glory with one's heart.[24] Ripley's appeal to Edwards' Sense of the Heart was made in the course of a vigorous polemic against the Unitarian Andrews Norton's argument that miracles are the *sole* evidence of the divine origin of Christianity, i.e. that the only evidence that we have for the belief that Christ was a messenger of God is the fact that Christ performed miracles. Norton, who was called the "Unitarian pope", had been influenced in this direction by Locke's view that we must give arguments for the belief that a revelation is divine. According to Locke, as we have seen in an earlier chapter, God may reveal a truth to a favored person; but we who do not have the benefit of what Locke calls such "original revelation" must have evidence that it came to such a person from God if we are to accept the revealed proposition as true. In this spirit Norton held that the fact that Christ performed miracles is the only evidence for his being a divine messenger. In opposing Norton, Ripley did not dispute the divine mission of Christ, nor did he deny that Christ had in fact made miracles.[25] For Ripley the issue was whether these miracles were the *only* evidence of the divine origin of Christianity, and this Ripley denied. There was also, he held, evidence that came from a direct inspection of Christ's character and moral doctrine as these emerge in Scriptures.

In the course of his theological attack on Norton, Ripley said several things that illuminate some of the social and political tendencies of Transcendentalism. In attacking the idea that a Christian's belief can be justified in only one way, he accused Norton of "exclusiveness"; and this was calculated to discredit Norton with those Unitarians who felt that the hallmark of their religion and of Protestantism itself was opposition to exclusiveness. In attacking the rationalism of Norton, Ripley also revealed the democratic animus in the theology of Transcendentalism. Norton had maintained that the investigations needed for supporting Christian belief were beyond the capacities of the majority of men, and that these men must rest on the authority of the learned in religion much as they must rest on the authority of physicists when accepting Newtonian mechanics.[26] In denying this, Ripley once again appealed to Edwards in a passage that shows not only the link between Edwards and the Transcendentalists but also certain

reservations in their attitude toward him. Ripley, after reporting that he knew many sincere Christians who could not appreciate the Argument from Miracles, says of Edwards: "This
experience is confirmed by the testimony of an eminent man,
already quoted, who, whatever portion of truth he might have
failed to perceive, it would be extreme folly to doubt, was
conversant with the workings of the soul, in the affairs of religion, as few have ever been, in our country, or in any
other".[27] And then Ripley quotes the following from Edwards
in support of the idea that religious truth may come more easily out of the mouths of babes: "If the evidence of the Gospel
depended only on history, and such reasonings as learned men
only are capable of, it would be above the reach of far the
greatest part of mankind. But persons with but an ordinary
degree of knowledge are capable, without a long and subtile
train of reasoning, to see the divine excellency of the things of
religion. They are capable of being taught by the spirit of
God, as well as learned men. The evidence, that is this way
obtained, is vastly better and more satisfying, than all that can
be obtained by the arguings of those that are the most
learned, and the greatest masters of reason. And babes are as
capable of knowing these things, as the wise and prudent; and
they are often hid from these when they are revealed to
those". [28]

In the same spirit, Ripley telescoped a series of remarks
made by James Walker in the *Christian Examiner* and produced the following passage around which he put quotation
marks, without any indications of deletions, though he accu-
rately reported the gist of Walker's thought: "Christianity embodies a collection of moral and vital truths, and THESE
TRUTHS, apart from ALL HISTORY or philosophy, constitute
Christianity itself. Instead, therefore, of perplexing and confounding the young with what are called the evidences of
Christianity, give them Christianity itself. Begin by giving
them Christianity itself, as exhibited in the life and character

of the Lord Jesus, as illustrated by his simple, beautiful, and touching parables, and as it breathes through all his discourses. They will FEEL IT TO BE TRUE. Depend upon it, paradoxical as it may sound, children will be much more likely to believe Christianity without what are called the evidences, than with them; and the remark applies to some who are not children. Why talk to one about the argument from prophecy, or the argument from miracles, when these are the very points and the only points on which his mind, from some peculiarity in its original constitution, or from limited information, chiefly labors".[29]

Orestes Brownson—the on-and-off Transcendentalist—was even more explicit (when he was on) in identifying feeling as the faculty that gave man access to dark and mysterious truth.[30] In his review of Benjamin Constant's *De la Religion,* he subscribed wholeheartedly to the author's view that "religion and morality rest not on the understanding, not on logical deductions, but on an interior sentiment"; [31] and he felt obliged to make an extended comment on the mysterious: "We may be told, that to admit, that the feelings, the sentiments, are worthy of reliance, is to go off into the mysterious, to stop we know not where. We know many are very coy of mystery. We know there are many who say, 'Where mystery begins, there religion ends;' and we know, also, that in saying it, if they mean what is inexplicable to the understanding, properly so called, they pronounce a general sentence of condemnation upon all that is elevated, generous, and touching in human nature. We can explain to the understanding, none of the workings of the sentiments of the heart, none of the emotions, the affections of the soul. Indeed, we do not wish to explain them. We are not afraid of the mysterious. It is one of the glories of our nature, and one of the strongest pledges of its immortal destiny, that it delights in the mysterious; that it has cravings which go beyond what is known; that it dares rush off into the darkness, trusting to its own instincts for guidance; and that it has powers, which can out-travel the understanding, and which can seize and shadow forth to its own eye a perfection, which reason cannot comprehend, of which it does not even dream. To condemn the mysterious, were to bring the soul down from the beautiful and the holy, to the merely useful,—were to kill poetry, to wither the fine arts, to discard all the graces, for all these have something of the mysterious, are enveloped in mystic folds, offensive it may be to the understanding, but enchanting to the soul . . .".[32] All of this fitted in with Brownson's view "that the sentiments are as worthy of reliance, as the understanding; that, to speak in popular language, the testimony of the heart is as legitimate, as that of the head".[33] And when he says that we may rely on our sentiments and that they give testimony to something, he means that they give testimony to truth. Not simply to the truth that the sentiments themselves exist. That would be a trivial contention, for it is obvious that if we have a sentiment of sadness, then it is true that we have such a sentiment. Nor was Brownson merely urging that men should cultivate their feelings as well as their intellect and in that way become whole men. He was rather urging that they could legitimately appeal to their feelings or emotions in trying to decide the truth of a proposition which did not say anything about those feelings. Thus their *hope* that a proposition was true could be enough evidence for its truth. Brownson's doctrine, therefore, was not the innocuous doctrine that man should be not only a knower of truth but also a feeler of feelings. It was the typically Transcendentalist doctrine that feelings may by themselves certify knowledge about something other than feeling. This doctrine appealed to Brownson's contemporary Emerson, as it appealed to all Romantic anti-intellectualists, including William James, as we shall see in a later chapter.

*The Persistence of the Scottish Influence
in Theology and Ethics*

Although the Transcendentalists' basic impulses were religious, they were not content to rely on mystical theology alone. They were prepared not only by familiarity with Edwards' Sense of the Heart to accept the Coleridgian Reason that Emerson loved; they were also prepared by the Scottish Philosophy of Common Sense that Emerson had studied as an undergraduate at Harvard—even though Marsh was critical of that philosophy. Emerson and his friends were especially familiar with the views of Thomas Reid's disciple, Dugald Stewart, who held that there are "primary truths, a conviction of which is necessarily implied in all our thoughts and in all our actions; and which seem, on that account, rather to form constituent and essential *elements* of reason, than objects with which reason is conversant". Among these elements of Reason —a phrase which he preferred to Reid's "principles of Common Sense"—Stewart included mathematical axioms like "The whole is greater than a part" and "Things equal to the same thing are equal to one another", both of which he described as being supposed or implied in arithmetic and geometry. If such truths were ever called into question, Stewart held, arithmetical and geometrical reasoning would become impossible. Hence he argued that acceptance of them virtually defines rationality or reason. Among the components of Reason he also included what he called *"metaphysical* or *transcendental* truths". These, he said, "form a part of those original *stamina* of human reason, which are equally essential to all the pursuits of science, and to all the active concerns of life", for example, the propositions *"I exist; I am the same person to-day that I was yesterday; the material world has an existence independent of my mind; the general laws of nature will continue, in future, to operate uniformly as in time past"*. In short, Stewart maintained that a belief in such truths identified a man as a rational being.[34]

Because some of the Scottish philosophers maintained that such beliefs could be uncovered by what they called "consciousness", by what Locke called "reflection", and by what is now called "introspection", the beliefs were coveted as examples by Transcendentalists in rebellion against Unitarianism.[35] The method of introspection or consciousness was, the Transcendentalists thought, a potent ally of the method of internal evidence in theology, because they thought that deeply important truths are not discovered by the use of sensory experience. Thus Ripley held in his review of Martineau's *Rationale of Religious Enquiry* that "our own consciousness assures us that a revelation of great spiritual truths is made to the soul. There are certain primitive and fundamental ideas which compose the substance of reason, that exist, with more or less distinctness, in every intelligent mind. These ideas are the intuitive perceptions on which all moral and religious truth is founded . . .".[36] After these Scottish remarks, Ripley went on to say that primitive and fundamental ideas like "the perception of the Just, the Holy, the Perfect, the Infinite" are not created by us but are put into us by God, and furthermore that there are some minds in which "the essential ideas of religious truth exist in signal perfection, independent of human agency".[37] Such minds are *super*naturally inspired. We may say this of Christ without any limitation; and though the Apostles were inspired to a lesser degree, they were more inspired than ordinary men are. However, the ordinary man's basis for knowing that Christ and his Apostles were divinely inspired "can be no other than its agreement with the primitive and universal dictates of the absolute reason in man. In this way and in no other, can it be distinguished from the fancies of enthusiasm, or the reveries of superstition. Every thing which claims to be of an immediate divine origin in history, must be brought to the test of that which is admitted to be of immediate divine origin in the facts of consciousness". At this point Ripley's democratic sentiments are once again evident, for he goes on to assert that "as a common degree of poetical genius is qualified to decide upon the merits of the great masters of song, so the divine sense of truth which is the property of the race, must pass sentence on the claim of its prophets and teachers to supernatural endowments".[38] In other words, the people know that Christ and the Apostles were inspired by God because the people can see from the Scriptures without the help of learned theologians that Christ and the Apostles had in high degree the spiritual ideas and beliefs that the people themselves have in lesser degree. Such a "proof" of the supernatural inspiration of Christ and the Apostles was very different from Norton's external proof by miracles because the latter was too dependent on learning about the distant past and, more importantly, because it was addressed to the Lockeian senses. Since Ripley deemed "it an error, under any circumstances, to rest a system of spiritual truth addressed to the soul, upon the evidence of miracles addressed to the senses",[39] he appealed only to Scottish "consciousness", the descendant of Locke's reflection.

So did James Walker, who, although he was a Unitarian, had won the admiration of the Transcendentalists by defending religious ideas that were congenial to them. As an editor of the Unitarian *Christian Examiner* he published their work, and he employed Scottish philosophy for purposes of which they approved highly.[40] Walker defined faith scripturally as the substance of things hoped for, the evidence of things not seen, but he also called it a faculty by which "we can and do regard many things, which lie beyond the sphere of our senses and actual experience, as really existing".[41] A little reflection, he went on to say, will show everyone "alive to noble thoughts and sentiments" that such a spiritual faculty exists in the soul of man. It is "attested and put beyond controversy, by the *revelations of consciousness*".[42] Its existence is not established by sensation since we cannot see, feel, taste, or smell a mental faculty—nor, he adds for good measure, can we sense the existence of a moral sentiment or an idea.[43] Plainly showing the influence of the Scottish philosophers, Walker maintained that neither sensation nor logic can prove even the existence of one's own being and personality, for only consciousness can show that.[44] Only by introspection can we see that we ourselves exist, establish the existence of faith as a faculty, and show that we have a capacity for veneration and devotion. Religion for him was a manifestation and development of faith and of the capacity for veneration; and because our idea of a perfect man requires the development of these religious faculties, Walker believed they should be developed to the full.

Walker maintained that faith should be encouraged even in the face of possible logical difficulties, but he quickly assured his readers that all such difficulties could be surmounted. His reasoning was once again Scottish: "From the acknowledged existence and reality of spiritual impressions or perceptions, we may and do assume *the existence and reality of the spiritual world;* just as, from the acknowledged existence and reality of sensible impressions or perceptions, we may and do assume the existence and reality of the sensible world".[45] Continuing his Scottish argument, Walker pointed out that skeptics have been led to extravagance by insisting on a kind of evidence which the nature of the case does not admit. He agrees that "if we are to believe in nothing but the facts of sensation, and what can be *logically* deduced" from them, then we should not believe in the existence of the spiritual world *or* the sensible world. "For what logical connexion is there between a fact of sensation, between an impression or perception, and the real existence of its object, or of the mind that is conscious of it? None whatever." We believe in both worlds "only because we are so constituted as to make it a matter of intuition. . . . our conviction of the existence of the sensible world does not rest on a logical deduction from the facts of sensation, or of sensation and consciousness. It rests on the constitution of our nature. It is resolvable into a fundamental law of belief. It is held, not as a logical inference, but as a first principle. With the faculties we possess, and in the circumstances in which we are placed, the idea grows up in the mind, and we cannot expel it if we would".[46] If we are asked, "On what evidence does a devout man's conviction of the existence and reality of the *spiritual world* depend?", we must answer, Walker said: "On the very same" evidence as that on which our belief in the sensible world depends.[47]

The Transcendentalists appealed to Scottish intuitionism not only in theology but also in ethics. There Ripley once again proves to be one of our most helpful sources, especially in his lengthy review of James Mackintosh's *A General View of the Progress of Ethical Philosophy,* where Ripley sharply attacked utilitarianism and advanced a form of ethical intuitionism.[48] He began by denying that our "perception" of the useful is the same thing as our perception of the right. He went on to argue, as he echoed Moral Sense theorists, that the useful and the right "differ in the kind of impression, which they produce upon the mind" because "the one [the useful] is addressed principally to the understanding, and the other always terminates upon the feelings". We determine whether or not an action is useful by an exercise of judgment just as we determine the properties of a circle or triangle, and therefore the perception of utility "is not an emotion and does not necessarily involve one". By contrast, he said, the perception of Right "always involves the sentiment of moral approbation". So much so, he adds, that the perception of Right and the sentiment of moral approbation are often confused. What, then, is the connection between them? Ripley answers that the quality of the right action "excites" the understanding's perception of right, and also "touches the feelings" and "creates a vivid sentiment". This sentiment, he continues, "possesses a character of its own, unlike any other, and is evidently altogether and absolutely distinct from the calm conclusions of the intellect, which determine whether or not an action is useful".[49] From this we can see that according to Ripley the perception of the rightness of an action contains what a twentieth-century philosopher might call a descriptive and an emotive component. Indeed, if Ripley had been inclined to use more linguistic terminology, he might have claimed in the manner of certain twentieth-century philosophers that the *word* "right" has both a descriptive meaning and an emotive meaning and that its emotive meaning sharply distinguishes it from the word "useful". Instead, Ripley says that the *quality* rightness produces both an idea in the understanding and a sentiment of approbation. By producing this sentiment of approbation, the quality of rightness was distinguished, Ripley thought, from utility.

Ripley continued his attack on utilitarianism by pointing out that there are many things which are useful but excite no emotion of moral approbation. For example, no inanimate object excites the emotion of moral approbation. "The very supposition of its being virtuous is ludicrous. . . . who ever thought of asking a question concerning the virtue of the most valuable machine?"[50] Ripley also maintains that no quality of a brute will create or excite the emotion of *moral* approbation. Having offered this criticism, he considers the view of those utilitarians who admit that our moral sentiments are never called forth except by the actions of rational and voluntary agents, but who then argue that the perception of the Right and the Useful are the same when we are considering human actions. This Ripley regards as a confession of defeat since it abandons the utilitarian thesis of the *identity* of the useful and the right. His point is that to be useful and to be right cannot be really identical if they are said to be identical only in the case of human actions. From the statement that being a useful *human action* and being a right *human action* are identical, we cannot infer that the attribute of being useful as such is identical with the attribute of being right as such. Attributes are identical only if they are possessed by exactly the same things. Moreover, he holds that even the qualified utilitarian thesis of identity is false, simply because there are human actions that are useful but not virtuous. Here he makes the familiar point that we may perceive an action to be useful without examining the intention of the agent, and therefore we may see that a useful action is not virtuous after discovering the evil intention with which it was performed. Conversely, Ripley points out, there are actions which excite the emotion of moral approbation before we have perceived them to be useful.

Having argued that "the conception of the Right and the conception of the Useful . . . are by no means one and the same", Ripley goes on to ask what we mean by "right". Once again he gives evidence of a degree of logical power that one does not find in Emerson. In effect Ripley holds that the concept, quality, or idea of right is unanalyzable. First he says: "If it be now asked what we mean by a right action, it may be as difficult to give a general answer, as to the question, what we mean by a true proposition".[51] And then he says, in a long passage that deserves quotation: "A true proposition is one which must be believed; a right action, one which must be done. This is the simple Idea of Right. Turn it which way we will, we cannot get rid of it. We may think we have resolved it into something else, that it consists in a regard to our own greatest happiness, in the pursuit of the general good, in obedience to the divine will, in propriety, and so on, but all these expressions only describe particular right actions; they shed no light on the general and absolute Idea of Right, which we can carry no further than this, namely,—that, which *must* be done, which *ought* to be done, which we are *obliged* to do, which it is *wrong* to omit; all which are clearly equivalent expressions for the same thing, differing only in form, as statements of one fundamental idea".[52] In other words, every effort to analyze or define the idea of Right introduces that very idea into the putative definition, which is therefore circular. And this is tantamount to maintaining that the idea of Right is undefinable, unanalyzable, or simple.

Ripley grants that although the idea of Right may be simple, all right actions may have something in common that constitutes what he calls a criterion of rightness. "What," then, he asks, "is the common quality in those actions, by which the idea is suggested? What is the criterion by which we may determine whether or not an action or mental disposition is Right?" [53] He imagines a utilitarian asserting in reply that even though the idea of right is simple, it may be "suggested by" a common quality that all right actions possess, namely, utility. But at this point Ripley reiterates that the extensions—to use logical terminology—of the terms "Right" and "Useful" are not identical, i.e. that some right actions are not useful and that some useful actions are wrong; and then takes the occasion to deal with an effort of Paley to circumvent such an objection to utilitarianism. Paley imagines an objector to utilitarianism saying: "Suppose that an old man of worthless character is in possession of a large fortune, which I can attain by putting him to death, and employ for my own benefit and that of mankind. Why should not I knock the rich villain in the head, and do good with the money, of which he makes no use? The action, by the very terms of the statement, will be a beneficial one. My intentions in committing it, are with a single view to the benefit it will produce. If utility is the criterion, the old miser must die. There is no other way". In reply to this objection, Paley says that the action would be wrong because a *general rule* to sanction such actions would be injurious. But Ripley says in criticism of Paley's version of utilitarianism: "We cannot see how a general rule, formed from a particular beneficial action can be injurious. The general rule would comprehend only such actions as are precisely similar to the one upon which it is founded. If it be useful in a given case to take the life of an old man because I can make a better use of his money than he does himself, it would also be useful to take the lives of ten, twenty, thirty, or as many as were in similar circumstances. If the utility of one action makes it Right, it is impossible that the utility of ten, twenty, or thirty actions precisely similar, should not also make them Right. If the particular case be beneficial, the general rule must be beneficial also".[54]

It must be observed that Ripley, in his review of Mackintosh, does not advocate Kant's doctrine of the Categorical Imperative. Ripley asserts that if we wish to know whether to perform a given action, "we refer it to a general maxim of conduct, the truth of which is intuitively perceived by the mature reason, and this, we will suppose in the present case, determines the action to be right".[55] Here there is no Kantian insistence that the validity of our maxim must be established by appealing to what Kant called The Supreme Categorical Imperative. Ripley's Scottish idea was that the maxim should be seen to be true intuitively without using a criterion as elaborate as Kant's, and this intuitionism brought him closer to the Scottish philosophers than to either Kant or mysticism. Like other Transcendentalists, Ripley associated his own view with that of the Moral Sense theorists, and concluded his review of Mackintosh with a reference to the "sublime sentiment of Duty" that explained much about the social philosophy of Transcendentalism. This peroration should be read while remembering that its author was the presiding spirit of Brook Farm socialism: "We ought, perhaps, to offer an apology for occupying so many of our pages with a subject relating to the abstract philosophy of ethics, which cannot be supposed to possess the same interest for others, which we take in it ourselves. We may be permitted, however, to say, that there is a far more intimate connexion between sound theoretical principles, and the advancement and prosperity of society, than is generally imagined. It has been abundantly verified by experience, that when the primitive and sublime sentiment of Duty, engraved by the finger of God on the heart of man, has been lost sight of, or merged in an inferior order of principles, a slow but fatal poison has preyed upon the vital interests of the community".[56]

However, even that individualistic non-Brook Farmer, Henry Thoreau—who had less concern for "the community" —supported his civil disobedience by means of a philosophical theory that was intuitionistic and anti-utilitarian. He asked rhetorically in his famous essay, "Civil Disobedience": "Must the citizen ever for a moment, or in the least degree, resign his conscience to the legislator?" and he answered: "It is not desirable to cultivate a respect for the law, so much as for the right".[57] Although Thoreau's essay was not a notable contribution to analytical ethics, the one moral philosopher he chooses to attack in that essay is the very Paley whom Ripley and other Transcendentalists also attacked for his utilitarianism, which they associated with empiricism and State Street commercialism. Thoreau's chief complaint against Paley is that he "resolves all civil obligation into expediency". Moreover, Thoreau maintained that "Paley appears never to have contemplated those cases to which the rule of expediency does not apply, in which a people, as well as an individual, must do justice, cost what it may. If I have unjustly wrested a plank from a drowning man, I must restore it to him though I drown myself. This, according to Paley, would be inconvenient. But he that would save his life, in such a case, shall lose it. This people must cease to hold slaves, and to make war on Mexico, though it cost them their existence as a people".[58] In some respects, of course, Thoreau's philosophical thoughts resembled Kant's, but he uses no Kantian machinery in defense

of them. His defense is more like that offered by Ripley and
the Scottish philosophers, and also by Jacobi, described by
Emerson as "the Transcendental moralist" who refused "all
measure of right and wrong except the determinations of the
private spirit".[59]

5 · Ralph Waldo Emerson: Overseer of the Oversoul

"Reason . . . never reasons, never proves,
it simply perceives; it is vision."

Thoreau's name naturally brings to mind Emerson, and so it is time to return to the most revered American sage. He was born in Boston in 1803, a century after the birth of Jonathan Edwards and forty-five years after Edwards' death. Emerson entered Harvard in 1817 and was graduated four years later without making a distinguished record. In 1829 he was ordained a Unitarian minister, but in 1832 he resigned as pastor of the Second Church in Boston because he felt that he could no longer conscientiously administer the Lord's Supper. In 1833 Emerson traveled to Europe—where he met Wordsworth, Carlyle, and Coleridge—and soon after his return settled in Concord, Massachusetts, in 1834. The year 1836 saw the appearance of his first important work, *Nature;* 1837 called forth his famous Phi Beta Kappa oration, "The American Scholar"; and 1838 was the year in which his "Divinity School Address" started a theological storm in Boston. Upon leaving the Second Church, Emerson had preached a sermon on the Lord's Supper in which he gave eloquent voice to views that reveal his attachment to some of the Transcendentalist ideas we have already examined. He declared: "If I understand the distinction of Christianity, the reason why it is to be preferred over all other systems and is divine is this, that it is a moral system; that it presents men with truths which are their own reason, and enjoins practices that are their own justification; that if miracles may be said to have been its evidence to the first Christians, they are not its evidence to us, but the doctrines themselves . . .".[1] Two years later he penned the hallelujah to Reason which appeared in the letter to his brother [2] and launched his career as a seer who was better at moral vision than at the philosophical theory of moral vision.[3]

Emerson's Theory of Vision

In the last chapter we saw some of the more proximate sources of Emerson's hallelujah to Reason; but we do him too much justice and too little justice if we think that he was an epistemologist who was deeply exercised about the differences between, say, Locke and Kant on intuition, or between Reid and Stewart on Common Sense, or between the various versions of the contrast between intuitive and discursive reason. The comparatively superficial level at which Emerson was concerned with these concepts is best illustrated by the following passage from his lecture "The Transcendentalist", which followed Ripley's review of Mackintosh by ten years and preceded Thoreau's "Civil Disobedience" by about seven: "It is well known to most of my audience that the Idealism of the present day acquired the name of Transcendental from the use of that term by Immanuel Kant, of Königsberg, who replied to the skeptical philosophy of Locke, which insisted that there was nothing in the intellect which was not previously in the experience of the senses, by showing that there was a very important class of ideas or imperative forms, which did not come by experience, but through which experience was acquired; that these were intuitions of the mind itself; and he denominated them *Transcendental* forms. The extraordinary profoundness and precision of that man's thinking have given vogue to his nomenclature, in Europe and America, to that extent that whatever belongs to the class of intuitive thought is popularly called at the present day *Transcendental*".[4] This simple equation of the intuitive with the transcendental, however, needed no elaborate Kantian terminology for its exposition or defense, since Emerson might just as well have found his version of the equation in Dugald Stewart, who labeled Reid's intuitive principles of common sense as "transcendental truths". As we have seen, the Scottish philosophers believed that there are intuitive truths—as Locke did—so that if all Emerson meant by "transcendental" was "intuitive", he most certainly need not have relied on Kant for that notion.[5] Moreover, whenever Emerson spoke of the Reason as a faculty exercised in the expression of moral sentiment, he departed from Kant's absolutistic and anti-naturalistic ethics as well as from the rationalistic ethics of Locke and Reid. Whereas Kant held that the principles of morality may be certified on purely formal grounds by the application of the Supreme Categorical Imperative, and whereas Locke held that the first principles of natural law may be seen to be true by the exercise of the same intuitive reason that perceives the truth of mathematical axioms, Emerson appealed to something quite empirical when he appealed to moral sentiment as a test of moral truth, namely, the actual feelings of men.[6]

However, it is a thankless task to pursue the origins and the confused windings of Emerson's views of Reason. It is sufficient for our purposes to note that he thought that moral and religious beliefs are supported by Reason viewed as a faculty of feeling; and therefore that he represented a very influential chapter in the transformation of Lockeian Reason from a purely intellectual faculty to one which may be exercised in a person's having sentiments. For Emerson, Reason was primarily a power of the mind to feel moral and religious truth,

though, in his confused way, he also regarded it as a faculty
for the detection of any kind of truth that transcended historical fact. This tendency to think that Reason can go beyond historical fact led him to avoid fine distinctions among
thinkers and sages of anti-empirical bent: ancient Greek and
Indian philosophers, Neoplatonic mystics, English Platonists,
Scottish intuitionists, French eclectics, German and English
transcendentalists. Whatever non-empirical truths they saw,
he allowed his Reason to see, for his Reason apprehended Plato's ideas and Plotinus's One, knew most of the propositions
of Scottish Common Sense, saw that Kant's things-in-them-
selves existed, discerned the truth of moral principles, knew
that Kant's synthetic *a priori* propositions were true, and saw
the glory that Paul saw in the face of Jesus.[7]

And yet, despite the wide-ranging prodigious powers of
Emerson's Reason, he was primarily interested in asserting
religious and moral truth without argument.[8] Religion, Poetry, and Honor were the things Emerson really cared about;
and that is why he emphasized in his letter of 1834 to his
brother that *they* "belong to Reason" and that the distinction
between Reason and Understanding was a "key" that would
help in the Church, in Literature, and in Life. In his earliest
days he had said that St. Paul marked the distinction and
"counteraction" between the Understanding and the Reason
by using the expressions "natural man" and "spiritual man",
and that the conflict between the Reason and the Understanding was formulated in St. Paul's sentence, "The Carnal mind
is enmity against God". In those days Emerson had maintained that the dualism between Understanding and Reason
is a philosophical counterpart of Law versus Gospel in Luther
and St. Paul, of Swedenborg's love of self versus love of Lord,
and of William Penn's World versus Spirit; but as his interest
in the religion of the churches declined, he was more inclined
to use Reason in moral criticism than in theology.[9]

Emerson, however, made no contribution at all to what is

now called the analysis of ethical concepts. He merely took over a variety of ethical intuitionism that he could find in the writings of others. We may therefore say of him what he himself once said of Cicero in an undergraduate prize essay: "Cicero, though the ornament and herald of philosophy in his age, did little for the advancement of its principles. . . . His usefulness to moral science is the same in kind, though superior in degree, to that of modern essayists; his elegant effusions inspired a delight to investigate the topics of which they treated".[10] The eighteen-year-old Emerson was well aware of the distinction between the sage and the philosophical analyst. "In contemplating the science of morals," he announced, "we have only to speak of the classifiers and theorists who have analyzed, not the sages who have recommended and applied it. A sketch of the science has no more concern with the beautiful sentiments it contains or occasions, than the nature of the soil with the different owners through which its title had passed." [11] Ironically, therefore, the youth was condescending to the man he was to become, for Emerson was at his best not as a classifier or a theorist who analyzed, but as a sage who sought to apply the results of analysis, an essayist who expressed and occasioned beautiful moral sentiments as he reflected on the pressing issues of personal and social life. The sentence in Emerson's Bowdoin Prize Essay that foretold the role he was later to play, was the one that read: "It is ennobling . . . to place ourselves on an eminence from whence we survey at once the whole history of legislation and refer to our knowledge of ethical truth in judging of the good or bad spirit of laws".[12]

Emerson's Vision

From 1821 on, Emerson strove to place himself on such an eminence so that he could survey not only the history of American legislation but also the whole history of American

society, referring to a knowledge of ethical truth that supposedly could be acquired only by the use of Reason. Because he
later thought he had the appropriate kind of Reason at his
command, he confidently made many judgments on concrete
issues, judgments that he might never have made had he not
felt that he was resting on a solid and deeply supported epistemological platform. Once he mounted this Germano-Coleridgian device, he was helped to attain that eminence of which
he had spoken at eighteen. By the time he was thirty-three in
1836, he no longer felt like a slave of historical fact and probability but rather like a master of immutable morality that
could be supported by sentiment. Now he thought he could
be really sure of his ethical knowledge, and he expressed this
assurance in a series of memorable essays beginning with *Nature* of 1836, continuing with "The American Scholar" of
1837, and reaching a climax in his attack on Unitarianism in
the "Divinity School Address" of 1838. By that time he had
surveyed American politics, religion, education, letters, and
social life, hammering away at a number of notes that had
been sounded by the Transcendentalists while expressing
doubts in "The Transcendentalist" of 1842 about the excesses
of the comrades of his youth. By 1844 he had securely established his reputation as the sage of New England, as a penetrating critic of American culture, as a philosophically oriented student of the whole of American civilization, especially
of religion, law, politics, poetry, and education. Emerson's
version of the distinction between the Reason and the Understanding was a godsend to a writer who could not argue. He
welcomed the idea that there is such a thing as an emotionalized Reason which could issue those *pensées,* those "infinitely
repellent particles", that fill his pages without being bound
together by any logical structure. Emerson's distinction between the Reason and the Understanding also influenced the
substance of his moral criticism and his comments on American civilization. This is most evident in his letter to his

brother Edward, where he maintained that by contrast to the Reason, the Understanding dwells in the expedient and the customary.

No one communicated this aspect of Transcendentalism more clearly than its popularizer, Theodore Parker, another of Emerson's contemporaries who illuminates his thought. According to Parker, the basic idea of Transcendentalism was that the partisan of the Understanding, that is to say, the sensationalist or the empiricist, is a slave of historical fact. In politics, according to Parker, the doctrine of sensationalism knows nothing of absolute right and absolute justice. It knows only of historical justice because sense experience cannot let the idea of absolute justice into the intellect. " 'There is no right but might,' is the political philosophy of sensationalism. It may be the might of a king, of an aristocracy, of a democracy, the might of passions, the might of intellect, the might of muscle,—it has a right to what it will. It appeals always to human history, not human nature. Now human history shows what has been, not what should be or will be. . . . Political expediency is the only right or justice it knows in its politics. So it always looks back, and says 'it worked well at Barcelona or Venice,' or 'did not work well.' It loves to cite precedents out of history, not laws out of nature. It claims a thing not as a human right, but as an historical privilege received by Magna Carta or the Constitution; as if a right were more of a right because time-honored and written on parchment; or less, because just claimed and for the first time and by a single man. The sensationalist has no confidence in ideas, so asks for facts to hold on to and to guide him in his blindness." [13] In ethics, said Parker as he forgot his Locke, the sensationalist knows no first truths; and here again he is a slave of historical fact. We ask: "How shall I know what to do in a matter of morals? by referring to a moral sense?", and the sensationalist replies: "Not at all". Only by observation, by experience, by learning what works well in the long run, referring to history, can we answer this question. We must study the history of mankind, and find what has worked well, and follow that because it has worked well. If we say: " 'But human history only tells what has been and worked well, not what is right. I want what is right!' ", the sensationalist answers: " 'It is pretty much the same thing' ".[14]

Parker's summary of Transcendentalism and his highly tendentious account of empiricism illuminate the connection between Emerson's epistemology and his philosophy of civilization.[15] Although Emerson was capable of writing extremely penetrating history and biography, his writing is filled with hostility toward those who worship the past and those who think that knowledge of the past exhausts all knowledge. This antipathy is connected in his mind with the idea that mere inductive examination of past instances is not enough to establish a principle and with the idea that what happens to have been the case must be distinguished from what ought to be the case; and by means of a philosophical pun, Emerson identified what was established—in the sense of empirically established—with the Establishment. Past fact and unquestioned power he associated with historical study and the Understanding, whereas what must be and what ought to be he identified with the Reason. And so it is not surprising that Emerson's first lines in his first published work, *Nature,* were the following: "Our age is retrospective. It builds the sepulchres of the fathers. It writes biographies, histories, and criticism. The foregoing generations beheld God and nature face to face; we, through their eyes. Why should not we also enjoy an original relation to the universe? Why should not we have a poetry and philosophy of insight and not of tradition, and a religion by revelation to us, and not the history of theirs? Embosomed for a season in nature, whose floods of life stream around and through us, and invite us, by the powers they supply, to action proportioned to nature, why should we grope among the dry bones of the past, or put the living generation into masquerade out of its faded wardrobe? The sun shines to-day also. There is more wool and flax in the fields. There are new lands, new men, new thoughts. Let us demand our own works and laws and worship".[16] This early manifesto set a tone that Emerson never abandoned. Being retrospective, biography, history, seeing through someone else's eyes, basing religion on past miracles in the manner of Unitarian scholars seeking external evidence, the poetry and philosophy of tradition—these are all bad. But beholding God and nature face to face with our own eyes, having an original relation to the universe, writing a poetry and philosophy of insight, espousing a religion of revelation based on internal evidence, new lands, new men, new thoughts, *our own* works and laws and worship—these are good because they transcend the past or the study of it.

Emerson's attack on retrospection in *Nature* was connected with his denigration of the Understanding—or what Coleridge called "the faculty of judging according to sense"—and it had corollaries throughout Emerson's philosophy of civilization. Its most immediate effect may be seen in the following remark on science: "Empirical science," Emerson said in *Nature,* "is apt to cloud the sight, and by the very knowledge of functions and processes to bereave the student of the manly contemplation of the whole. The savant becomes unpoetic. But the best read naturalist who lends an entire and devout attention to truth, will see that there remains much to learn of his relation to the world, and that it is not to be learned by any addition or subtraction or other comparison of known quantities, but is arrived at by untaught sallies of the spirit, by a continual self-recovery, and by entire humility. He will perceive that there are far more excellent qualities in the student than preciseness and infallibility; that a guess is often more fruitful than an indisputable affirmation, and that a dream may let us deeper into the secret of nature than a hundred concerted experiments".[17] This pronouncement is

not intended as an attack on all science—for Emerson respected scientific investigation and its results—but rather as
an attack on *empirical* science, by which Emerson meant a factual, historical study of particulars. In the same vein he said
that "the very announcement of the theory of gravitation, of
Kepler's three harmonic laws, and even of Dalton's doctrine
of definite proportions, finds a sudden response in the mind,
which remains a superior evidence to empirical demonstra-
tions".[18] And Emerson's remarks in *Nature* about the savant
becoming unpoetic and about how a dream may be superior
to a hundred experiments are clearly related to his idea that
science at its theoretical level is very close to, if not identical
with, poetry, since he insists: "Whoever discredits analogy and
requires heaps of facts before any theories can be attempted,
has no poetic power, and nothing original or beautiful will be
produced by him. Locke is as surely the influx of decomposition and of prose, as Bacon and the Platonists of growth. The
Platonic is the poetic tendency; the so-called scientific is the
negative and poisonous". By the *so-called* scientific tendency
he meant that philosophy of science which was excessively at-
tached to the empiricism of Locke and Hume.[19] One is hardly
surprised therefore to find no mention of John Stuart Mill's
Logic in Emerson's *English Traits*. Nor is one surprised to
find that Mill was not very impressed with Emerson when he
first met him in 1833.[20]

Emerson's distrust of retrospection, the chief activity of the
Understanding, is also evident in his philosophy of education.
In "The American Scholar" of 1837 he made Europe the symbol of the dead past, and books he saw merely as tools. He
therefore encouraged the American scholar to liberate himself
from a slavish dependence on Europe and to regard books
merely as instruments to be used by an inventive thinker who
trusts himself to arrive at the truth by the use of Reason.
Here, however, Emerson calls upon other doctrines in order
to encourage the lonely, courageous thinker who would take

his advice and fly beyond the secure confines of the Understanding. One was the doctrine that each man's Reason is
Universal Reason and that our souls are parts of a huge Oversoul much as harbors are parts of the ocean; the other was the
Swedenborgian doctrine of correspondence that led him to believe that the laws of nature have counterparts that are laws of
the soul. In this way Emerson tried to assure the student who
would use Reason for himself that he could avoid the perils of
subjectivity while ceasing to rely on the settled conclusions of
old books, old authors, and the old country. By advocating a
kind of pre-established harmony between the scholar's impression of truth and the truth itself, by advocating a latter-day
version of the view that God will not deceive a man who
trusts his own judgment, Emerson tried to encourage the
American scholar. The scholar will learn, he says, that "in
going down into the secrets of his own mind he has descended
into the secrets of all minds" and that "he who has mastered
any law in his private thoughts, is master to that extent of all
men whose language he speaks, and of all into whose language
his own can be translated".[21] Emerson gave substantially the
same advice to every American, whether scholar or not, in his
essay "Self Reliance": "To believe your own thought, to believe that what is true for you in your private heart is true for
all men,—that is genius. Speak your latent conviction, and it
shall be the universal sense; for the inmost in due time becomes the outmost, and our first thought is rendered back to
us by the trumpets of the Last Judgment".[22] In this essay
Emerson again contrasts believing one's own thought with reliance on external authorities who look to the foreign past in
the manner of, say, Andrews Norton: "If therefore a man
claims to know and speak of God and carries you backward to
the phraseology of some old mouldered nation in another
country, in another world, believe him not. Is the acorn better than the oak which is its fulness and completion? Is the
parent better than the child into whom he has cast his rip-

ened being? Whence then this worship of the past? The centuries are conspirators against the sanity and authority of the
soul".[23]

This theme of "Self Reliance" was also sounded in the "Divinity School Address" of 1838, Emerson's most famous statement of his philosophy of religion and a work that cannot be
thoroughly understood without awareness of the Transcendentalists' attitude toward the Argument from Miracles.
With George Ripley, who had denied that miracles supplied
the *sole* evidence of the divinity of Christ and had indicated
pretty clearly that he thought better of internal evidence and
sentiment, Emerson was in close agreement. He insisted with
his predecessors who had emotionalized Locke's intuitive Reason where morals were concerned, that the essence of being
religious was to have an "intuition of the moral sentiment",
that this intuition was one of Reason, that "there is no doctrine of the Reason which will bear to be taught by the Understanding",[24] that the appeal to miracles was an appeal to
the Understanding, and therefore that such an appeal was
monstrous. Historical Christianity, because it was taught by the
Understanding, was brought down to a phenomenal level; and
therefore it concentrated on the less spiritual aspects of God
and on ritual. Historical Christianity had abandoned an interest in the Moral Law—the deliverance of the Reason—and
had sunk into formalism and traditionalism. No passage in
the "Divinity School Address" more clearly indicates Emerson's anti-historical orientation than the following: "It is still
true that tradition characterizes the preaching of this country;
that it comes out of the memory, and not out of the soul; that
it aims at what is usual, and not at what is necessary and eternal; that thus historical Christianity destroys the power of
preaching, by withdrawing it from the exploration of the
moral nature of man; where the sublime is, where are the resources of astonishment and power".[25] The historical church,
he argued, is the slave of historical fact in two senses: first of

all, the pulpit has been usurped by the formalist who worships past forms; and, secondly, this usurper delivers only those truths that come to him from his empirico-historical Understanding.[26] Therefore, the pulpit must be restored to Reason, which can perceive the moral and eternal through sentiment and which can free the pulpit from ritualism and narrow empiricism.

This attitude, which dominated Emerson's philosophy of science, education, and religion could hardly be kept out of his philosophy of law. In 1851 he spoke out eloquently against the Fugitive Slave Law, and from a philosophical point of view the most interesting thing about that essay is not the admirable passion with which Emerson attacked a political evil but the fact that he based his attack on an appeal to Natural Law. He told his audience: "A few months ago, in my dismay at hearing that the Higher Law was reckoned a good joke in the courts, I took pains to look into a few lawbooks. I had often heard that the Bible constituted a part of every technical law library, and that it was a principle in law that immoral laws are void. I found, accordingly, that the great jurists, Cicero, Grotius, Coke, Blackstone, Burlamaqui, Montesquieu, Vattel, Burke, Mackintosh, Jefferson, do all affirm this. I have no intention to recite these passages I had marked: —such citation indeed seems to be something cowardly (for no reasonable person needs a quotation from Blackstone to convince him that white cannot be legislated to be black), and shall content myself with reading a single passage. Blackstone admits the sovereignty 'antecedent to any positive precept, of the law of Nature,' among whose principles are, 'that we should live on, should hurt nobody, and should render unto every one his due,' etc. *No human laws are of any validity, if contrary to this.*' 'Nay, if any human law should allow or enjoin us to commit a crime' (his instance is murder), 'we are bound to transgress that human law; or else we must offend both the natural and divine' ".[27] Throughout this

1851 address on the Fugitive Slave Law and throughout an 1854 lecture on the same subject, Emerson spoke of the Natural Law as expressing a moral sentiment; and it was clear that he thought that the Natural Law was discerned by the Reason rather than the Understanding. Once again we find him appealing to the felt eternal truths of Reason in an effort to condemn a mere fact of the past. The Natural Law stands to positive law for him as the intuitions of moral sentiment stood to the positive, formal, phenomenal matters that he identified with historical Christianity.

Emerson's insistence that moral sentiment plays a part in the discernment of Natural Law may explain why, when he listed the advocates of the Higher Law in his attack on the Fugitive Slave Law, he did not mention Locke. In "The Transcendentalist" Emerson described Transcendentalism as a reply to "the skeptical philosophy of Locke", and in his *English Traits* he not only said that "the dull men will be Lockists" but also lamented that English genius had fallen low in the days of Locke, that after Bacon its "heights were followed by a meanness and a descent of the mind into lower levels; the loss of wings; no high speculation. Locke, to whom the meaning of ideas was unknown, became the type of philosophy, and his 'understanding' the measure, in all nations, of the English intellect".[28]

As we have seen, Emerson's disapproval of Locke was linked with Emerson's disapproval of the empirical Understanding, "that wrinkled calculator" which dwelt on the customary and the expedient; and with his attack on bookworms in their studies, on formalists in their pulpits, and on lawyers who never looked up at the Higher Law. It was also linked with his distaste for the urban civilization that was spreading over the garden paradise of his America. He identified the Reason with the country he loved and the Understanding with the city he usually despised. Urban civilization, he held—except when he was sentimental about his Boston clubs—is the home of convention, artifice, fact, the past, the senses, and trickery. "The city delights the Understanding", whereas "the country . . . is the school of Reason". The city, Emerson insisted, is the place of memory: "Go into the city— I am afraid there is no morning in Chestnut Street, it is full of rememberers, they shun each other's eyes, they are all wrinkled with memory of the tricks they have played, or mean to play, each other, of petty arts and aims all contracting and lowering their aspect and character". By contrast, Nature is the place of the Reason, the true, the good, and the hopeful. It is the home of the poet, who in the last analysis is one with the true scientist, the true scholar, the true religious man, the true lawyer—all of them being ministers of the Reason and opponents of slavery to the historical past. In his essay "The Transcendentalist" Emerson reported that the Transcendentalists "feel the disproportion between their faculties and the work offered them, and they prefer to ramble in the country and perish of ennui, to the degradation of such charities and ambitions as the city can propose to them". They incline "to live in the country rather than in the town". In his essay *Nature* Emerson also attacked the city as the home of the Lockeian Understanding. Nothing could have been more attractive to rural, democratic, romantic America, which listened intently to Emerson as he sang of the future, the eternal, and the necessary: "Hallelujah to the Reason Forevermore".[29]

Emerson's Philosophical Legacy

It is a remarkable tribute to Emerson that he should have been admired by virtually all of the American philosophers who followed him. Even the severely scientific Chauncey Wright honored him; and William James, George Santayana, and John Dewey all wrote appreciations of him at the turn of the twentieth century. As one might expect, they did not regard him as a technician but rather as an inspiration and a sage; and this was as much of a tribute to them as it was to Emerson, since it showed that even though post-Emersonian American philosophy was tough, logical, and professional, its major representatives continued to respect the pursuit of wisdom. They were also large enough in spirit to forget that while they were empiricists, pragmatists, or naturalists, Emerson represented a form of the absolute idealism against which they all were in revolt. To them Emerson seemed to be above the battle of the *isms;* a source of higher wisdom.

What wisdom? What gnomic truths did they think he had seen? Emerson was a man of many sides; and being no small mind, he was not frightened by the hobgoblin of consistency. Therefore James, Santayana, and Dewey—upon whose interpretations I concentrate because they were the major American philosophers who wrote most fully about Emerson—made selections from the many thoughts of Emerson and, as we might expect, usually selected those that were congenial to their own ways of thinking. James was an individualist, so his Emerson was an individualist. The poetic Santayana understandably said that Emerson's imagination was the source of Emerson's wisdom. John Dewey was a democrat who condemned class-society and class-philosophy, so *his* Emerson was above all a democrat who wished to erase class-distinctions. Every one of these features of Emerson's thought is closely linked with features we have already observed. Emerson the critic of custom and conformity naturally encouraged the self-reliant individual—and especially the self-reliant artist or scholar—to assert his rights against them; Emerson the romantic idealist was surely a man of imagination; and Emerson the critic of State Street commercialism might easily be viewed as the democratic critic of class-society. Let us turn now to the details of Emerson's compound legacy to James, Santayana, and Dewey, for such details will reveal a little more about Emerson as we leave his philosophical world and will give us an introductory glimpse into the one that emerged after his death in 1882.

James on Emerson. Emerson revealed his individualism, James said, by defending the "indefeasible right to be exactly what one is, provided one only be authentic"; [30] and more particularly by defending the right of the artist and the scholar to report truth without being restrained by social or political responsibility. In a passage that succinctly expressed his own social philosophy, James praised Emerson for believing that "the present man is the aboriginal reality, the Institution is derivative, and the past man is irrelevant and obliterate for present issues".[31] James' admiration for Emerson's individualism was so great that he played down the fact that Emerson defended Absolute Idealism, a philosophy that James condemned when it was advocated by the more militant Royce. Emerson's Oversoul, an American ancestor of Royce's Absolute, did not seem to offend James. He acknowledged that Emerson believed in a great "Cosmic Intellect", but the edge of Emerson's idealism was blunted for James because Emerson held the individualistic doctrine that "the only way to be true to our Maker is to be loyal to ourselves".[32] James was not troubled by Emerson's idealistic metaphysics because James thought that according to Emerson "the point of any pen can be an epitome of reality; the commonest person's act, if genuinely actuated, can lay hold on eternity". "This vision," said James, "is the head-spring of all [Emerson's] outpourings; and it is for this truth, given to no previous literary artist to express in such penetratingly persuasive tones, that posterity will reckon him a prophet, and, perhaps neglecting other pages, piously turn to those that convey this message. His life was one long conversation with the invisible divine, expressing itself through individuals and particulars:—'So nigh is grandeur to our dust, so near is God to man!'." [33]

When James praised Emerson for seeing that the common-est person's act can lay hold on eternity, he seized on some-thing that John Dewey also had in mind when he de-scribed Emerson as *the* philosopher of democracy. Both of these pragmatic admirers of Emerson were no doubt thinking of passages like the following famous one in which Emerson embraced the common: "The literature of the poor, the feel-ings of the child, the philosophy of the street, the meaning of household life, are the topics of the time. It is a great stride. It is a sign—is it not?—of new vigor when the extremities are made active, when currents of warm life run into the hands and the feet. I ask not for the great, the remote, the romantic; what is doing in Italy or Arabia; what is Greek art, or Prov-ençal minstrelsy; I embrace the common, I explore and sit at the feet of the familiar, the low. Give me insight into to-day, and you may have the antique and future worlds. What would we really know the meaning of? The meal in the firkin; the milk in the pan; the ballad in the street; the news of the boat; the glance of the eye; the form and the gait of the body;—show me the ultimate reason of these matters; show me the sublime presence of the highest spiritual cause lurk-ing, as always it does lurk, in these suburbs and extremities of nature; let me see every trifle bristling with the polarity that ranges it instantly on an eternal law; and the shop, the plough, and the ledger referred to the like cause by which light undulates and poets sing;—and the world lies no longer a dull miscellany and lumber-room, but has form and order; there is no trifle, there is no puzzle, but one design unites and animates the farthest pinnacle and the lowest trench".[34]

Yet consider Emerson's command: "Show me the sublime presence of the highest spiritual cause lurking, as always it does lurk, in these suburbs and extremities of nature". This is very close to the optimistic idealism that James often lam-pooned for not recognizing the existence of evil, but James in his discussion of Emerson did not take the opportunity to criticize the failings of Absolute Idealism. James did not try to refute Emerson's idealism by telling—as he does elsewhere [35]—macabre stories of evil in the American city's streets. Such rhetoric James reserved for an attack on Hegel's, Royce's, and Bradley's versions of the idealistic idea that the highest spiritual cause is always lurking everywhere—in the cities as well as in the suburbs of nature. The point is that Emerson communicated thoughts and feelings to James which more than compensated for Emerson's attachment to absolute idealism. And therefore James was content to honor Emerson for seeing the value of authenticity; for seeing that the present man is the aboriginal reality whereas the Institution is derivative and the past man irrelevant and obliterate for present issues; and for seeing that the meal in the firkin and the milk in the pan can be more important than Greek art or Provençal minstrelsy.

Santayana on Emerson. It is very likely that George Santayana did not accept that judgment of the value of Greek art and Provençal minstrelsy, but he greatly esteemed Emerson even though he did not mince any words about his limitations as a technical philosopher. "At bottom," Santayana said flatly, "he had no doctrine at all. The deeper he went and the more he tried to grapple with fundamental conceptions, the vaguer and more elusive they became in his hands. Did he know what he meant by Spirit or the 'Over-Soul'? Could he say what he understood by the terms, so constantly on his lips, Nature, Law, God, Benefit, or Beauty? He could not, and the consciousness of that incapacity was so lively within him that he never attempted to give articulation to his philosophy. His finer instinct kept him from doing that violence to his inspiration." [36]

Santayana located the source of Emerson's power in Emerson's imagination. Santayana observed that Emerson, as an idealist, was given to thinking that the normal categories of thought might well have been different, and that if they had been different, we would have had a different world before us. Unlike the German idealists, however, Emerson did not try to build a *system* on this subjectivistic premise; and therefore "philosophy for him was rather a moral energy flowering into sprightliness of thought than a body of serious and defensible doctrines".[37] And since he held that all categories of thought are relative and surrenderable, he was subject, Santayana remarked, to the temptations of mysticism: "We are made to believe that since the understanding is something human and conditioned, something which might have been different, as the senses might have been different, and which we may yet, so to speak, get behind—therefore the understanding ought to be abandoned. We long for higher faculties, neglecting those we have, we yearn for intuition, closing our eyes upon experience. We become mystical".[38]

Because Santayana stressed Emerson's imaginative power and his proneness to mysticism, and because he found nothing in Emerson that resembled a systematic doctrine, Santayana summed up Emerson in a passage that we shall refer to once again in a later chapter on Santayana himself: "Emerson . . . was not primarily a philosopher, but a Puritan mystic with a poetic fancy and a gift for observation and epigram, and he saw in the laws of Nature, idealized by his imagination, only a more intelligible form of the divinity he had always recognized and adored".[39] However, even though Santayana regarded Emerson's subjectivism as an example of his imaginative powers, Santayana did not approve of that subjectivism; indeed he condemned it in his famous essay on the genteel tradition. Yet, as the following passage shows, Santayana admired the effort of which Emerson's subjectivism was a part: "Imagination, indeed, is his single theme. As a preacher might under every text enforce the same lessons of the gospel, so Emerson traces in every sphere the same spiritual laws of experience—compensation, continuity, the self-expression of the Soul in the forms of Nature and of society, until she finally recognizes herself in her own work and sees its beneficence and beauty. His constant refrain is the omnipotence of imaginative thought; its power first to make the world, then to understand it, and finally to rise above it. All Nature is an embodiment of our native fancy, all history a drama in which the innate possibilities of the spirit are enacted and realized. While the conflict of life and the shocks of experience seem to bring us face to face with an alien and overwhelming power, reflection can humanize and rationalize that power by conceiving its laws; and with this recognition of the rationality of all things comes the sense of their beauty and order. The destruction which Nature seems to prepare for our special hopes is thus seen to be the victory of our impersonal interests. To awaken in us this spiritual insight, an elevation of mind which is at once an act of comprehension and of worship, to substitute it for lower passions and more servile forms of intelligence—that is Emerson's constant effort. All his resources of illustration, observation, and rhetoric are used to deepen and clarify this sort of wisdom".[40]

Dewey on Emerson. Of the three distinguished philosophical commentators we have been discussing, only Dewey rejected the idea that Emerson was primarily a poet. Dewey thought this was far too condescending a view of the great man.[41] Always the opponent of sharp distinctions, Dewey refused to "make hard and fast lines between philosopher and poet".[42] He also refused to describe Emerson as a non-logical "recorder of brilliant insights and abrupt aphorisms", and added that those who viewed him in this way simply showed their "own incapacity to follow a logic that is finely wrought".[43] What, then, was Emerson's contribution to philosophy according to Dewey? First of all, he said, Emerson "takes the distinctions and classifications which to most philosophers are true in and of and because of their systems, and makes them true of life, of the common experience of the everyday man".[44] We get some notion of what Dewey had in mind when we see how he interpreted Emerson's idealistic idea that "we lie in the lap of immense intelligence which makes us organs of its activity and receivers of its truth". According to Dewey, this idea is not "an academic toy nor even a gleam of poetry, but a literal report of the experience of the hour as that is enriched and reinforced for the individual through the tale of history, the appliance of science, the gossip of conversation and the exchange of commerce".[45] Dewey construed Emerson's idealistic metaphysics as merely asserting that society is the scene of human communication, an observation which he repeated at the end of his *Public and Its Problems* (1927).

The second and more important contribution of Dewey's Emerson was the one that led Dewey to call him *the* philosopher of democracy. Dewey announced that "against creed and system, convention and institution, Emerson stands for restoring to the common man that which in the name of religion, of philosophy, of art and of morality, has been embezzled from the common store and appropriated to sectarian and class use".[46] For Dewey this was the highest praise, since it expressed a fundamental principle of Dewey's own approach to the history of philosophy and to the problems of social philosophy.

It is obvious that the interpretations of Emerson offered by James, Santayana, and Dewey confirm the familiar judgment that he was not an important systematic philosopher—if that judgment needs confirmation from such authority. Even Dewey, who at the beginning of his address on Emerson referred to a finely wrought logic in Emerson's thought that only gifted interpreters could discern, concluded his address as follows: "One may without presumption believe that even if Emerson has no system, none the less he is the prophet and herald of any system which democracy may henceforth construct and hold by, and that when democracy has articulated itself, it will have no difficulty in finding itself already proposed in Emerson".[47] Seer, artist, prophet, herald—whichever title is best bestowed on Emerson, it is perfectly clear that Matthew Arnold was right in saying that Emerson was not a Plato, an Aristotle, or a Kant. In a much-quoted phrase, Arnold called him "the friend and aider of those who would live in the spirit".[48] Yet high as this praise was meant to be, it did not delineate Emerson's position on the intellectual globe with enough accuracy. Emerson was less than Plato and more than a friend of those who would live in the spirit. As I have already said, it was the young Emerson who staked out the mature Emerson's field of most successful activity when the young Emerson distinguished between moral "theorists who have analyzed" and "sages who have recommended and applied" the science of morals. As a sage who recommended and applied that science, Emerson was—as we have seen from some of his writings and from the comments on them by philosophical admirers—a moving critic of retrospection, of dead morality, and of religious formalism, as well as an eloquent advocate of individualism, imagination, and democracy. Readers who are not primarily concerned with Emerson the philosopher may find other virtues in him but those I have mentioned are enough to explain the honor in which he came to be held by his broad-minded successors in American philosophy, even those who could not conscientiously put him in the same class with Plato, Aristotle, and Kant.

6 · Chauncey Wright: Empiricist Philosopher of Evolutionary Science

By 1876 Transcendentalism was a pattern of thought that was old enough to be the subject of a full-length historical work. A century after Independence and forty years after the appearance of Emerson's *Nature*, Octavius Brooks Frothingham published a sympathetic study of this intellectual movement whose official birth has often been identified with the appearance of Emerson's first book. Though still alive in 1876, Emerson had begun to lose his intellectual grip; and this probably caused Frothingham to remark lugubriously on the task he set himself: "In a little while it will be difficult to do it at all; for the disciples, one by one, are falling asleep; the literary remains are becoming few and scarce; the materials are disappearing beneath the rapid accumulations of thought; the new order is thrusting the old into the background".[1] The new order in the English-speaking world was dominated in great measure by Herbert Spencer and John Stuart Mill; and Frothingham rightly saw it as a revival of what he called the "Sensational" philosophy, a modernized version of the empiricism against which the Transcendentalists had rebelled. Natural science had put new weapons into the hands of the younger empiricists. Their views, Frothingham remarked, had been lent countenance by investigations in chemistry, biology, physiology, and psychology; and therefore they could strike more effectively against the philosophy which the Transcendentalists had favored in their struggle with the older empiricists and utilitarians. Among the new empiricists who by 1876 had helped thrust Transcendentalism into the background, there was an American of no great fame but one of considerable intellectual power, Chauncey Wright. He was born in 1830 in Northampton, he was graduated from Harvard College in 1852, and he died in Cambridge in 1875 without fulfilling the promise that many saw in him. He produced no large philosophical book but he wrote a number of articles and reviews, most of which were brought together in 1877 by his friend Charles Eliot Norton in a volume called *Philosophical Discussions*. Another good friend, the distinguished Harvard lawyer James Bradley Thayer, published in 1878 a privately printed volume entitled *The Letters of Chauncey Wright*.

These two volumes, which contain virtually everything of importance written by Wright, are dominated by views that one might have expected in an admirer of John Stuart Mill and Charles Darwin. Wright called himself an empiricist, a positivist, and a utilitarian; and therefore he did not himself add any strikingly new "ism" to the literature of Western philosophy. Like Edwards—who echoed Locke—and Emerson —who often echoed echoes of Kant—Wright was a representative of a foreign philosophical power; but, unlike his American predecessors, Wright attained no general fame for a variety of reasons. He was not a gifted writer and he was not the spokesman of a powerful religious tendency nor of a popular literary movement; and although he was one of the first American followers of Darwin and much respected by the master himself, Wright's inability to bark loudly made it impossible for him to become one of Darwin's bulldogs along with Huxley. Wright's firm grasp of the theory of natural selection, his philosophical acuteness, and his intellectual honesty made it impossible for him to inflate evolutionary biology into a world-view after the fashion of Herbert Spencer. Unlike Spencer's slavish American follower, John Fiske, Wright could not jump on the bandwagon of cosmic evolution.[2] Besides, Wright was a depressive who at times drank too much,[3] so everything seems to have conspired to keep him from becoming a prolific writer who could call a great deal of attention to himself and to the ideas he represented. Yet his philosophical bite was penetrating even if his bark was not loud; and if one reads him just after reading the Calvinists and the Transcendentalists, one sees that one is at last past the age of the quill, the wig, and the minister's cloth in philosophy. Twenty-seven years younger than Emerson, Wright was one of the first Americans to sound something like a twentieth-century philosopher, one of the first to abandon the parson's posture.[4] He was trained in mathematics, physics, and biology; and he had full control of the ideas in the *Origin of Species* and Mill's *System of Logic*. As the first American modern, Wright helped prepare the way for the pragmatism of his younger Cambridge contemporaries, Charles Peirce and William James. Although he is sometimes thought of as an early pragmatist, it is more accurate to think of him as an empiricist way-paver for pragmatism, one who did not subscribe to it but who encouraged it by his opposition to Transcendentalism, by fostering philosophical respect for scientific method, and by his wholehearted acceptance of Darwin's theory of natural selection.[5]

Wright's conversion to philosophical empiricism and his acceptance of Darwin's evolutionary biology were the two most important facts in his intellectual history. In coming to these views he recapitulated a good part of the history of early nineteenth-century thought. In college Emerson was his favorite author; and soon after leaving college in 1852 he took eagerly

to Francis Bacon, the British empiricist most admired by
Emerson and by Coleridge. After Bacon, Sir William Hamilton became Wright's intellectual hero, to be followed by Mill
and Darwin under the impact of the *Origin of Species* (1859)
and Mill's *Examination of Sir William Hamilton's Philosophy* (1865).[6] While at Harvard, Wright had been taught by
James Walker, who was in the habit of setting his students as
a subject for a "forensic" the question whether the faculties of
men and brutes differ in kind or degree. This question was
often discussed by Walker's Transcendentalist friends under
the influence of Coleridge; and like Coleridge they [7] answered
it by saying that the difference was one of kind, that man has
the faculty of Reason which raises him sharply above the
brutes. In a paper for Walker,[8] Wright argued that the difference was one of degree; and this early gradualism may have
prepared him not only for Darwin's biological message but
also for Mill's epistemology. Among all the empiricists Mill
was distinguished by his view that so-called necessary truths
are not epistemologically different in kind from contingent
truths, and therefore he did not need to postulate a Coleridgian Reason over and above the empirical Understanding. For Mill, neither the truths of mathematics nor those of
morals are sharply distinguished from the truths of physical
or social science, since he held that in the last analysis they
all rest on experience.

The "experiential philosophy" was adopted by Wright soon
after the appearance of Mill's *Examination of Sir William
Hamilton's Philosophy*. "Truths independent of all experience are not known to exist," said Wright, "unless we exclude
from what we mean by 'experience' that experience which we
have in learning the meanings of words and in agreeing to
definitions and the conventions of language, on the ground
that they depend solely, or may be considered as depending
solely, on a lexical authority, from which a kind of necessity
proceeds, independent of reality in the relations and connec-

tions of the facts denoted by the words." [9] Here Wright was obviously following Mill, who distinguished between what he called merely verbal propositions, like "All men are animals", which are essential predications because true by definition, and what he called the real propositions of physics, logic, and mathematics. All real propositions, like Newton's Law of Gravitation, the law of excluded middle, and "$7+5=12$", are in Mill's view supported by experience of nature, whereas he sometimes suggests that essential predications are supported by our experience of how men use words. Unlike the logical positivists of the twentieth century, however, he does not treat logic and mathematics as depending solely on definitions or "lexical authority". That Wright agreed with him on this point is evident from numerous passages in Wright's work. Wright subscribed to what he called Mill's far-reaching empiricism, according to which "particular experiences" are the tests "of all axioms logical or mathematical".[10] By the time Wright added his Millian empiricism to his Darwinian evolutionism, he came to play a formidable, though not widely heralded, role as a philosopher of science. Wright's main concerns were to defend science against the misinterpretations of theologians and cosmologists, to defend an empiricist theory of knowledge, to advance a "psychozoological" theory, as he called it, of the evolution of human rationality, and to assess the status of metaphysics and theology during the new order that dominated philosophy after the Civil War.

Against the Misinterpretation of Science

In Wright's own lifetime the theory of natural selection was the great example of current scientific achievement; and Wright, who was converted to it soon after reading the *Origin of Species,* was moved to defend the great work against misunderstandings that originated mainly among philosophers and theologians. He was so zealous in his defense that Darwin once wrote to him after reading his article "The Genesis of Species": [11] "I have hardly ever in my life received an article which has given me so much satisfaction. . . . I agree to almost every thing which you say. Your memory must be wonderfully accurate, for you know my works as well as I do myself, and your power of grasping other men's thoughts is something quite surprising".[12] Wright could not say the same of St. George Mivart, the Jesuit against whose misinterpretations of Darwin he relentlessly fired away in the article that Darwin understandably admired. Chief among Mivart's misunderstandings was his notion that the heritable variations which Darwin called "accidental", and which are today usually called "random", were thought by Darwin to be uncaused. Here Wright had an opportunity to reveal his power as a sort of philosophical lawyer for scientists not trained in metaphysics. He said of his client, "Mr. Darwin has undoubtedly erred in this respect. He has not in his works repeated with sufficient frequency his faith in the universality of the law of causation, in the phenomena of general physiology or theoretical biology, as well as in all the rest of physical nature. He has not said often enough, it would appear, that in referring any effect to 'accident,' he only means that its causes are like particular phases of the weather, or like innumerable phenomena in the concrete course of nature generally, which are quite beyond the power of finite minds to anticipate or to account for in detail, though none the less really determinate or due to regular causes".[13]

Wright accepted on Millian grounds a belief in the principle of universal causation like that accepted by Jonathan Edwards, though he never referred to Edwards on these matters. In fact, the most important thing that Wright ever said about accidental events, whether Darwinian variations or not— namely, that they "are relative to our knowledge of causes; that the same event, like the eclipse of the sun, might be an accident to one mind, and an anticipated event to another"—

may be found in the writings of the philosopher who
preached in Northampton a century before Wright was born
there.[14] Like Edwards, Wright thought that choices are subject to the principle of universal causation, and here once
again he used a favorite analogy, arguing that choices may,
like the weather, be caused even though it is practically impossible to know their causes and to predict them with certainty.[15] Wright also believed, as Edwards had, that moral
judgment does not presuppose the causelessness of our volitions,[16] so that he was in the tradition of British empiricism
on this subject as he was on most other subjects of fundamental philosophical import. Unlike other empiricists, however,
Wright spoke with authority about the content of physics and
biology, so that he could not be dismissed by scientists or rationalists as a Lord Chancellor writing about science—as
Bacon was—nor as a mere historian or an economist—as
Hume and Mill were respectively. One of Wright's main ser-
vices to the empiricist tradition was connected with his defense of scientific theories that had been formulated, like Darwin's, with the help of terms like "accidental". Given its long
philosophical history, such a term could easily be jumped on
and misconstrued by metaphysically tendentious readers, but
Wright could supply an empiricist answer to them, much to
the relief of Darwin, who complimented him on his power to
analyze words thoroughly.[17]

This power of analysis not only helped Wright to clear up
some confusions about accidental variations but also led him
to make some interesting remarks on the relationship between
the term "real species" as used by pre-Darwinian biologists
and the term "real kinds" as used by logicians like Mill.[18]
Wright pointed out that when some biologists spoke of the
reality of species they had in mind what followers of Linnaeus
called the fixity of species. In other words, they held that "all
the individuals propagated from one stock have certain distinguishing characters in common, which never vary, and which

have remained the same since the creation of each species",[19] whereas Darwin denied that species were fixed in this sense. For Darwin the so-called fixed species, Wright said, are fixed only as the fixed stars are fixed—which is to say that they change very slowly. The horse descended from *Eohippus* [20] by insensible steps of gradation over a very long time, and therefore the species *Eohippus* could not have been fixed or real in the Linnaean sense. Nevertheless, a Darwinian could accept the logical distinction between classes which are real kinds—like the class of men, the class of horses, and the class of oaks —and classes which are not real kinds, like the class of things that are an inch in length. Real kinds, Wright said under the influence of Mill, are classes of objects which necessarily agree with each other in many respects, as men do with each other because there are laws of nature that connect manhood with mortality, bipedality, and so on. By contrast, things that are one inch long do not of scientific necessity agree in many other respects. Thus, while all members of the species *Eohippus* were similar to each other in many respects and in that sense constituted a real kind for certain logicians, *Eohippus* was not a real or fixed species in the biologist's sense because it is not true to say that all individuals propagated from that stock never varied from the members of *Eohippus*.

After pointing this out, Wright said something about the use of the word "real" that may serve as a good example of his power of analysis. He says that in ordinary language we use two "marks" or "tests" of reality as applied to a concrete physical object. One he calls breadth of relationship and the other is fixedness in time. If I can see, hear, touch, smell, taste an object, and another person can, "then I know that the object is real, and not a mere hallucination or invention of my fantasy; though it may disappear immediately afterwards in an unexplained manner, or be removed by some unknown but supposable agency".[21] Here the test is breadth of relationship to my experience and sources of knowledge. On the other hand, "I may only *see* the object, and consult no other eyes than my own; but seeing it often, day after day, in the same place, I shall judge it to be a real object, provided its existence is conformable to the general possibilities of experience, or to the test of 'breadth.' Here the test of reality is 'fixity' or continuance in time".[22] Having made this distinction between two tests of reality in talk about physical objects, Wright now transfers it to talk about species and asserts that a species will be said to be real by the test of breadth if the individuals that are members of it are alike in an indefinitely large number of respects. By this test, which is the test employed by the logicians, he says, all natural species are real kinds. But then Wright remarks: "That they are real in the other sense, or fixed in time absolutely in respect to any of the particulars of their resemblance, whether these are essential (that is, useful for discrimination and classification) or are not, is far from being the axiom it has seemed to be. It is, on the contrary, highly improbable that they are so, though this is tacitly assumed . . . in criticisms of the theory of natural selection".[23] Wright's point was that while all biological species are real by the test of breadth which is employed by the logician when he is singling out natural kinds, none of them may be real by the test of fixity precisely because one real or natural kind may in time evolve into another. There are several difficult questions that may be raised about this analysis but it certainly shows more depth than one can find in most biologico-philosophical discussions of 1872, and it reveals Wright in a typical stance —using the lessons of works like Mill's *Logic* to defend the *Origin of Species* against misunderstandings like Mivart's, which were born of philosophical confusion and theological prejudice.

Mivart was not Wright's only victim in his campaign to keep science from being abused. Whereas he thought that Mivart misinterpreted Darwin in a way that blocked the progress of biology, he thought that Herbert Spencer was given to misreading science in a way that blocked the progress of philosophy. In trying to create a synthetic philosophy which would serve as a sort of super-science, Spencer proposed a law of cosmic evolution which would preside over lesser laws in physics, embryology, and sociology, much as Newton's law presided over physics and astronomy. Wright argued that Spencer had not succeeded because, for one thing, his law was too vague and, for another, he gave the appearance of gaining inductive support from the special sciences only by misconstruing their terms. Spencer, Wright insisted, transferred those terms from their original contexts in which they were clear, to others in which they were not. This led Wright to attack Spencer in 1865 with arguments that have become very familiar to twentieth-century philosophers and biologists who may never have heard of Wright. He pointed first of all to the obscurity of Spencer's concept of evolution, which was allegedly illustrated not only in biology but throughout the universe.[24] Then, speaking of Spencer's misuse of physics, Wright made an observation which has become standard in more recent discussions of the philosophy of science: "Terms which the real physicist knows how to use as the terms of mathematical formulas, and which were never even suspected of any heterodox tendencies, terms which have been of inestimable service both in formulating and finding out the secrets of nature, are appropriated by Mr. Spencer to the future elaboration of his vague definitions, and to the abstract description of as much in real nature as they may happen to apply to". Later Wright added: "Out of mathematical formulas these terms lose their definiteness and their utility. They become corrupting and misleading ideas".[25] Wright anticipated one of the slogans of twentieth-century philosophers of science when he said: "Mr. Spencer regards the ultimate ideas of science as unknowable; and in a sense the meanings of the abstractest terms are unknowable, that is, are not referable to any notions more abstract, nor susceptible of sensuous apprehension or representation as such. But the way to know them is to use them in mathematical formulas to express precisely what we do know".[26] Here Wright was probably pointing to the fact that a physical term like "mass" may not be definable in terms of something more fundamental, and may not be a sensory word like "blue" or "hard", but nevertheless we understand it insofar as it appears in formulae which express truths that we know and use in scientific inquiry.

Whereas Mivart misunderstood Darwin's biology and Spencer misused physics, Archdeacon Paley and other devotees of the Argument from Design exaggerated the power of anatomy to support the claims of theology. So here was another form of scientific waywardness for Wright to attack. Spencer sought to derive scientific laws from his very general law of cosmic evolution, but the natural theologians unsuccessfully sought to prove the existence of God by pseudo-inductive arguments. Wright pointed out that natural theologians began their arguments with the alleged fact that nature exhibits remarkable adaptations of means to ends—for example, that the eyebrow is a case of such adaptation because it keeps us from being blinded by sweat—and then moved inductively, or claimed they did, to the conclusion that nature must have been created by a designing God. Their argument, they held, was similar to one in which we move from the fact that a watch is an excellent means for telling time to the conclusion that it must have been created by a designing watchmaker. Wright argued, however, that the statement that the eyebrow is a *means* of protecting the eye from sweat is not, as construed by the natural theologian, a purely scientific statement. A biologist may observe that the eyebrow *causes* the sweat to be diverted, but he must go beyond the facts of biology to establish that the eyebrow is a means that is used by God to achieve an end. Furthermore, the assertion that it is a means to an end—the alleged premise of the natural theologian's allegedly inductive argument—virtually assumes what is to be shown by induction, since to say that something is a means to an end is to say in part that it was designed. Wright concluded that natural theology was not the positive science that it claimed to be, just as Spencer's cosmic philosophy was not.

In Defense of Empiricism

In addition to defending science from abuse and attacking pseudo-science, Wright resisted certain theories about the nature of scientific knowledge. Here he used Millian and Comteian doctrines against Transcendentalists who, as he thought, did not understand the logic of scientific inquiry. Wright's critiques of Transcendentalist pronouncements on science might well have been stimulated by Emerson's reflections on this subject, for the sage of Concord had maintained that the truth of Newton's theory was established by Reason, or what Coleridge called "the power of universal and necessary convictions, the source and substance of truths above sense". Transcendentalists maintained that Reason may be used to *verify* scientific theories; and therefore Wright warned the positivists of his day not to identify scientific method merely with the verification of theories, since that was not enough to distinguish their view from the view of Coleridge and Emerson.[27] He urged the positivists to make perfectly clear that it was verification *by the senses* that counted in science, and to say that "inasmuch as mankind are nearly unanimous about the testimony and trustworthiness of their senses, but are divided about the validity of all other kinds of authority, which they in a word call the reason, or internal sense, therefore verification by the senses produces absolute conviction, while verification by the reason settles nothing".[28] This appeal to verification by the external senses Wright characterized as "objective method" by contrast to what he called the "subjective method" of verification by the Transcendentalists' Reason, or internal sense.

In criticizing the subjective method, Wright demonstrated the modernity of his empiricism by arguing that those who thought that the Transcendentalists' Reason played a part in science failed to see that the origin of a scientific theory is irrelevant to its value. "Whatever be the origin of the theories of science", Wright reminded the partisans of subjective method, "whether from a systematic examination of empirical facts by conscious induction, or from the natural biases of the mind, the so-called intuitions of reason, . . . the *value* of these theories can only be tested, say the positivists, by an appeal to sensible experience, by deductions from them of consequences which we can confirm by the undoubted testimony of the senses".[29] By emphasizing that a scientific theory is evaluated, that is to say, tested, by presenting sensory evidence for it and not by tracing its origin, Wright disassociated himself from the geneticism of Locke's preoccupation with the *sources* of ideas, and from the Transcendentalists' preoccupation with finding transempirical *avenues* to truth. How we got our scientific ideas was for Wright irrelevant. The important thing was whether they were confirmed by sensory experience. Wright's use of this argument against the Transcendentalists was ironic, for he was in effect turning against them their own notion that concentration on past history—in this case the past history of a scientific theory—is a serious error when the value of the theory is at stake.

The Transcendentalists were not the only philosophers charged by Wright with a failure to look forward in the manner of scientists, and with a failure to see that scientific theories are to be tested by their predictive value. He leveled a similar charge against Spencer, whose lack of first-hand acquaintance with science he deplored, and he urged all philosophers of science to learn "how to make knowledge profitable to the ascertainment of new truths" so that they could see the central role of such ascertainment.[30] Wright explained that "by new truths must be understood such as are not implied in what we already know, or educible from what is patent to common observation. However skillfully the philospher may apply his analytical processes to the abstraction of the truths involved in patent facts, the utility of his results will depend not so much on their value and extent as mere abstractions, as on their capacity to enlarge our experience by bringing to notice residual phenomena, and making us observe what we have entirely overlooked, or search out what has eluded our observation. Such is the character of the principles of modern natural philosophy, both mathematical and physical. They are rather the eyes with which nature is seen, than the elements and constituents of the objects discovered. It was in a clear apprehension of this value in the principles of mathematical and experimental science, that the excellence of Newton's genius consisted; and it is this value which the Positive Philosophy most prizes. But this is not the value which we find in Mr. Spencer's speculations".[31] Spencer's effort to formulate a law of cosmic evolution was, Wright continued, not only faulty but pernicious and misleading because "nothing justifies the development of abstract principles in science but their utility in enlarging our concrete knowledge of nature. The ideas on which mathematical Mechanics and the Calculus are founded, the morphological ideas of Natural History, and the theories of Chemistry are such working ideas,—finders, not merely summaries of truth".[32] This passage, although sometimes cited as an illustration of Wright's pragmatism or as an anticipation of pragmatism, is rather an expression of his sympathy with empiricism and what he called the Positive Philosophy, and of his antipathy to the thought of Herbert Spencer. He was not defending what Peirce called a pragmatic theory of meaning, nor what James called a pragmatic theory of truth—as we shall see more clearly when we come to discuss them. He was merely pointing out that a scientific theory is predictive in character, that it goes beyond the evidence actually in hand; and he was insisting with Mill that the principles of mechanics—a natural science—and the calculus—a part of pure mathematics—are accepted because of their capacity to predict experience.[33] By contrast, Herbert Spencer regarded the "primordial truth" from which he hoped to deduce all of science—the law of persistence of force, as he called it, or the principle of conservation of energy as it is known today—in a decidedly non-empirical way.[34] Spencer held that the test of his primordial truth was the fact that "its opposite was inconceivable"; and when his American disciple, John Fiske, enthusiastically embraced this test of truth, Fiske showed how strong a grip the rationalistic Lockeian conception of science continued to have on the American mind. When Fiske leapt to the defense of Spencer against John Stuart Mill's criticism of Spencer's views on this subject, Fiske revealed his attachment to the idea that strict science is a deductive system the axioms of which are seen to be true independently of the kind of empirical evidence which Darwin was bent on collecting in support of the theory of natural selection. By contrast to Darwin's theory, Spencer's cosmic theory—the basic proposition of his synthetic or, as Fiske preferred to call it, cosmic philosophy—was superscientific: Spencer and Fiske supposed it to be fundamentally different in kind from the truths of the special sciences.[35]

This difference in kind led Spencer and Fiske to think that one who served as the custodian of a cosmic truth was an especially regal or pontifical intellectual figure. This meant that he was in a very important respect superior not only to scientists like Darwin but also to methodologists of science like Wright. Fiske made perfectly clear that he regarded Wright as inferior because he was at most a methodologist of science;[36] and probably it was this attitude of Fiske which led William James to hope that Fiske would not be assigned the task of writing an introduction to the volume which appeared as Wright's *Philosophical Discussions*.[37] Wright's antipathy to the idea that Spencerian cosmologists had privileged access to primordial truth was not unconnected with his antipathy to the intuitionism of the Transcendentalists. He was therefore put in the position of attacking two dominant philosophical positions of Anglo-American philosophy in the early nineteenth century. Partly for this reason, he had to wait to receive his due posthumously from those who had more sympathy with his philosophy of science than was common in the heydays of Emerson and Spencer. For the same reason, Wright was unknown to thousands of lay readers who thought the philosophy of science was what Fiske wrote about in the lively but unoriginal pages of his *Outlines of Cosmic Philosophy*.

Science, Metaphysics, Theology, and Poetry

As we have seen, the two main components of Wright's thought—his Darwinian biology and his empiricist or positivist philosophy of science—were often combined for negative, polemical purposes; but in one of his longest essays, his "Evolution of Self-Consciousness",[38] he showed that he was more than an empiricist lawyer for Darwin and more than a positivist policeman on the lookout for hasty and obscure generalizers and logically wayward Transcendentalists. This was a sixty-eight-page essay on the evolution of man's rationality, that is to say, man's capacity to engage in science with the awareness that he is doing so. This capacity distinguishes him from the most intelligent of the lower animals and even, Wright ventured, from "the lowest of the human race". Wright was here discussing the evolution of logic, as it were, rather than the logic of evolution and was working mainly in what he called "psychozoology". His essay also illustrates Wright's propensity to combine the lessons of Darwin and Mill, for it is in great measure a study of how scientific thinking, as conceived by Mill, evolved according to a Darwinian pattern.

Wright's Darwinian interest in the evolution and logic of

scientific method was paralleled by an interest in the motives that led men to engage in unscientific speculation. The latter was probably stimulated by his reading in Comte. Although Wright diverged sharply from Transcendentalism, he always maintained an interest in the origin and function of metaphysics and theology. For him they represented intellectual activities that could not be brushed aside as worthless, even by one who had committed himself wholeheartedly to the more scientific pursuits of psychozoology and critical epistemology. Therefore, he thought much about how to draw a line of demarcation between his own main interests and those of metaphysicians and theologians. The history of Wright's thinking on this matter began with the idea that whereas science describes nature, transcendental metaphysics deals with the psychological origin and logical nature of scientific belief, and religious faith is exercised when we adopt non-scientific beliefs about the creation of the universe as a whole.[39] Therefore Wright held that science is never in conflict with the other two; and he maintained this to the end of his life. He emphasized that whereas the motive for science is objective curiosity about the ways of nature, the motive for both metaphysics and religion is subjective and emotional. Our desire to know about nature underlies scientific inquiry, whereas certain of our feelings and desires prompt us to engage in metaphysics and theology. Ultimately, this line of argument led him to the conclusion—more popular in the twentieth century than in his day—that the relationship between metaphysico-religious discourse and science is analogous to the relationship between poetry and science.

Before coming under the influence of Mill, Wright spoke praisingly of Sir William Hamilton's efforts to "secure a ground for belief in truths which are inconceivable, or truths of which the terms cannot be united in a judgment either by proofs from what is really known or by intuition".[40] Hamilton maintained that the proposition that the whole of space is limited is inconceivable because our idea of space is such that we must think of every space as contained within another space and hence as unlimited. But then, Hamilton added, we cannot conceive the contradictory of that proposition, viz., that space has no limit, because when we characterize space in any way, we must regard it as limited insofar as we put it under some wider concept. We need not tarry over the cogency of Hamilton's analysis of these two propositions because that is not crucial; but we must observe that Hamilton held, with the approval of the pre-Millian Wright, that in spite of the fact that both of these propositions are inconceivable, one of them must be true because a logical principle says so. As soon as Hamilton reached the logical claim "It is true that space is limited or not limited", Hamilton appears to have supposed that he had arrived at a truth which is inconceivable because it is an alternation of two contradictory propositions which are inconceivable.[41] Therefore, Wright said in sympathetic summary of Hamilton's view, "we have the feeling that there is truth beyond the power of knowledge, or that 'the domain of our knowledge is not co-extensive with the horizon of our faith;' for a principle of truth—the principle of non-contradiction—is seen to extend where sense and imagination and our powers of conception cannot follow".[42] In this way Hamilton tried to show that a principle of logic could not be regarded as a generalization from experience, and with this Wright seemed to have some sympathy in 1865. In trying to reason about inconceivable propositions—to conclude, for example, that one of a pair of them must be true—Hamilton was trying, Wright said, to "bring the objects of religious feeling, partially at least, within the scope of our thoughts".[43] "Such," Wright said, "are the motives for metaphysical philosophy, and such indeed are the only grounds for metaphysics. Philosophy converts practical reasons or final causes into theoretical reasons, and postulates a faculty where there is only a feeling. But after all, that which the Best in us most prizes is not so much the service of Philosophy as that for which this service is undertaken." [44] Even if metaphysics should fail to arrive at truth, Wright argued, there is a certain dignity and absolute worth in the pursuit itself because it involves an "exercise of powers which, though they should fail of their end, are regarded as the noblest and the most distinctive of the tendencies native to the human mind".[45]

In 1865 Wright was evidently willing to encourage philosophers to seek metaphysical truth and knowledge in this quixotic manner, but by 1866—probably after reading Mill's *Hamilton*—he spoke of Hamilton's "somewhat sentimental view of the value of metaphysical studies".[46] From then on he seems to have begun a retreat from the idea that transcendental metaphysics could be defended as a cognitive enterprise and to have adopted the view that it was akin to poetry. In "The Evolution of Self-Consciousness", published in 1873, Wright examined Hamilton's ontology and metaphysics from an evolutionary point of view and concluded that "the languages employed by philosophers are . . . lessons in ontology, and have, in their grammatical structures, implied conceptions and beliefs common to the philosopher and to the barbarian inventors of language".[47] It must be noted that Wright, like others involved in this discussion at the time, defined ontology as the science of the supernatural or the non-phenomenal. With this definition in mind, he singled out for special attack Hamilton as a philosopher whose "ontological faith" or "ontological feeling or passion" was "a survival of the barbarian's feelings and notions of phenomena as the outward show of hidden powers and things".[48] The barbarian, according to Wright, did not distinguish clearly between persons and things since he thought of heavenly bodies as personal and of fire as an animal or a spirit. Therefore the barbarian thought of the phenomenal or observable qualities of a planet as manifestations of its hidden personality; and for

him, an abstract name like "redness" names a power within a
thing that makes it red. Unfortunately, Wright lamented, the
most advanced metaphysicians of his time had inherited such
barbaric beliefs or a tendency to them. Sir William Hamilton's belief in the existence of hidden metaphysical substrata,
both material and mental, was a survival of such barbarism;
and so was the tendency of some metaphysicians to ask why an
ultimate law of nature holds, since they aim to show that the
question cannot be answered and that all science rests on mystery. They ask the question "from the feelings that in the barbarian or the child forbid or check inquiry"; [49] and these feelings, according to Wright, should not be honored. He grants
that "the feelings of loyalty and reverence, instinctive in our
natures, and of the utmost value in the history of our race, as
the mediums of cooperation, discipline, and instruction, are
instincts more powerful in some minds than in others, and,
like all instincts, demand their proper satisfaction. From the
will, or our active powers, they demand devotion; from the intellect, submission to authority and mystery".[50] So much did
the Wright of 1873 concede to the Hamiltonian Wright; but
then, in a manner much less concessive to obscurantism, he
warned that feelings of loyalty and reverence "like all instincts . . . may demand too much; too much for their proper
satisfaction, and even for their most energetic and useful service to the race, or to the individual man".[51] Wright would
therefore not invent occult powers or noumena in deference
to these feelings and would not feign hypotheses in order to
satisfy the ontological passion. He granted that mystery still
had its uses as an ally of inquisitiveness and that devotion
could be useful in what he called its active forms. But metaphysics, he said, fosters the sentiments of mystery and devotion in their passive and attitudinal forms. "These attitudes,
which are symbolized in the forms of religious worship, were
no doubt needed to fix the attention of the barbarian, as they

are still required to fix the attention of the child upon serious contemplations and purposes"; but they are no longer useful in the service of the race.[52]

By 1873, then, Wright no longer defended transcendental metaphysics as a cognitive enterprise and argued that the relationship between science and metaphysics was *analogous*—I emphasize the word—to that between science and poetry, because the latter pair also represented a contrast that did not involve conflict: "A contrast of tendencies analogous to [the contrast between science and metaphysics], which involves, however, no necessary conflict, is shown in the opposition of science and poetry; the one contemplating in understanding and in fixed positive beliefs the phenomena which the other contemplates through firmly established and instinctive tendencies, and through interests, which for want of a better name to note their motive power, or influence in the will, are also sometimes called beliefs".[53] A whole philosophy underlay Wright's remark that the instinctive tendencies and interests through which poetry contemplates phenomena are called "beliefs" *for want of a better name.* He therefore advised his reader to lay aside the word "belief" because it is ambiguous and to recognize that *so-called* poetic beliefs—"convictions of half-truths, or intimations of truth, coupled with deep feeling, and impressed by the rhythms and alliterations of words, are obviously different from those connections which logic and evidence are calculated to establish in the mind".[54] Poetry, Wright thought, expressed such convictions and intimations, whereas science established connections by the use of logic and evidence. The poet, he went on to say, is the descendant of the noble, pre-scientific savage; his "productions are . . . , in part, reproductions, refined or combined in the attractive forms of art, of what was felt and thought before language and science existed; or they are restorations of language to a primeval use, and to periods in the history of his race in which his progenitors uttered their feelings, as of gallantry, defiance, joy, grief, exultation, sorrow, fear, anger, or love, and gave expression to their light, serious, or violent moods, in modulated tones, harsh or musical; or later, in unconscious figures of speech, expressed without reflection or intention of communicating truth".[55]

In this period of his thought, Wright continued to grant a certain authority to religious faith, provided that it was regarded as he said St. Paul regarded it—namely, as a sentiment, not as a faculty of knowledge.[56] At this time Wright did not praise efforts like Hamilton's to secure intellectual "grounds" for belief in truths which are inconceivable. "The test of a true faith," Wright now said, "is emotional and moral, not intellectual"; [57] and that is why it does not conflict with science.[58] He wrote Grace Norton in 1875 of an exchange with William James in which he, Wright, admitted that "unproved beliefs, unfounded in evidence, were not only allowable, but were sometimes even *fit, becoming, or appropriate* to states of feeling or types of character, which are deserving of approval, or even of honor. This fitness does not, however, amount to an obligation of duty".[59] Wright held that a man might say "I believe that God exists"—thereby expressing a certain favorable sentiment toward the proposition —without being prepared to say "I know that God exists", because saying the latter would imply that he had scientific evidence for the proposition that God exists. Wright did not observe a peculiarity of the phrase "I believe but I do not know that . . .", which grows out of the fact that some persons might hesitate to say "I believe" if they were not prepared to say "I know". Had Wright been confronted with his observation, he might have made a distinction between two uses of the word "believe", one for faith and one for science. The former use, he might have held, registers an attitude toward a proposition without implying the possession of evidence sufficient to justify saying that one knew the proposition to be true; the latter registers an attitude supported by scientific evidence which *did* justify saying "I know". Perhaps Wright wished to resolve the alleged conflict between religion and science in this way, that is to say, by showing that it was not a conflict but a contrast analogous to that between poetry and science.

Throughout the foregoing discussion I have emphasized that Wright never *says* that metaphysics and theology are forms of poetry, but at most that the contrasts between each of them and science are *analogous* to the contrast between poetry and science. There is some evidence, however, that he may have been willing to take the deeper plunge. There is first of all his use of the word "conviction" when he is characterizing poetry in the passage quoted earlier—a word that he himself calls a theological term. And then there is his use of the word "intimation" in the same passage, a fact that assumes some significance when we find him writing to Charles Eliot Norton in 1866 that a manuscript by W. T. Harris lacked "the genuine transcendental merit of suggestiveness". In this letter he went on to say, even more significantly: "I am not so much a positivist as to deny that mystical and poetical philosophies are valuable products of human genius; but then they must be works of real genius,—of a Plato, a Hegel, or an Emerson. No being is prosier than the uninspired disciple of the mystic. All that is stimulating—all the glorious vision— has melted away. Instead of clouds, we have left mere idiocy; blank staring at emptiness".[60] Is it too farfetched to suppose, then, that Wright saw the "genuine transcendental merit of suggestiveness" in those works of Emerson in which he found "convictions of half-truths, or intimations of truth, coupled with deep feeling, and impressed by the rhythms and alliterations of words"? Is it too farfetched to suppose that he regarded Emerson as a poet in metaphysical clothing? I do not think so.

Wright was therefore a member of the new order whom the Transcendentalists need not have feared altogether. He may have helped to thrust their movement into the background, but he allowed room enough for faith to keep one element of their tradition alive. He was a positivist and an empiricist in revolt against Transcendentalism; but in allowing that feeling may be used to justify beliefs which are non-scientific, he was perpetuating to a certain extent the tradition of Edwards' Sense of the Heart and Emerson's Reason, and approving in some measure what James was to call "The Right To Believe". However, Wright's insistence that unfounded religious beliefs which are fit, becoming, and appropriate do not express knowledge, brought him a long way from the theological doctrines of Edwards. In underscoring the similarity between religion and poetry on the ground that both of them are not primarily interested in communicating knowledge,[61] Wright was anticipating a view which Santayana was to make the cornerstone of his philosophy of religion. In this respect Wright was very different from Peirce, James, and Royce—all of whom were much more anxious than Wright to support the claims of theology and metaphysics as cognitive enterprises, that is to say, as disciplines which aim at and achieve knowledge of the truth.

7 · Charles Peirce: Pragmatist and Metaphysician

Because Edwards was a Calvinist representative of Locke, Emerson an admirer of Kant as expounded by Coleridge, and Wright a Darwinian follower of John Stuart Mill, we may say that up to the Civil War, America had to be content with philosophers who imported their main ideas from abroad. It is true that they packed these importations in their own boxes before offering them to the American public, but the main contents of those boxes should have been marked "Made in Europe", and they usually were, since Edwards duly paid his respects to Locke and Calvin, Wright paid his to Darwin and Mill, and Emerson characteristically paid his respects to almost everybody.[1] Acknowledgment of so great an indebtedness to foreigners was no longer necessary when Charles Peirce and William James made their appearance on the American scene, because, in spite of their familiarity with foreign philosophy and their debt to it, those lifelong friends and partners in pragmatism produced and distributed the one philosophy that could honestly be stamped "Made in America". Both of them were far more original than any of their American predecessors though, of course, they owed a great deal to some of those predecessors and to the intellectual atmosphere around Boston in their youth. They had been exposed to their friend Chauncey Wright's empiricism, his nominalism, his Darwinism, and his generally suspicious attitude toward theology, metaphysics, and cosmology. However, because Peirce and James were the sons of intellectuals who traveled in Emersonian circles, they had also been exposed to continental and anti-empirical influences that played a comparatively small part in the mature thinking of Wright. Peirce's father was Benjamin Peirce, the leading American mathematician of his day and a father who caused his son to learn the *Critique of Pure Reason* almost by heart. James was the son of the Swedenborgian, Henry James, Sr., who could be expected to raise a child with much more sympathy for religion and ghost-seeing than the agnostic Wright could tolerate.

As the sons of their fathers, neither Peirce nor James was militantly opposed to some of the ideas espoused by the Transcendentalists. Peirce was drawn to the metaphysical system-building that Emerson admired, and James was always concerned to defend the possibility of religious knowledge. For this reason anyone who wishes to situate Peirce and James in the history of American thought must acknowledge a certain tension in their thinking. They had both been trained at Harvard's Lawrence Scientific School and they both respected some of the deflationary tendencies in nineteenth-century positivism, but neither of them could ruthlessly dismiss the kind of speculation for which Emerson propagandized so eloquently. Not that they learned any technical philosophy from the Concordian, but they were more receptive to the kind of metaphysical and religious thinking he admired than most nineteenth-century philosophers who had as much training as Peirce had received in logic, mathematics, chemistry, and physics, and as much as James had received in medicine, physiology, and psychology. It is true that they anticipated a good

deal of twentieth-century positivistic doctrine, but their anticipations of it exist side by side with doctrines and ways of
thinking that are distinctively anti-positivistic in animus. Of
the two pragmatists, James was more conscious of the need to
harmonize what he called the tender-minded and the tough-
minded philosophies, or the two souls at war within his own
breast; but it is important to recognize that Peirce also tried
to meet the demands of science on the one hand and those of
metaphysics and religion on the other.

The Two Souls of Charles Peirce

If Wright was the first American modern, then Charles Peirce
may be called the first American contemporary. Peirce was
not only a philosopher of science but also a creative mathematical logician whose pages bristle with the logical terminology and symbolism that have become so common in recent
philosophy. Peirce's mathematical and scientific credentials
were even more impressive than Wright's. He was one of the
distinguished logicians of the nineteenth century; he began
the study of chemistry at eight and by twelve he was conduct-
ing experiments in quantitative analysis; he studied zoology
under the eminent Louis Agassiz; the only job he ever had for
an extended period of time was with the U.S. Coast and Geodetic Survey; and the only book he ever published was entitled *Photometric Researches*. These credentials combined
with Peirce's philosophical and logical powers to make him
one of the most acute methodologists of science in the nineteenth century.

Peirce's interest in the logic of science did not prevent him
from exercising a penchant for cosmological speculation that
would have horrified the positivistic Wright; and unlike
Wright, Peirce often put his scientific and logical tools to
work in behalf of doctrines that had their origin in ancient,
medieval, and German philosophy. Peirce was much more

widely read in the history of philosophy than Wright was, much more sympathetic to anti-empiricist figures in that history, and in general a broader-gauged intellect than Wright. Speaking of his upbringing under his father, Peirce gives us some idea of the range of intellectual experience to which he had been exposed as a boy: "My father was universally acknowledged to be by far the strongest mathematician in the country, and was a man of great intellect and weight of character. All the leading men of science, particularly astronomers and physicists resorted to our house; so that I was brought up in an atmosphere of science. But my father was a broad man and we were intimate with literary people too. William Story the sculptor, Longfellow, James Lowell, Charles Norton, Wendell Holmes, and occasionally Emerson, are among the figures of my earliest memories".[2]

In spite of his connection with Emerson, however, Peirce avowed that he was not consciously influenced by the Transcendentalists. He announced in 1892 at the beginning of one of his more speculative essays: "I may mention, for the benefit of those who are curious in studying mental biographies, that I was born and reared in the neighborhood of Concord—I mean in Cambridge—at the time when Emerson, Hedge, and their friends were disseminating the ideas that they had caught from Schelling, and Schelling from Plotinus, from Boehm, or from God knows what minds stricken with the monstrous mysticism of the East. But the atmosphere of Cambridge held many an antiseptic against Concord transcendentalism; and I am not conscious of having contracted any of that virus. Nevertheless, it is probable that some cultured bacilli, some benignant form of the disease was implanted in my soul, unawares, and that now, after long incubation, it comes to the surface, modified by mathematical conceptions and by training in physical investigations".[3] By whatever route the probable influence of the Transcendentalists was exerted on Peirce, it is clear that there were many intellectual affinities between him and them. To begin with, he espoused what he called a "Schelling-fashioned idealism which holds matter to be mere specialized and partially deadened mind".[4] He also held that feeling is a sounder guide in life than logic and that the heart is more to be trusted than the head; that ideas as Platonic essences are more important than actions since the general is more valuable than the particular; that the outer world and the inner world are both manifestations of God; that reality is one and not many; that evil is seen to be good when properly viewed under the aspect of eternity. Like Walt Whitman, Peirce was large and contained multitudes, so large that it has been argued by Professor Goudge that there are two irreconcilable Peirces, one a naturalist and the other an anti-naturalist who cannot be unified into a single consistent philosopher by exegetical magic.[5] On the one hand Peirce insists that scientific method is the only way of obtaining knowledge but on the other he says that feeling or instinct is a more important source. We find him stressing the value of precise logical analysis and then doubting the possibility of analyzing the most important philosophical ideas. Sometimes he adopts a scholastic realism concerning universals and sometimes he jeers at ontological metaphysics. Sometimes he regards system-building with suspicion and sometimes he embraces it as his own life-task. Sometimes he praises common sense to the skies and sometimes he thinks it must be transcended.

Peirce's attachment to metaphysics may be partly explained by saying that he was, in Sir Isaiah Berlin's Archilochian metaphor, a logical fox who wanted to be a metaphysical hedgehog.[6] Peirce once said that he wanted "to erect a philosophical edifice that shall outlast the vicissitudes of time" and "to make a philosophy like that of Aristotle . . . a theory so comprehensive that, for a long time to come, the entire work of human reason, in philosophy of every school and kind, in mathematics, in psychology, in physical science, in history, in sociology, and in whatever other department there may be, shall appear as the filling up of its details".[7] This hedgehoggish ambition may explain the pathos of Peirce. He made no small plans in philosophy but died at seventy-five without ever publishing a single philosophical book. He owes his fame in great measure to his admiring editors: Morris R. Cohen, who brought out the first posthumous collection of Peirce's papers in 1923 under the revealing title of *Chance, Love and Logic,* revealing because it alludes to the less positivistic side as well as to the logical side of Peirce's thought; Charles Hartshorne and Paul Weiss, who consummated their prodigious editorial labors with a monumental six-volume set of Peirce's *Collected Papers* published in the early thirties; and Arthur Burks, who added two more volumes to that set in 1958.

These posthumous volumes and the unpublished literary remains of Peirce have been ransacked by several generations of Ph.D. candidates; and philosophers of different persuasions have sought aid, comfort, and anticipations in his merest scraps of paper. It is fair to say, however, that only in the field of logic, broadly conceived as including his pragmatic analysis of empirical knowledge, do they find finished work. There he helped lay a visible foundation upon which others have built, whereas his sketches of cosmology and metaphysics have at best earned him a following of scholars who can only speculate as to how Peirce would have finished and furnished the higher stories of his system. Still, it is always worth bearing in mind that Peirce was not only a pragmatic logician but also a highly speculative mind who combated the positivistic, nominalistic, empiricistic, deterministic tendencies of the nineteenth century. In this respect he had much more in common with his junior friend, James, than with his senior friend, Wright.

The Logic of Peirce's Pragmatism

The year 1877 may be thought of as that in which American
pragmatism was officially launched, for it was then that
Charles Peirce began to publish a series of articles called "Illustrations of the Logic of Science", of which the second,
"How To Make Our Ideas Clear", was destined to become a
classic in the history of American philosophy. Although
Peirce's pragmatism had been germinating for some time, it
was in this article that he first formulated what he called his
pragmatic maxim, the primary purpose of which was to clarify
language in which claims to knowledge are made and to has-
ten the day when scientific and philosophical disputes would
be settled by the use of a more rational method. It is not surprising that the maxim should first have been unveiled by
Peirce before the Metaphysical Club, an intellectual group
like many that sprang up around Boston in the nineteenth
century but one that was very different from earlier literary
clubs that concentrated, according to Emerson, on oysters and
wine.[8] Unlike the clubs that attracted Emerson, who, as we
know, despised argument, this one was composed mainly of
persistently argumentative lawyers like Oliver Wendell
Holmes, Jr., and Nicholas St. John Green, and dialectically
oriented men of scientific background like Peirce, Wright,
and William James. So, if Emerson's Saturday Club was
where the fall leaves of Transcendentalism were being raked
together in the eighteen-seventies, the Metaphysical Club
was where a philosophical spring was beginning with more logical buds. Whereas the Transcendentalists were mainly
littérateurs, the Cambridge pragmatists were scientifically
trained men who helped launch a philosophy that was far
more original and far more valuable in its influence than anything the Transcendentalist philosophers had given to the
world. The pragmatists were not philistines but they were less

interested in saying things well than in saying what was true, especially Peirce. In spite of his bragging about the literary men who frequented his father's house, he proudly reported that when William Dean Howells had once criticized one of his articles for lacking rhetorical elegance, he said to Howells (with characteristic exaggeration), "Mr. Howells, it is no part of the purpose of my writings to give readers pleasure". Such an idea, Peirce went on to say, "was quite out of Howells' horizon".[9] One may add that the fact that it was, symbolized a developing gulf between American philosophy and American literature, and the beginning of an era in which philosophers rarely published their more technical contributions in the kind of general periodical which men like Howells controlled. It was also the beginning of an era in which the most important American philosophers were to be professors, as they had not been before the 1870's, though lesser and safer figures did hold chairs. Edwards had been a minister, Emerson earned his livelihood by writing and popular lecturing, Chauncey Wright was a computer for the *Nautical Almanac* and only an occasional lecturer at Harvard; and so, when William James became an instructor in physiology and anatomy at Harvard in 1872, he became the first of the main figures treated in this book to be launched on an academic career that was to be permanent.

Such a career was denied to the brilliant Peirce in spite of James' efforts in his behalf. The American philosophical profession was not ready for a prickly mathematical logician, and many a Victorian university would not welcome an eccentric who would go so far as to divorce a woman. For much of his life, therefore, Peirce lived in hardship and even in squalor, was forced at times to earn his living by engaging in poorly paying journalism, never completed any of the grandiose philosophical books he planned, and was not accorded in his lifetime the degree of recognition that his talent and his work deserved. It was not until 1898, when Peirce was fifty-nine, that his philosophical work began to receive some general acclaim, for it was then that the ever-generous James told a California audience how much he had learned from "an American philosopher whose home is in the East, and whose published works, few as they are and scattered in periodicals, are no fit expression of his powers. I refer to Mr. Charles S. Peirce, with whose very existence as a philosopher I dare say many of you are unacquainted. He is one of the most original of contemporary thinkers; and the principle of practicalism—or pragmatism as he called it, when I first heard him enunciate it at Cambridge in the early '70's—is the clue or compass by following which I find myself more and more confirmed in believing we may keep our feet upon the proper trail".[10]

James was complimenting Peirce primarily on views to be found in his essay "How To Make Our Ideas Clear".[11] In that essay Peirce wrote mainly in psychological terms of clarifying *ideas* and *beliefs;* but in later formulations he came to speak more and more of pragmatism as a logical maxim that tells us how to translate a singular *statement* like "This piece of butter is soft" into another one which expresses its meaning in a form applicable to human conduct, that is to say, in a form of statement which reports the result of an individual's deliberately doing something to an object. In the later formulations of his pragmatism, Peirce held that the statement that a piece of butter is soft has as its pragmatic translation the statement that if a normal person were to try to scratch the piece of butter, he would succeed and hence see an indentation on it. According to Peirce, the main virtue of this mode of translation is that it leads us to see how we should settle certain disputes about the truth of statements and hence to achieve what he called the third or highest grade of clearness. There is, he held, a first grade of clearness in which we may know how to identify, say, lithium but not be able to tell anyone what we mean by the word "lithium", and hence not be able to contribute articulately to a dispute about whether something is or is not a specimen of lithium. If, in an effort to attain greater clarity, we should turn to a chemistry book and read that lithium is the element whose atomic weight is nearly 7, this would bring us only to the second degree of clearness, one that is characteristic of what Peirce invidiously called abstract definition, which is inadequate, he said, for the settlement of serious disputes. Therefore, the pragmatist insists that we move on to a third grade of clearness which can be attained only by translating the statement that something is a specimen of lithium into a statement that if a normal person were to perform certain operations on the specimen, he would have certain experiences. When we reach this kind of translation, we have, Peirce claims, a mode of statement that two disputants understand in the clearest possible way because they can test it by performing the indicated operations and then determining whether the predicted sensible consequences ensue. This kind of translation, Peirce holds, brings us to a level on which normal men can discover with greater ease whether the translated statement is true or false.

By focusing on Peirce's pragmatic theory of meaning, we can see the most important general features of the more fully developed parts of his philosophy. First of all, there is his emphasis on the importance of publicity. He thinks we must go beyond the first grade of clearness in which the speaker merely has a grasp of what it is to be lithium but cannot express the meaning of the word "lithium". That is why the philosophically minded scientist and the philosopher must make explicit the meaning of the term by presenting a more complex term that will communicate to another person what the speaker has in mind. It was this part of Peirce's thought that won him the applause of analytical philosophers in the twentieth century; but unlike some analytical philosophers Peirce says that this making explicit of the meaning will not go far enough if it issues in a definition or analysis that makes use of excessively abstract terms. After illustrating such excessive abstractness by the definition of "lithium" as "the element whose atomic weight is nearly 7", Peirce offers as an example of a superior pragmatic definition or analysis of "lithium" the following statement of what one would experience if one performed certain operations: "If you search among minerals that are vitreous, translucent, grey or white, very hard, brittle, and insoluble, for one which imparts a crimson tinge to an unluminous flame, this mineral being triturated with lime or witherite rats-bane, and then fused, can be partly dissolved in muriatic acid; and if this solution be evaporated, and the residue be extracted with sulphuric acid, and duly purified, it can be converted by ordinary methods into a chloride, which being obtained in the solid state, fused, and electrolyzed with half a dozen powerful cells, will yield a globule of a pinkish silvery metal that will float on gasolene; and the material of *that* is a specimen of lithium".[12]

In other places, and more typically, Peirce contrasts the pragmatic kind of definition or translation with the abstractness of the genus-and-differentia definition offered by scholastics. According to the scholastic method, we provide a definition of "canary" by differentiating canaries from other birds, and if we are asked for a definition of "bird", we proceed to differentiate birds from other vertebrates. And so, Peirce says: "Rising through *birds, vertebrates, animals, living creatures, natural objects, things,* we come, in the ninth remove from *canary-birds,* to *substances*" in our chain of definitions.[13] Peirce objected to the fact that the scholastics introduced more and more abstract terms into their definitions as they moved from lower to higher species in this chain. By contrast, he thought that his pragmatic method of translation led to more concrete terms that referred to human actions and their observable results; and that is why he thought it led to the highest or third degree of clearness.

Peirce's attachment to concreteness and observability in pragmatic analysis went hand in hand with his emphasis on the public nature of scientific knowledge. He insisted that a pragmatist is not concerned to report in his translation the private images that a man might have in mind when he utters or hears sentences like "This is lithium", "This is a canary", or "This is soft". Nor did Peirce hold that the meaning of "This is soft" consists in sensations that the speaker wishes his listener to have when the latter hears the utterance. Because Peirce held that the meaning is expressed in a statement of the form: "If a normal person were to perform an operation of kind O on the specimen, he would observe results of kind R", Peirce keeps insisting that the pragmatic maxim is a recipe for extracting the "intellectual purport" of the analyzed statement and not for presenting the sensations or images associated with it.[14] For Peirce, reference to an operation performed is as essential when one is translating a statement as reference to a result experienced.

Peirce insisted, especially in his later writings, that a singular statement like "This is soft" has the same meaning as a statement of the form: "If anybody who is normal were to perform an operation of kind O on this, he would observe a result of kind R"; and Peirce's use of the phrase "if anybody who is normal were" is intended to make clear that a pragmatic translation refers to a possible community of investigators. When I assert that a piece of butter is soft, I am not merely saying that if I should perform a certain operation on it, I would observe a certain result. That would destroy the element of publicity in what I communicate when I say "This is soft" because it might have the unwanted effect of making the sentence mean something different for different investigators. You might observe something else because your vision is abnormally poor. Moreover, when Peirce insists on translating "This is soft" as he does, he prepares the way for his doctrine of fallibilism. Though this term is ambiguously used in his writings, it sometimes refers to his contention that we can be mistaken in any statement we make. The point is taken to be quite evident in the case of statements which explicitly formulate laws, because they obviously imply statements that may turn out to be false. For example, the explicitly universal statement that every diamond is hard implies that each diamond that has existed, does exist, or will exist is hard; but since it is logically possible that some as yet unexamined diamond may turn out not to be hard, Peirce takes this possibility into account by saying that we could be mistaken in asserting that every diamond is hard. If we now add to this Peirce's pragmatic doctrine that singular statements like "This is a diamond" and "This is hard" covertly express laws because they are translatable into universal statements like "If anyone who is normal were to try to scratch this, he would see no indentation on it after trying", or "Any normal person who tries to scratch this, will see no indentation on it after trying", we see that in Peirce's view both singular and explicitly universal statements of empirical science fall under the sway of his fallibilism because of their predictive character. They both refer to an indefinite number of possible experiments, any one of which might give a negative result.

Since Peirce thought the singular statement "This diamond is hard" is equivalent to the universal statement "Any normal person who tries to scratch this, will see no indentation on it after trying", Peirce also thought that "This diamond is hard" had as its consequences statements like "If James, a normal person, were to try to scratch it, he would see no indentation on it after trying", "If Dewey, a normal person, were to try to scratch it, he would see no indentation on it after trying", and so on for every normal person who might try the experiment. These are consequences of the universal statement; so, if "This diamond is hard" is equivalent to the universal statement, the consequences of the universal statement are also consequences of "This diamond is hard". However, these consequences are *logical* consequences of "This diamond is hard" and of its equivalent; and when we recognize this we can see why Peirce's pragmatic theory of meaning was very different from James' pragmatic theory of meaning. It is advisable to explain this difference between Peirce and James now, since it will help us understand why Peirce often disassociated himself from James on this crucial question as well as prepare us for some of James' views in the next chapter.

By contrast to Peirce, James tended to formulate his pragmatic theory of meaning by focusing on the meaning of an act of adopting a given proposition as true. James says at one point while discussing "the Pragmatic Rule" that "in obeying this rule we neglect the substantive content of the concept, and follow its function only".[15] This is better understood when we know that James distinguished between *what* a man believes when he believes that this diamond is hard—the proposition—and his act of adopting a believing attitude toward the proposition. One difference between Peirce's approach to meaning and James' may be seen by returning to Peirce's (by now familiar) example about the diamond. If a man says "I believe that this diamond is hard", Peirce is mainly concerned to examine the meaning of the sentence after the word "that"—the proposition or the substantive content of the man's belief. But James is mainly interested in the *function* of the man's having adopted a believing attitude toward the proposition. When James focuses on this function, he asks what *causal* consequences ensue from the man's adopting this attitude—particularly what ensues in the man's own history when he takes this plunge. Because James concentrated on this act, his notion of pragmatic consequence is causal; because Peirce concentrated on the proposition, his notion of pragmatic consequence is logical. In James' view, my act of adopting the belief that this diamond is hard may have many different kinds of causal consequences. It may bring about the fact that I can now explain many things that I could not explain before. It may also bring about a certain esthetic pleasure by ordering previously disordered phenomena. And it may even bring me the pleasure of agreeing with someone I admire. Furthermore, since James regards the totality of these consequences as "the meaning" of my act of adopting a believing attitude toward the proposition, he maintains that I am entitled to perform that act if these consequences are on balance favorable. Peirce, in keeping with his more puritanical approach, insists that the only thing that entitles me to accept the proposition is a series of successful experiments showing that anyone who tries to scratch the diamond will fail.

Because James did not advocate a logical analysis of "the substantive content" of statements, he did not require that the statement "God is real" be translatable into Peirceian terms before it could be regarded as a candidate for belief. James did not require that such a statement be translated into one which reports the sensible consequences that would follow the performance of a Peirceian experiment on a diamond or a rose. And because James did not adopt this stringent requirement for, so to speak, nominating a belief as meaningful, James thought he was able to move directly to the question whether it should be, to continue the metaphor, elected as true. For this reason, James' version of the pragmatic rule is very different from Peirce's and from later, Peirce-like, positivistic theories of meaning which identify the meaning of a statement with verifiable logical consequences of it. Consequently there is a danger that those who read only, as it were, positivistically expurgated versions of Peirce, may get the impression that the more puritanical Peirce was the only Peirce. This, however, is not true. No matter how tough and deflationary he was in many of his declarations about meaning— especially when he was chastising James for his deviations from the True Pragmatic Church—Peirce was tougher on James than he was on himself. It is a great mistake to suppose that Peirce, because he advocated a more scientifically oriented pragmatic theory of meaning than James, was on that account less favorable to metaphysics and religion. Moreover, when the reader has finished this chapter and the next one on James, he will see the superficiality of historical analyses which treat either Peirce's or James' pragmatism as a mere cultural expression of American capitalism or American technology, as a philosophy which is incapable of rising to anything above science and engineering. When Bertrand Russell said in 1922 that he found the "love of truth obscured in America by commercialism of which pragmatism is the philosophical expression", John Dewey rightly replied that this was comparable to saying that Russell's own realistic philosophy at that time was a reflection of the snobbish aristocracy of the English, or to saying that French dualism is an expression of an alleged Gallic disposition to keep a mistress in addition to a wife.[16] The pragmatism of Peirce and that of James left them a remarkable amount of room for metaphysical and theological doctrines that are as high-flown as any advocated in the history of Western thought. I shall now turn to some that appear in the writings of Peirce.

The Metaphysics of Peirce: Freedom, Universals, and God

As Peirce grew older, the cultured bacilli of which he speaks when he describes his youthful contact with Transcendentalism, began to have more visible effects on his thinking. The clearest of them appear in his indeterminism, his scholastic realism and essentialism, and his theism.

Indeterminism. Peirce believed in what he called absolute chance and in a freedom of the will that Edwards would have called Arminian. Peirce rejected what he called the common belief that every single fact in the universe is explained by a reference to deterministic laws and statements of initial conditions, and in particular he rejected the belief that every act of

the will is so explicable.[17] He associated his views with those
of Epicurus and with Aristotle's remarks on chance in the
Physics, and he condemned the Stoics for giving a big boost to
necessitarianism and materialism by returning to the mechan-
istic determinism of Democritus. The Stoic view, Peirce said,
was favored during the revival of learning and was encouraged later by the great discoveries in classical mechanics; but
determinism did not meet with general acceptance before the
nineteenth century because of its incompatibility with a belief
in freedom of the will and in miracles. These obstacles were
removed in some degree, he said, when the rise of associa-
tionist psychology encouraged a deterministic theory of motives and when the emergence of a variety of historical criticism exploded the doctrine of miracles. Therefore, when
Peirce published his "Doctrine of Necessity Examined" [18] in
1891, he believed that the doctrine of necessity was unfortunately in greater vogue than it had ever been before; and he
attacked it with the feeling that he was taking on a lion of an
idea. He did not attack it on moral grounds as James Marsh
had, but bearded it in its own den of science. Peirce did not
follow the lead of Kant—or that of William James, as we shall
see—by arguing that determinism should be rejected or qualified simply because it conflicts with our moral feelings and
moral judgments. Instead he tried to show that a careful examination of the method of science itself would show that determinism is not one of its presuppositions or postulates. He
argued further that it is not supported by empirical evidence,
and that it cannot be established on *a priori* grounds. Peirce
maintained that the conclusions of science make no pretense
to being more than probable, and furthermore "that a probable
inference can at most only suppose something to be most frequently, or otherwise approximately, true, but never that anything is precisely true without exception throughout the universe".[19] Peirce seems to have held that science should not
make absolutely universal statements like "All men are mor-

tal" but should content itself with advancing statistical or probabilistic claims like "The probability is .99 that any given human being is mortal". Here, of course, he was defending something like the contemporary view that the laws of quantum mechanics are inherently statistical in character and, to be consistent, would find it necessary to revise the universal statement into which he translated "This piece of butter is soft".[20]

Scholastic Realism and Essentialism. Peirce's pragmatism was, he thought, quite compatible with scholastic realism. Indeed, around 1890 he began to think that the pragmatic theory of meaning *leads to* a metaphysical belief in the reality of universals—a view which is not consonant with some of the things he had written in his earliest papers on pragmatism.[21] By a universal he meant an attribute or property that many individuals could have in common, and he held that the reality of universals follows from the translatability of a statement like "This piece of butter is soft" into its pragmatic equivalent. Peirce held that such translatability proves the reality of a universal because it shows that a soft thing has a disposition, namely, scratchability. Scratchability, he held, is a universal by contrast to the particular, concrete piece of butter which has it as a disposition. He also held that if the probability that a given coin will fall heads is 0.5, then this probability-statement attributes a disposition to the coin. In this way, his realism was made compatible with his indeterminism. Even if "This piece of butter is soft" must be translated into a statistical statement, it still attributes a disposition.

When Peirce said that a statement like "This piece of butter is soft" is equivalent to one which attributes a disposition, he was deliberately allowing for the possibility that no one had ever tried to scratch the piece of butter and that no one had ever observed a result of the predicted kind. Even though this piece of butter *has* the disposition, the disposition might

never be manifested; and therefore Peirce held that the statement which the pragmatist offers in translation is not a mere
summation of past historical events that Emerson would have
said required nothing more than the empirical Understanding for their detection. Peirce's pragmatic equivalent of "This
is soft" does not assert that on all past occasions trying to
scratch the piece of butter was in fact followed by success.
The statement "If any normal person were to try to scratch
this piece of butter, he would succeed" does not assert that
every time a normal person tried to scratch the piece of
butter, he *did* succeed, since, by hypothesis, no one may have
ever tried to scratch this piece of butter. Because "This is
soft" asserts or implies that the piece of butter has a certain
disposition or potentiality, the pragmatic translation of "This
is soft" makes explicit the fact that there is a lawful connection between trying to scratch the piece of butter and succeeding. This is different, of course, from a mere statement of
what happened on a finite number of occasions in the past.

Peirce did not merely depart from certain varieties of nominalistic empiricism by defending the reality of connections in
nature and the reality of universals. He also went further in
disassociating himself from the British tradition when he
maintained that the universal, habit, or disposition possessed
by the piece of butter is not only real but also what he called
a real *agency*. Here he turned his back on the view that a
mere power or disposition cannot be the cause of anything.
Peirce rejected Chauncey Wright's notion that it is barbaric
and unscientific to think that redness is a power in a red
thing which causes it to appear red. At many places Peirce
argued that whenever you succeed in scratching a soft thing,
your success is explained by the fact that the piece of butter
has an abstract power which *causes* your success. Hence he
called that power or universal a real agency. He was quite
aware of the bad odor in which such a view was held by those
who rejected what they called occult qualities, but he was

forthright in defense of it: "Abstractions have been a favorite butt of ridicule in modern times. Now it is very easy to laugh at the old physician who is represented as answering the question, why opium puts people to sleep, by saying that it is because it has a dormitive virtue. It is an answer that no doubt carries vagueness to its last extreme. Yet, invented as the story was to show how little meaning there might be in an abstraction, nevertheless the physician's answer does contain a truth that modern philosophy has generally denied: it does assert that there really is in opium something which explains its always putting people to sleep. This has, I say, been denied by modern philosophers generally. Not, of course, explicitly; but when they say that the different events of people going to sleep after taking opium have really nothing in common, but only that the mind classes them together—and this is what they virtually do say in denying the reality of generals—they do implicitly deny that there is any true explanation of opium's generally putting people to sleep".[22] When Peirce said that there really is in opium *something* which explains its always putting people to sleep, he referred to a universal or a property, and not, as Locke had, to the concrete atomic constituents of opium.

From what I have said so far, it would seem that Peirce was torn apart by the nineteenth-century conflict between science on the one hand and religion and metaphysics on the other. His pragmatic theory of meaning, which represented the scientific strain in his thinking, seemed to put both metaphysics and theology in jeopardy, but the older Peirce grew, the more he thought otherwise. Not only did he think that his pragmatism was *compatible* with scholastic realism but he insisted that it logically implied that metaphysical doctrine. We may go even further and say that his pragmatism also led to a version of the scholastic doctrine of essential truth. He held, as we have seen, that *the* meaning of a statement like "This is hard" or "This is lithium" can be presented in only one way, namely, in a statement linking human operations and their observable results. What we may call Peirce's essentialism is best illustrated in his spurning the statement "This is a specimen of an element whose atomic weight is nearly 7" as a translation of "This is a specimen of lithium", and in his insisting upon translating the latter into his long statement that begins with the phrase "If you search among minerals".[23] Although he grants that a given statement will have "myriad" [24] equivalents—and presumably the statement "This is a specimen of lithium" has as one of its equivalents the statement "This is a specimen of an element whose atomic weight is nearly 7"—he seems to think that there is among the myriad equivalents one which is special because it expresses "the very" or "the whole" meaning that is expressed by the statement itself. In making this invidious distinction between two kinds of equivalents, Peirce perpetuated an old tradition according to which "rational animal" expresses the essence expressed by the term "man", whereas "featherless biped" does not—a tradition which in different terminology says that the equivalent "rational animal" has the same meaning or connotation as "man", whereas the equivalent "featherless biped" merely has the same denotation or extension as "man". A similar view is expressed in Kantian terminology by saying that "All and only men are featherless bipeds" is synthetically and not analytically true.

Therefore we may say that if Peirce differed from scholastics who distinguished between an essence-stating equivalence and one which is not, it was only because he thought that the scholastics used a wrong formula for picking out the one term that expresses the meaning or essence expressed by the term to be clarified. Peirce did not mind the scholastics' view that *one* equivalent of the word "man" expresses its very essence, so much as their view that the essence is always expressed by a term which is the compound of a so-called genus-term, like "animal", and a differentia-term, like "rational". The scholastic was not condemned for believing in essences but for describing them wrongly. Thus we see that there is a close connection between Peirce's belief in the reality of universals and his idea that only one equivalent formula expresses the very meaning of a term like "lithium". For if one believes as he did that there is a real attribute of being lithium which is possessed by every specimen of lithium, one may be moved to say what that attribute or universal is, to analyze it. One may then maintain that the attribute of being lithium is *not* identical with the attribute of being a specimen of an element whose atomic weight is nearly 7 but that it *is* identical with the attribute expressed in Peirce's previously quoted long statement beginning with "If you search among minerals".[25] In the same vein, certain philosophers say that the attribute of being a man is *not* identical with the attribute of being a featherless biped but that it *is* identical with the attribute of being a rational man. Similarly, if one holds, as Peirce held, that the statement that a Jacqueminot rose really is red means the same as the statement that if such a rose is put before a normal eye in the daylight it will look red,[26] and if one denies that it means that such a rose emits light of a certain wavelength, one may hold that the attribute of being red is identical with the attribute of looking red to a person with normal eyes in daylight, but deny that it is identical with the attribute of emitting light of a certain wavelength.[27]

Because Peirce's pragmatism led in his own mind to a theory of universals according to which they are not only real but causally efficacious, and to a closely related theory of essential truth, his pragmatism is not as clear, as sunny, and as empirical as some of his more positivistic admirers may wish to think. And even though he was the most powerful logician of all American philosophers of his time, his logical power did not protect him from the kind of tension that I have mentioned. In trying to defend the reality of universals by appealing to pragmatism, Peirce resembled James. Though we shall see that James' defense of his metaphysical and religious beliefs was different from Peirce's defense of his, it is worth observing that both of them were upset by what they regarded as the arrogance of certain varieties of empiricism, and to that extent perpetuated the tradition of Edwards and Emerson. Calvinism, Transcendentalism, and Pragmatism all found room for knowledge of religious and metaphysical truth; and in Peirce's case there was special irony in the fact that the scientifically oriented pragmatic theory of meaning which he invented in order to kill ontological metaphysics became the instrument of its resurrection.

Theism. It is appropriate at this point to remark that Peirce believed in the reality of God. Furthermore, he explicitly associated this belief with the doctrine he came to call "pragmaticism". He coined that ugly word, as he called it, in order to disassociate himself from what he regarded as the defects in James' pragmatism. Some of those defects Peirce connected with James' excessive emphasis upon satisfaction to the believer—which emphasis helped James defend *his* religious beliefs, as we shall see in the next chapter—but it must not be concluded that Peirce was more diffident than James about defending religious beliefs. He was just as interested in defending the existence of the supernatural, only he characteristically wanted to do it in his own *pragmaticist* way. Peirce announced: "If a pragmaticist is asked what he means by the word 'God,' he can only say that just as long acquaintance with a man of great character may deeply influence one's whole manner of conduct, so that a glance at his portrait may make a difference, just as almost living with Dr. Johnson enabled poor Boswell to write an immortal book and a really sublime book, just as long study of the works of Aristotle may make him an acquaintance, so," Peirce continues, "if contemplation and study of the physico-psychical universe can imbue a man with principles of conduct analogous to the influence of a great man's works or conversation, then that analogue of a mind—for it is impossible to say that *any* human attribute is *literally* applicable—is what he means by 'God' ".[28] For Peirce, then, God is a mind that imbues certain contemplators of the physico-psychical universe with certain principles of conduct; and it is analogous to the mind that a scholar of Aristotle regards as real on the basis of study of his works, or that a friend of Johnson supposes to be real on the basis of acquaintance with him.

After Peirce offers a "pragmaticist" definition of the word "God", he asks whether there really *is* such a divine mind. And Peirce answers in the affirmative because he thinks that just as there is reason to conclude that Aristotle's mind is real on the basis of the responses of scholars to books that are supposed to have been written by him, so there is reason to conclude that God is real on the basis of the conduct of priests courageously living in leper colonies. Peirce also says that "the discoveries of science, their enabling us to *predict* what will be the course of nature, is proof conclusive that, though we cannot think any thought of God's, we can catch a fragment of His Thought, as it were".[29] In some places, Peirce's argument for the reality of God resembles his argument for the reality of universals. We have seen that he holds that "there really is in opium *something* which explains its always putting people to sleep" and that nominalists deny that there is when they deny the reality of universals. They maintain, he says, that the different events of people going to sleep after taking opium have really nothing in common, but that the mind merely classes them together. Reasoning similarly, Peirce says that the question whether there really *is* such a being as God is "the question whether all physical science is merely the figment—the arbitrary figment—of the students of nature",[30] thereby suggesting that those who do not believe in the reality of God share a failing of nominalists who think that universals are not real. Peirce also identifies the question whether there really is a God with the question "whether the *one* lesson the Gautama Boodha, Confucius, Socrates, and all who from any point of view have had their ways of conduct determined by meditation upon the physico-psychical universe, be only their arbitrary notion or be the Truth behind the appearances which the frivolous man does not think of; and whether the superhuman courage which such contemplation has conferred upon priests who go to pass their lives with lepers and refuse all offers of rescue is mere silly fanaticism, the passion of a baby, or whether it is strength derived from the power of the truth".[31] It would seem that Peirce, when he *argued* for the reality of God, held that science must be regarded as a figment—which it is not—if God is not real, and that only by supposing that God is real can we explain the conduct of the courageous priests and wise men he mentions.

It must be added, however, that just after Peirce has reasoned in this way, he draws back and asserts: "But whatever there may be of *argument* in all this is as nothing, the merest nothing, in comparison to its force as an appeal to one's own instinct, which is to argument what substance is to shadow, what bed-rock is to the built foundations of a cathedral".[32] This appeal to instinct is, of course, not unrelated to the Scottish Philosophy of Common Sense; [33] and when we read other things by Peirce on God, we instantly recognize an affinity between him and our old friend Jonathan Edwards. Consider, for example, the following paragraph from Peirce: "Where would such an idea, say as that of God, come from, if not from direct experience? Would you make it a result of some kind of reasoning, good or bad? Why, reasoning can supply the mind with nothing in the world except an estimate of the value of a statistical ratio, that is, how often certain kinds of things are found in certain combinations in the ordinary course of experience. And scepticism, in the sense of doubt of the validity of elementary ideas—which is really a proposal to turn an idea out of court and permit no inquiry into its applicability—is doubly condemned by the fundamental principle of scientific method—condemned first as obstructing inquiry, and condemned second because it is treating some other than a statistical ratio as a thing to be argued about. No: as to God, open your eyes—and your heart, which is also a perceptive organ —and you see him".[34]

In conclusion, I must say that Peirce's view that the heart is a perceptive organ is not very different from the view of Edwards; nor is it very different from the view of the young George Ripley. Well might Peirce have said that some form of Transcendentalism may have been planted in his soul and that after long incubation it came to the surface, modified by mathematical conceptions and by training in physical science. However, Peirce's efforts to use his genius in defense of a metaphysics and a theology are far less interesting than his contributions to mathematical logic and the methodology of natural science. His work in pure logic is beyond the purview of this book, but I hope I have said enough about his conception of science to reveal his originality and his great philosophical powers. In the good company of his most famous admirer, William James, I find much of Peirce's writing full of flashes in a Cimmerian darkness,[35] a darkness created by Peirce himself. The most important philosophical flash he issued was his pragmatic theory of meaning, and the most important bit of darkness he created may be found in his announcement that the heart is a perceptive organ. In this announcement, of course, one of our most original philosophers reveals what we now know to be an old habit in American philosophy—a habit more remarkable in a logician and scientist than it is in a theologian like Edwards, a lawyer like Wilson, and a poet like Emerson. Presently we shall see that the psychologist-philosopher William James was also subject to it in very considerable degree.

8 · William James: Pragmatism and the Whole Man

While Charles Peirce was measuring the value of gravity as an employee of the U.S. Coast and Geodetic Survey, serving as a wandering lecturer, and writing reviews and dictionary entries to keep body and soul together, the Harvard Department of Philosophy was going through what is sometimes called its Golden Age without him. William James began to teach philosophy at Harvard in 1879, Josiah Royce in 1882, and George Santayana in 1889; so, from the eighties roughly to the First World War, Cambridge was the scene of a three-ringed philosophical circus that commanded the respect and admiration of other philosophers and the world outside of professional philosophy. The audience consisted of adoring Harvard undergraduates who became adoring alumni, of scholars working in other fields, and of all people who read books. For books flowed freely from the pens of this prolific trio, some on the problems of technical philosophy and others on religion, loyalty, or poetry. As book-writers, the golden three differed from Emerson, who was primarily an essayist, and from Wright and Peirce, who imitated the paper-writing habits of scientists; James, Royce, and Santayana believed in voluminously demonstrating their technical expertise, their learning, their wisdom, and their sensibility. A well-established tradition dictated that philosophers should study logic, metaphysics, epistemology, and ethics; and although James, Royce, and Santayana carried out the dictates of that tradition in their more academic moods, they believed that philosophers should also address the world outside the lecture hall. Some will feel that they overextended themselves in their zeal to be both scholars and pundits, and that their age should be called not golden but merely glistering because of its over-vaulting ambition and its pretentiousness, whereas those who disagree will cite the depth, richness, and relevance of what they produced. Whichever judgment is correct, there is no doubt that they created a monumental style in American philosophy, and that they spoke not only to each other but also to the world.[1]

Their era was in many respects typified by William James' employment of philosophy to justify his religious beliefs. Like Edwards, he responded to the demands of American society for a usable philosophy of religion; and this explains to some extent why he was known to the general public whereas his friends Wright and Peirce were not. The general public was understandably more interested in those philosophers who were interested in its problems; and nobody was more interested in its problems than James, who in 1897 described religion as "the great interest of my life".[2] James' sympathetic interest in religion was reminiscent not only of Edwards' but also of Emerson's, except that Emerson was not as well equipped as James or Edwards to deal with the logic of religious belief. James knew, as his father before him knew, that Emerson was no dialectical spokesman for the claims of religion. Emerson had once said to the elder Henry James: "I am awed and distanced a little by [an] argumentative style: every technical *For* and *Suppose* and *Therefore* alarms and extrudes me",[3] and William James himself observed that Emerson was a seer of whom "we must not expect . . . too rigorous a consistency".[4] Yet James expected much more of himself in the way of rigor and he had a right to do so. Having entered philosophy by way of physiology and psychology, he could appreciate far better than Emerson the value of science and of logical argument.

However, in spite of being a better arguer than Emerson, James was just as prepared as the Concordian to give sentiment a central place in his theory of knowledge. Although James followed Locke on certain issues in his *Principles of Psychology* of 1890, James in that work gave sentiment a decisive, unLockeian role in the acceptance of metaphysical beliefs. In *The Will To Believe,* a collection of essays, published in 1897, he gave sentiment a similar role in religion. In his *Pragmatism* of 1907 he went further and made sentiment a factor in the acceptance of *all* beliefs; and in *A Pluralistic Universe,* published in 1909, one year before he died, James defended a form of anti-intellectualism which was very close to that of Bergson and the tradition of philosophical Romanticism. In *Pragmatism* James went well beyond Edwards and Emerson in making claims on behalf of the heart and the "whole man", and thereby brought to a climax one of the most powerful strains in the history of philosophy in America. We shall see how he came to this view by turning first to the period of his thought before *Pragmatism* appeared, when Locke's philosophy was a more powerful influence on him than it was to be in later years.

The outline of James' development was roughly as follows. In his *Psychology* he announced that he was a Lockeian insofar as he distinguished truths which may be established merely by examining concepts from those that require sensory evidence. Except for certain ambiguities to be noted later, he assigned the conceptual truths of logic and mathematics to pure science and the truths of disciplines like physics, biology, and chemistry to natural science. James then parted company with Locke in a manner reminiscent of Edwards and Emerson by saying that the justification of theological and moral beliefs involves an appeal to sentiment. Finally, in his most original departure from Locke, he held that metaphysical principles are also based on sentiment. In the eighteen-eighties and nineties, James distinguished among three different and coordinate methods of establishing belief—reason, experience, and feeling—each of them associated with different departments of human thought. If Locke may be called a dualist because he appealed to (1) intuitive reason in defense of axiomatic beliefs in immutable truths and to discursive reason in defense of other immutable truths, and (2) to experience in defense of what he called probable opinions, then James may be called a *trialist* for adding sentiment to Locke's two factors and letting it prevail in the establishment of beliefs in metaphysics, morals, and religion. As we shall see, however, James did not hold to this simple trichotomy to the end of his life. In *Pragmatism* he continued to appeal to a variety of factors in arriving at beliefs but did not consistently associate reason with belief in one kind of proposition, experience with belief in a second kind, and feeling with belief in a third kind. Instead, he tended to argue in some parts of his *Pragmatism* that all three of these considerations enter into the assessment of a whole "stock" of beliefs which contains logical beliefs, beliefs of natural science, of morals, of metaphysics, and of religion. In the following sections I shall trace James' progress toward this position.

James, Locke, and Necessary Truth

In the last chapter of his *Principles of Psychology* James addressed himself to the classical problem of necessary truth. He began by assuming that there are necessary propositions like the proposition that the opposite sides of a parallelogram are equal, and contingent ones like the proposition that tomorrow will be rainy. His main problem was to account for the fact that there are necessary propositions.[5] In dealing with this problem James interwove discussions of two kinds. One was "psychogenetic" insofar as it involved James in trying to show how the human race has come to have beliefs in necessary truths; the other was more epistemological because in it James concentrated on the method of justifying such beliefs. On the psychogenetic level James was primarily concerned to dispute the views of Herbert Spencer, whereas on the epistemological level James was eager to show that he was not a follower of John Stuart Mill but rather of John Locke.

Herbert Spencer had defended what he called the "experience-hypothesis" about the origin of beliefs in necessary truths by saying that they are caused by the accumulation of experiences which the whole human race has had.[6] Spencer maintained that the nervous structures of numberless generations of our ancestors had been affected by numberless experiences and that we, as their descendants, had inherited from them an organic mental structure with built-in knowledge which had been brought about by the action of those experiences. Spencer's putative explanation of the fact that we know *a priori* that $2+2=4$, that opposite sides of a parallelogram are equal, or that a proposition is either true or not true, is analogous to the Lamarckian explanation that giraffes have tall necks because their ancestors had been stretching their necks for innumerable years to get food from high trees. According to the Spencerian explanation, our knowing that $2+2=4$ without bothering to consult experience, is an acquired characteristic which is inherited, whereas we ourselves must have sensory experience of external reality in order to find out that fire burns and that water wets. Spencer held that the experience of our ancestors plays a part in our acquisition of *a priori* knowledge but that we, the beneficiaries of their experience, no longer have to consult experience when we believe that $2+2=4$. We are like today's giraffes, who are blessed with long necks without having to repeat their ancestors' stretching; and that is why we know certain propositions to be true without looking, touching, smelling, tasting, and listening in the manner of our ancestors. In explicit opposition to Spencer, James—a Darwinian—held that in some unknown manner knowledge that $2+2=4$ arose as a random variation in the minds of one or more of our ancestors, and that it was then selected for its usefulness in the struggle for existence and passed on as a heritable variation. By contrast, our knowledge that fire burns, according to both James and Spencer, is something which we acquire by our own sensory experience of the external world, by copying relations which hold in it.

It should be emphasized that even though James disagreed with Spencer's explanation of how we come to have *a priori* knowledge of necessary truth, James held that we do *have* such knowledge. Therefore he was obliged to oppose John Stuart Mill's view that there is no sharp distinction between necessary and contingent truths. The only distinction between them, Mill had held, was one of degree. For him the truths of logic and mathematics were simply more general than those of physics and economics; they were based on a wider range of experience. In opposition to Mill, James sided with Locke; and when James came to summarize his views in the last chapter of his *Psychology,* he wrote: "In truth I have done nothing more in the previous pages than to make a little more explicit the teachings of Locke's fourth book" [7] (of the *Essay Concerning Human Understanding*). In agreeing with Locke, James maintained that the truths of logic and mathematics are necessary and immutable, and that they are seen to be true merely by examining what James called "ideal conceptions". [8] We compare these ideal conceptions and on the basis of that comparison arrive at beliefs such as those that comprise logic and mathematics. For this reason James maintains that "the pure sciences" establish their truths as ordinary men establish the truth that no white thing is black. Here he is obviously and avowedly Lockeian in his view, maintaining that "to learn whether black and white differ, I need not consult the world of experience at all; the mere ideas suffice. *What I mean* by black differs from *what I mean* by white, whether such colors exist *extra mentem meam* or not. If they ever do so exist, they *will* differ. White things may blacken, but the black of them will differ from the white of them, so long as I mean anything definite by these three words".[9] James then goes on to say, in effect, that the logical statement that if Socrates is a man and every man is mortal, then Socrates is mortal, is true on the basis of "our insight into the very meaning of the word *is*" (there is no mention of insight into the meaning of "every" and "and").[10] Similarly, he holds that arithmetical beliefs like the belief that $2 + 2 = 4$ are established merely on the basis of our insight into the meaning of numerical expressions.

James and Rationalism: A Digression

It is important to bear in mind that in summarizing Locke's view on necessary truth, some philosophers, like James, identify it simply with the doctrine that there is a sharp distinction between necessary and immutable axioms on the one hand, and contingent truths like "Fire burns" on the other; the former being established by an examination of concepts and the latter not. If one understands Locke in this way, one disregards his view that some necessary truths are self-evident axioms and others theorems; and one also disregards Locke's idea that even principles of natural science may be self-evident. Yet Locke, as I have emphasized in my chapter on him, seems to have held that ideally natural science, like pure mathematics, would seek principles which might serve as axioms seen to be true immediately by examining the concepts expressed in them, in spite of his doubts about the possibilities of atomic physics. Therefore the question arises: Which Locke did James follow in his *Psychology?* Was

James content to associate himself merely with Locke's view that *some* principles are necessary and immutable while he, James, insisted that there is no such thing as a principle of *natural* science of this kind? Or did James go on to espouse some form of rationalism? The main part of James' discussion of necessary truth in the *Psychology* would lead us to say that he took the former path, but it is essential to add that there are passages in that book where his own unclarity might give the impression that he inclined toward rationalism.

In the main part of his discussion it is clear that James wishes to say two things about the theories of natural science: (1) that they are like truths of pure mathematics and logic in *not* being forced upon us by external reality, and hence fundamentally different from the belief that fire burns; but (2) that although theories of natural science are like mathematical theories in not being forced upon us by external reality, they differ from mathematical theories in having to "harmonize" with empirical truths like "Fire burns", "Water wets", and "Glass refracts". Had James said nothing more about theories of natural science, we might conclude that he agreed with Hume and twentieth-century positivists in holding that there is a sharp distinction between the way in which we justify the *a priori* truths of logic and mathematics on the one hand, and the *a posteriori* truths of physics on the other. True, we would have to acknowledge that he thought that physical theories and mathematical theories are similar *in origin*, but then add that this did not mean that he failed to see that physical theories, however abstract, are to be *justified* on empirical grounds.

Nevertheless, there *are* places in the *Psychology* where James comes very close to holding that physical theories like the wave-theory of light and theories of pure mathematics are alike not only in being "spontaneous variations" but also in being "rational propositions". It is worth calling attention to this tendency in James' writing if only because it may help us

understand similar lapses toward rationalism in the writings
of James' pupil, Santayana, and his admirer, Dewey.[11] It is
true that James insists that although pure science asserts necessary truths like $7+5=12$, arithmetic does not tell us
whether her "7's, 5's, and 12's are to be found". That task he
assigns to natural science, which "thinks that she has discovered the outer realities in question".[12] But James becomes
fuzzy when he begins to speak of what can be achieved once
science does discover these outer realities. For example, he asserts: "Atoms and ether, with no properties but masses and ve-
locities expressible by numbers, and paths expressible by analytic formulas, these at last are things over which the
mathematico-logical network may be flung, and by supposing
which instead of sensible phenomena science becomes yearly
more able to manufacture for herself a world about which rational propositions may be framed".[13] But what "rational
propositions" does James have in mind here?

It would seem that he thought that physics could frame
these new rational propositions by using mathematics. But let
us consider a famous physical proposition which is formulated
with the help of mathematical notions, Newton's universal
law of gravitation. In textbooks it is written: "$F = G\dfrac{m_1 m_2}{d^2}$",
meaning that each particle of matter is attracted by every
other particle with a force, F, which is directly proportional
to the product of their masses, m_1 and m_2, and inversely proportional to the square of the distance, d, between them. How
would James have viewed Newton's law itself? It is clear that
James thought that the discovery that Newtonian particles
exist in outer reality is an empirical affair, but would he have
regarded Newton's *law* as a "rational proposition"? His words
suggest that he might have; and if he did, he was a rationalist
in the sense I have in mind. The point is that although the
formulation of Newton's law with the help of mathematical
expressions permits us to "fling" a mathematical network over
it and logically derive from it other statements formulated

with the help of mathematical expressions, the law itself is not on that score to be regarded as a "rational proposition" in James' sense, i.e. one we can establish merely by comparing concepts. Yet James also holds that natural science "strives after . . . a mathematical world-formula, by which, if all the collocations and motions at a given moment were known, it would be possible to reckon those of any wished-for future moment, by simply considering the necessary geometrical, arithmetical, and logical implications. Once we have the world in this bare shape, we can fling our net of *a priori* relations over all its terms, and pass from one of its phases to another by inward thought-necessity".[14] The last sentence might lead one to suppose that he thinks that a physical theory which says something of the form: "Whatever particle is in state S_1 at time t_1 will be in state S_2 at time t_2" is an *a priori,* necessary truth; and it is just such a view that would make him a rationalist. I suspect that James was confused on the point. He might have meant that from a general law of the above form *and* the statement that a particular particle was in state S_1 at an earlier time, we may pass by an "inward thought-necessity" of logic to the conclusion that the particular particle will be in state S_2 at a later time. But this does not mean that the general law of *physics* expresses an "inward thought-necessity". What does express such a necessity is the law of logic which asserts that if the law of physics is true *and* the particle is in the first state at the earlier time, then the particle will be in the second state at the later time. Hence we do not pass from one of the *phases of the world* to another by a logical necessity; but only from the premises of a logical argument to its conclusion.

I strongly suspect that throughout James' discussion of natural science in his *Psychology* there is an element of rationalism which rests on a confusion of the kind I have described. But it should be clear that whether or not James was what I have called a rationalist, he certainly held in his *Psychology* that there is a sharp distinction between rational and non-rational propositions, even if he did not think that physical principles may be rational propositions. We may now return to the point we had reached before our digression. We must now describe how James departed from Locke's views on metaphysical principles and religious beliefs by allowing sentiment to play a decisive role in their acceptance.

Sentiment and Metaphysics: Against Determinism

Let us begin by observing how James diverged from Locke on the status of metaphysical principles. As we have seen,[15] Locke regarded as self-evident the metaphysical principle that whatever begins to exist has been produced by something, yet James decisively abandoned such an approach not only in his *Psychology* but also in his collection *The Will To Believe,* the title-essay of which is one of his most famous pieces. In his *Psychology* he held that there are metaphysical propositions which are neither rational nor verified by sensory experience, hence out of the domain covered by science, whether pure or natural. They are formulated, he pointed out, in such "axioms as 'The Principle of things is one;' 'The quantity of existence is unchanged;' 'Nature is simple and invariable;' 'Nature acts by the shortest ways;' *'Ex nihilo nihil fit;'* 'Nothing can be evolved which was not involved;' 'Whatever is in the effect must be in the cause;' 'A thing can only work where it is;' . . . 'Nature makes no leaps;' 'Things belong to discrete and permanent kinds;' 'Nothing is or happens without a reason;' 'The world is throughout rationally intelligible;' etc., etc., etc.".[16] Such principles, according to James, "are properly to be called *postulates of rationality,* not propositions of fact. If nature *did* obey them, she *would* be *pro tanto* more intelligible; and we seek meanwhile so to conceive her phenomena as to show that she does obey them. . . . They have a fertility as ideals, and keep us uneasy and striving always to recast the world of sense until its lines become more congruent with theirs".[17] James offered the principle "Nothing can happen without a cause" as an example of such a postulate of rationality and in effect said that the best we can do is *hope* such principles will turn out to be true. But if this is the best we can say for the principle of causality, it is clear why James did not hesitate to pit the doctrine of free will against it in "The Dilemma of Determinism",[18] without fearing that he was running up against the wall of logical necessity or *a priori* truth. "Many of the so-called metaphysical principles are at bottom only expressions of aesthetic feeling. Nature is simple and invariable; makes no leaps, or makes nothing but leaps; is rationally intelligible; neither increases nor diminishes in quantity; flows from one principle, etc., etc.,—what do all such principles express save our sense of how pleasantly our intellect would feel if it had a Nature of that sort to deal with? The subjectivity of which feeling is of course quite compatible with Nature also turning out objectively to be of that sort, later on." [19] And also, of course, with its *not* turning out objectively to be of that sort.

With such a point of view about the status of the principle of causality, it is not surprising that James was not afraid to challenge the determinists of his day. In his campaign he was joined, we already know, by Charles Peirce; but James characteristically appealed to moral feeling in his defense of free will, whereas we have seen that in "The Doctrine of Necessity Examined" Peirce appealed primarily to the logic of scientific explanation and inference.[20] Whatever their differences, however, both would have pleased their spiritual uncles in the Transcendentalist movement if only because they showed that younger American philosophers with scientific training were prepared to defend freedom and even God.

In "The Dilemma of Determinism" of 1884, James emphasized that the issue between determinism and free will could not be settled by an appeal to what he called "evidence of an

external kind" or facts, thereby moving the metaphysical battle to a ground like that to which he later moved the theological battle in "The Will To Believe". Yet he held that both
determinism and indeterminism are about external matters,
just as theism and atheism are. Determinism says that every
event is necessitated by some other, whereas indeterminism
flatly denies this and defends the existence of chance events.
Therefore, the issue between them "is a perfectly sharp one.
. . . The truth *must* lie with one side or the other, and its
lying with one side makes the other false".[21] In order to show,
however, that we cannot establish the truth of determinism or
indeterminism by an appeal to facts, James argues that the
issue concerns possibilities and therefore cannot be established by an appeal to existing facts. The question, he says, is
whether one volition having occurred, another *could* have occurred in its place. The determinists say no and the indeterminists say yes. "Now," James asks, "can science be called in
to tell us which of these two point-blank contradicters of each
other is right? Science professes to draw no conclusions but
such as are based on matters of fact, things that have actually
happened; but how can any amount of assurance that something actually happened give us the least grain of information
as to whether another thing might or might not have happened in its place? Only facts can be proved by other facts.
With things that are possibilities and not facts, facts have no
concern. If we have no other evidence than the evidence of
existing facts, the possibility-question must remain a mystery
never to be cleared up." [22] This passage makes us wonder how
James viewed ordinary scientific laws and their confirmation.
In the *Psychology,* as we have seen, he held that generalizations like "Fire burns" and "Glass refracts" are confirmed by
an appeal to facts. But, then, it would seem plausible to say
that such statements express laws of nature. In that case
"Glass refracts" should be equivalent to "It is impossible for a
piece of glass not to refract". But if it is, then for James it can-

not be "based on matters of fact". It would appear, then, that James is involved in an inconsistency here.

Apart, however, from this inconsistency about whether such scientific generalizations are based on matters of fact, James was convinced that philosophers do not appeal to facts when they become determinists or indeterminists. "Sure enough, we make a flourish of quoting facts this way or that; and if we are determinists, we talk about the infallibility with which we can predict one another's conduct; while if we are indeterminists, we lay great stress on the fact that it is just because we cannot foretell one another's conduct, either in war or statecraft or in any of the great and small intrigues and businesses of men, that life is so intensely anxious and hazardous a game. But who does not see the wretched insufficiency of this so-called objective testimony on both sides? What fills up the gaps in our minds is something not objective, not external. What divides us into possibility men and anti-possibility men is different faiths or postulates,—postulates of rationality. To this man the world seems more rational with possibilities in it,— to that man more rational with possibilities excluded; and talk as we will about having to yield to evidence, what makes us monists or pluralists, determinists or indeterminists, is at bottom always some sentiment like this." [23] For James, then, this great issue of metaphysics went the way of the great issue of theology, as we shall see when we come to "The Will To Believe". The question whether there are chance events, like the question whether there is a God, is settled and should be settled, he held, by each man according to his sentiments. James therefore called attention to certain unpleasant consequences of accepting determinism, hoping in this way not to *prove* the freedom of the will but to induce his audience to follow his example "in assuming it true, and acting as if it were true".

Before returning to his efforts at inducement, I should remark that James did not think very much of the attempts at

reconciliation represented in the view that freedom is only necessity understood, or in the view that "bondage to the highest is identical with true freedom", or in the view that to be
free is to act without external restraint. He labeled them as
examples of what he called "soft determinism", dismissed soft
determinism as "a quagmire of evasion", and claimed that the
soft determinist's freedom presents no problem at all because
in all of the soft determinist's senses of "free" it is obvious
that sometimes we are free and sometimes we are not.[24] Why
did James say this? I shall try to spell out what he thought in
particular of the soft determinist view that a free act is one
which is done without external restraint. Because such a view
is close to Edwards' doctrine, dilating on James' attitude toward it may help clarify the relationship between the two
main commentators on free will treated in this volume. Why
did James say that accepting a soft determinist's conception of
freedom and holding that sometimes we are free and sometimes we are not, led to "a quagmire of evasion under which
the real issue of fact has been entirely smothered"? [25] For Jonathan Edwards it was obvious that some acts are free or voluntary and others not, and he held that one virtue of his analysis
of free action was that it provided for this fact. But what *other*
issue of fact did James think was smothered by the soft determinist view of freedom? Obviously, it was the great issue of
determinism versus *in*determinism. The reader of my chapter
on Edwards will recall that although Edwards was a determinist, he did not think that an analyst of freedom *had* to raise
the question of whether all choices are determined. In Edwards' view, therefore, the issue of determinism versus indeterminism could be avoided by the analyst of free or voluntary action. But because James held a view like that of the
Arminians he thought the issue *had* to be raised. A moral philosopher who is asked "Do you believe in determinism or indeterminism?" must pick one or the other; whereas a moral
philosopher who is asked "Do you believe in determinism or

in free will as construed by soft determinists?" may reasonably reply that he believes in both. He may assert that some acts—the free ones—are performed in accordance with the agent's choice though some are not; and at the same time assert that every event, and therefore every choice, is caused.

It was this method of showing free will to be compatible with determinism that James opposed because he was sympathetic to one of the doctrines associated by Edwards with Arminianism—namely, that some events are not caused. James said that when we accept soft determinism we make "a pretence of restoring the caged bird of liberty with one hand, while with the other we anxiously tie a string to its leg to make sure it does not get beyond our sight".[26] In a manner reminiscent of those philosophers whom Edwards had attacked one hundred and thirty years earlier, James insisted that when we regret the performance of an action we *must* think that the agent's volition is an undetermined event and therefore that moral judgeability implies or presupposes a belief in indeterminism.

This led him to expound the dilemma which provided him with the title of his essay, a dilemma which he hoped would induce the determinist to mend his ways. James pointed out that we constantly have to regret the occurrence of certain things, to believe that something else would have been better in their places. Determinism, however, asserts that nothing could have replaced them. James' example of an action he regretted—brilliantly selected for its horror and macabre humor—is that of a Brockton murderer who, to get rid of his boring wife, inveigled her into a deserted spot, shot her four times and then, as she lay on the ground and said to him, "You didn't do it on purpose, did you, dear?", answered, "No, I didn't do it on purpose", as he raised a rock and smashed her skull. What, asks James, are we to think of a universe which contains the regretted Brockton murder? Are we to say that it would have been a better universe with something different from the Brockton murder in it, even though we say as determinists that a universe without the Brockton murder *could not have existed*? This seems like the natural thing to say, and yet it leads us to a kind of cosmic pessimism because it implies that the universe as a whole contains an incurable taint, or irremediable flaw. If we regret the murder, we must, to be consistent determinists, says James, "regret . . . that whole frame of things of which the murder is one member".[27]

"The only deterministic escape from pessimism," James continues, "is everywhere to abandon the judgment of regret" [28] and then to adopt an optimism according to which even such matters as the Brockton murder are right from a higher point of view. But this escape, he contends, leads directly to what he calls the dilemma of determinism. If we hold to determinism and try to escape from pessimism to some higher optimism about the universe, we must say that the *judgments* of regret we make are wrong. They are wrong, according to the optimist, because they falsely assert that "right" actions like the Brockton murder are wrong. Yet, if our judgments of wrongness are wrong, other judgments, presumably judgments of approval, ought to be in their places. However, the original judgments of wrongness are themselves necessitated and therefore *cannot* be replaced. So once again we are faced with a universe in which what ought to be appears impossible. First it was impossible to have a universe in which the *wrong Brockton murder* is replaced by a *right action;* now it is impossible to have the optimist's universe in which the *wrong moral judgment* that the Brockton murder is wrong is replaced by the *right moral judgment* that the murder is right.

James examines the possibility that determinists might be able to escape pessimism by finding some way of consistently holding that the Brockton murder is right and that regretting it is also right, but rejects that possibility and concludes that the only way out is to reject determinism and to accept indeterminism. "What sense can there be in condemning ourselves for taking the wrong way," he asks, "unless we need have done nothing of the sort, unless the right way was open to us as well? . . . I cannot understand regret without the admission of real, genuine possibilities in the world." [29] James admits that "to a reader who says he is satisfied with a pessimism, and has no objection to thinking the whole bad, I have no more to say: he makes fewer demands on the world than I, who, making them, wish to look a little further before I give up all hope of having them satisfied". [30] James reiterates that he cannot "offer any arguments which could be coercive in a so-called scientific fashion" in favor of indeterminism and that "the most any one can do is to confess as candidly as he can the grounds for the faith that is in him, and leave his example to work on others as it may".[31] He agrees that a mind "possessed of the love of unity at any cost" would be sickened by his pluralistic universe in which the past does not determine every part of the future. He reports that he had a friend who once told him that the thought of a pluralistic universe did make him sick, "like the sight of the horrible motion of a mass of maggots in their carrion bed". The figure allowed James to express concretely his view that what makes us determinists or indeterminists, is at bottom always some sentiment. "While I freely admit that the pluralism and the restlessness are repugnant and irrational in a certain way, I find that every alternative to them is irrational in a deeper way. The indeterminism with its maggots, if you please to speak so about it, offends only the native absolutism of my intellect,— an absolutism which, after all, perhaps, deserves to be snubbed and kept in check. But the determinism with its necessary carrion, to continue the figure of speech, and with no possible maggots to eat the latter up, violates my sense of moral reality through and through. When, for example, I imagine such carrion as the Brockton murder, I cannot conceive it as an act by which the universe, as a whole, logically and necessarily expresses its nature without shrinking from complicity with such a whole. And I deliberately refuse to keep on terms of loyalty with the universe by saying blankly that the murder, since it does flow from the nature of the whole, is not carrion. There are *some* instinctive reactions which I, for one, will not tamper with." [32]

Sentiment and Religion: Against the Agnostics

Just as James held in his *Psychology* and "The Dilemma of Determinism" that sentiment determines the acceptance of metaphysical beliefs, so he held in other writings of the same period that sentiment determines the acceptance of religious beliefs. This brought him into direct conflict with British agnosticism, which played the part of whipping boy in James' philosophy of religion much as British nominalism did in Peirce's reflections on the problem of universals. James was determined in 1896 to do combat with tough characters like T. H. Huxley and W. K. Clifford as he had with Chauncey Wright on the same question twenty years earlier. Huxley had written: "My only consolation lies in the reflection that, however bad our posterity may become, so far as they hold by the plain rule of not pretending to believe what they have no reason to believe, because it may be to their advantage so to pretend, they will not have reached the lowest depth of immorality". [33] And Clifford, whom James called "that delicious *enfant terrible*", had gravely warned: "Belief is desecrated when given to unproved and unquestioned statements for the solace and private pleasure of the believer. . . . Whoso would deserve well of his fellows in this matter will guard the purity of his belief with a very fanaticism of jealous care, lest at any time it should rest on an unworthy object, and catch a stain which can never be wiped away. . . . If [a] belief has been accepted on insufficient evidence [even though the belief be true, as Clifford on the same page explains] [34] the pleasure is a stolen one. . . . It is sinful because it is stolen in defiance of our duty to mankind. That duty is to guard ourselves from such beliefs as from a pestilence which may shortly master our own body and then spread to the rest of the town. . . . It is wrong always, everywhere, and for every one, to believe anything upon insufficient evidence".[35]

It was against such stern moral decrees that James rebelled when he published his famous essay "The Will To Believe" in 1896. In opposition to Clifford, he tried to establish the moral proposition that under certain circumstances a man may *rightly* accept a proposition for which he does not have the support of reason or experience. He described "The Will To Believe" as "an essay in justification *of* faith, a defence of our right to adopt a believing attitude in religious matters, in spite of the fact that our merely logical intellect may not have been coerced".[36] In defending his faith, James resembled Edwards, who also thought he saw a road to religious truth which was neither logical nor empirical. In other words, James' Will To Believe was in the same tradition as Edwards' Sense of the Heart and Emerson's Reason, not to speak of Peirce's view that the heart is a perceptive organ.

In "The Will To Believe" James pled eloquently for the view that the adoption of belief is not governed solely by the rules of scientific evidence-gathering. Six years earlier he had written in his *Principles of Psychology:* "Nothing is commoner than to hear people discriminate between their different selves of this sort: 'As a man I pity you, but as an official I must show you no mercy; as a politician I regard him as an ally, but as a moralist I loathe him;' etc., etc.".[37] In keeping with this observation, James held in "The Will To Believe" that as a scientist one has the right to believe a proposition only if it is established by evidence; but as a man with hopes, fears, and desires one may, under certain circumstances, believe a proposition which is not established by scientific evidence. James argued that sometimes a man is obliged to decide whether a proposition is true even though he cannot adduce scientific evidence for it or its negation, and James acknowledged that he himself was in this condition with regard to the fundamental propositions of religion. The agnostics told him that he should suspend judgment—neither believe nor disbelieve those propositions, neither assert them nor deny them—but James insisted that even though as a scientist a man is obliged to suspend judgment on the truth of a proposition in the absence of evidence, as a whole man he may believe it in deference to the demands of his "passional nature". Therefore, James flatly rejected Clifford's statement that it is always wrong to believe anything upon insufficient evidence. As we shall see, James tried to produce counter-examples to this supposedly absolute moral principle. He responded to Clifford as he might have to someone who had said that it is always wrong to tell a lie, to steal, to commit adultery, or to kill.

In later years James came to regret his use of the phrase "The Will To Believe" and preferred to speak only of "The Right To Believe".[38] Yet it is important to see how the will entered his argument. In his paper James was polemicizing mainly with Clifford, who had announced his stern principle in a paper called "The Ethics of Belief",[39] and James, as I have said, was also concerned to make a moral point about belief. The main subject of this moral debate was something that both parties regarded as a human act, namely, the act of adopting a certain kind of attitude toward a proposition like the proposition that God exists. And therefore James wished to make explicit the fact that such acts of adopting attitudes had to be voluntary or the products of willing if they were to be subject to moral judgment. However, James also wished to make perfectly clear that he did not maintain that we can believe *any* proposition just by choosing or trying to believe it. Just as there are some overt actions which we cannot perform by willing to perform them, so there are some acts of adopting attitudes toward propositions which we cannot perform. James asked: "Does it not seem preposterous on the very face of it to talk of our opinions being modifiable at will? Can our will either help or hinder our intellect in its perceptions of truth? Can we, by just willing it, believe that Abraham Lincoln's existence is a myth, and that the portraits of him in McClure's Magazine are all of some one else? Can we, by any effort of our will, or by any strength of wish that it were true, believe ourselves well and about when we are roaring with rheumatism in bed, or feel certain that the sum of the two one-dollar bills in our pocket must be a hundred dollars? We can *say* any of these things, but we are absolutely impotent to believe them; and of just such things is the whole fabric of the truths that we do believe in made up,—matters of fact, immediate or remote, as Hume said, and relations between ideas, which are either there or not there for us if we see them so, and which if not there cannot be put there by any action of our own".[40]

In this passage James said explicitly that no one could, by using his will, believe away, so to speak, the established propositions of history and mathematics. He agreed with Hume that all propositions formulated in the language of science and mathematics are tested by examining matters of fact or relations between ideas. They are tested by the intellect—by experience or reason—but by contrast, James thought, there are non-scientific and non-mathematical propositions which we may believe and which are not, he said in "The Will To Believe" as he had said in the *Psychology,* capable of being established or refuted by experience or reason. They form powerful counter-examples, he thought, to Clifford's view that we should believe only propositions for which scientific or mathematical arguments are available. One class of such counter-examples is the class of moral propositions, and James asserted: "A moral question is a question not of what sensibly exists, but of what is good, or would be good if it did exist.

Science can tell us what exists; but to compare the *worths,* both of what exists and of what does not exist, we must consult not science, but what Pascal calls our heart".[41] In addition, James asserted that what we would today call the meta-ethical question as to whether any moral beliefs are true or false, is also to be decided by the heart.[42] Even the question as to whether we should be skeptics in the theory of knowledge is not, according to James, a purely intellectual question.[43] And finally, he said that religious questions cannot be settled by a Humeian appeal to experience or to the relations between ideas. Neither an affirmative nor a negative answer to moral, metaphysical, and theological questions, then, can come from science or mathematics; and therefore we have the right to answer those that we feel obliged to answer by appealing to our hearts.

It is highly significant that James repeated the doctrine of his *Psychology* by distinguishing moral, metaphysical, and (this time) theological questions from those of natural science and mathematics by saying, with Hume,[44] that the former are not settled by appealing to matters of fact nor to relations between ideas. It is significant for one thing because James also had it in mind to *dispute* a certain contention of Hume's, namely, that statements that are neither empirical nor mathematico-logical should be burned up. I am thinking of a famous passage in Hume which twentieth-century positivists have cited with hearty approval. Hume declared: "When we run over libraries, persuaded of these principles, what havoc must we make? If we take in our hand any volume; of divinity or school metaphysics, for instance; let us ask, *Does it contain any abstract reasoning concerning quantity or number?* No. *Does it contain any experimental reasoning concerning matter of fact and existence?* No. Commit it then to the flames: for it can contain nothing but sophistry and illusion".[45] By contrast, James argued in "The Will To Believe" for our right to accept, on non-empirical and non-logical grounds, just such religious statements as Hume wished to burn, just such statements as a twentieth-century positivist would declare "cognitively meaningless". When Hume was not for burning them, he asserted ironically that religious statements should be defended by an appeal to revelation; [46] but James maintained with utmost seriousness that they could be defended by an appeal to faith.

It follows that James does not adopt anything like a twentieth-century positivist's criterion of meaning. He never says that statements which are neither empirical nor mathematical must be cognitively meaningless. He maintained that they could be true and therefore meaningful even though our scientific intellects could not discover them to be true. In 1895, a year before "The Will To Believe" appeared, he published an essay called "Is Life Worth Living?", in which he gave an illustration of the sort of non-scientific proposition he had in mind and an illustration of the non-intellectual ground on which it could be accepted. "I wish to make you feel," he wrote, ". . . that we have a right to believe the physical order to be only a partial order; that we have a right to supplement it by an unseen spiritual order which we assume on trust, if only thereby life may seem to us better worth living again." [47] In the same essay he also said of the religious propositions with which he was concerned: "Religion has meant many things in human history; but when from now onward I use the word I mean to use it in the supernaturalist sense, as declaring that the so-called order of nature, which constitutes this world's experience, is only one portion of the total universe, and that there stretches beyond this visible world an unseen world of which we now know nothing positive, but in its relation to which the true significance of our present mundane life consists. A man's religious faith (whatever more special items of doctrine it may involve) means for me essentially his faith in the existence of an unseen order of some kind in which the riddles of the natural order may be found ex-

plained".[48] And James conveyed his attitude toward the bearing of science on all of this in the following passage: "There is
included in human nature an ingrained naturalism and materialism of mind which can only admit facts that are actually
tangible. Of this sort of mind the entity called 'science' is the
idol. Fondness for the word 'scientist' is one of the notes by
which you may know its votaries; and its short way of killing
any opinion that it disbelieves in is to call it 'unscientific.' It
must be granted that there is no slight excuse for this. Science
has made such glorious leaps in the last three hundred years,
and extended our knowledge of nature so enormously both in
general and in detail; men of science, moreover, have as a
class displayed such admirable virtues,—that it is no wonder
if the worshippers of science lose their head. In this very University [Harvard], accordingly, I have heard more than one
teacher say that all the fundamental conceptions of truth have
already been found by science, and that the future has only
the details of the picture to fill in. But the slightest reflection
on the real conditions will suffice to show how barbaric such
notions are. They show such a lack of scientific imagination,
that it is hard to see how one who is actively advancing any
part of science can make a mistake so crude. Think how many
absolutely new scientific conceptions have arisen in our own
generation, how many new problems have been formulated
that were never thought of before, and then cast an eye upon
the brevity of science's career. It began with Galileo, not
three hundred years ago. Four thinkers since Galileo, each in-
forming his successor of what discoveries his own lifetime had
seen achieved, might have passed the torch of science into
our hands as we sit here in this room. Indeed, for the matter
of that, an audience much smaller than the present one, an
audience of some five or six score people, if each person in it
could speak for his own generation, would carry us away to
the black unknown of the human species, to days without a
document or monument to tell their tale. Is it credible that

such a mushroom knowledge, such a growth overnight as this, *can* represent more than the minutest glimpse of what the universe will really prove to be when adequately understood? No! our science is a drop, our ignorance a sea. Whatever else be certain, this at least is certain,—that the world of our present natural knowledge *is* enveloped in a larger world of *some* sort of whose residual properties we at present can frame no positive idea".[49]

When James acknowledged that science could not establish the truths of religion, he was of course rejecting the claims of natural religion, as his friend Chauncey Wright had. "There were times when Leibnitzes with their heads buried in monstrous wigs could compose Theodicies, and when stall-fed officials of an established church could prove by the valves in the heart and the round ligament of the hip-joint the existence of a 'Moral and Intelligent Contriver of the World.' But those times", he went on to inform his YMCA audience, "are past; and we of the nineteenth century, with our evolutionary theories and our mechanical philosophies, already know nature too impartially and too well to worship unreservedly any God of whose character she can be an adequate expression." [50] James was prepared to admit that some men could conclude from the failures of natural theology that they should accept the counsel of "agnostic positivism" and believe neither that a supernatural God exists nor that he does not exist. "If a thinker had no stake in the unknown, no vital needs, to live or languish according to what the unseen world contained, a philosophic neutrality and refusal to believe either one way or the other would be his wisest cue. But, unfortunately", James said as he described his own predicament and that of other men, "neutrality is not only inwardly difficult, it is also outwardly unrealizable, where our relations to an alternative are practical and vital." [51] Here he reached a very important step in his argument. If science is unable to assert that God exists and unable to assert that God does not exist, James conclud-

ed that science necessarily left open what he called a *live*
option [52] for whole men who felt the need to believe religious
propositions.

James then said in one of the most crucial steps in his argument, that such men were also faced with what he called a
forced option, in other words, that they had the option of believing that God exists or not believing that God exists, and
that they had no third alternative.[53] The agnostic, of course,
would characterize the situation differently. He would say
that when a man is confronted with any proposition, he may
(*1*) *believe* it; or (*2*) *disbelieve* it—which means believe its
negation; or (*3*) *neither believe it nor disbelieve it,* which is
to say doubt it, because he has no evidence to support either
belief or disbelief. There is, of course, no logical conflict between James' and the agnostic's ways of characterizing the situation in which we find ourselves when confronted with any
proposition. There is no more logical conflict than there
would be if one person said that the spectrum was divisible
into violet and non-violet regions, whereas another said it was
divisible into violet, blue, green, yellow, orange, and red regions. The first person—the counterpart of James—could say
that if he had to put an object somewhere on a spectrum, he
would have the option of putting it on the violet part or not
putting it on the violet part, the latter being equivalent to
putting it on the non-violet part. The second person—the
counterpart of the agnostic—could say that *he* had the option
of putting it on just one of *six* parts. Why, then, did James
insist on the two-part division of possible attitudes toward a
religious proposition, namely, belief and non-belief, and
thereby disregard the agnostic's distinction between *two forms
of non-belief,* namely, disbelieving on the one hand and
doubting on the other? The following passage gives us some
idea of James' reasoning: ". . . belief and doubt are living attitudes, and involve conduct on our part. Our only way, for
example, of doubting, or refusing to believe, that a certain

thing *is,* is continuing to act as if it were *not.* If, for instance, I refuse to believe that the room is getting cold, I leave the windows open and light no fire just as if it still were warm. If I doubt that you are worthy of my confidence, I keep you un-informed of all my secrets just as if you were *un*worthy of the same. If I doubt the need of insuring my house, I leave it un-insured as much as if I believed there were no need. And so if I must not believe that the world is divine, I can only express that refusal by declining ever to act distinctively as if it were so, which can only mean acting on certain critical occasions as if it were *not* so, or in an irreligious way. There are, you see, inevitable occasions in life when inaction is a kind of action, and must count as action, and when not to be for is to be practically against; and in all such cases strict and consistent neutrality is an unattainable thing".[54]

We here see that James' basic contention is that proposi-tional attitudes like believing, disbelieving, and doubting have counterparts which are overt actions like shutting win-dows but that among overt actions we cannot make distinc-tions as fine as those we make among propositional attitudes. For example, the attitude of disbelieving a proposition and the attitude of doubting it—the (2) and (3) of the agnostic— are fused by James on the level of action. He cannot find an action-counterpart of doubting which is different from the ac-tion-counterpart of disbelieving. That is why he says that "our only way . . . of doubting, or refusing to believe, that a cer-tain thing *is,* is continuing to act as if it were *not*", from which it would follow that our only way of doubting, or of being agnostic about God's existence, is continuing to act as if God does not exist. In this way James amalgamates the posi-tions of the agnostic and the atheist. From a practical point of view, he says, they are both *against* the proposition that God exists because neither of them is for it. A man who merely doubts that God exists may, of course, distinguish himself from the atheist when asked the question: "What is your attitude toward the proposition that God exists?" by *saying* "I neither believe it nor disbelieve it", since the atheist will *say,* in answer to the same question, "I disbelieve it". But such a speech-act on the part of the agnostic is disregarded by James. He looks rather at the non-verbal behavior of the agnostic and comes to the conclusion that because the agnostic, like the atheist, does not *do* the things that the theist does, they are both in the same boat. What James failed to recognize, however, is that the disbelieving atheist might express his disbelief by burning churches, whereas the doubting agnostic might express his doubt by letting them stand and not attending them. Not everyone who is neither for nor against a proposition shows by his action that he is against it.

James also failed to recognize that when he described the forced option as between belief in God on the one hand, and disbelief-or-doubt on the other, he was using only one method of transforming the agnostic's trichotomy into a dichotomy. James did not seem to realize that he might have transformed it into the forced option of disbelief on the one hand and belief-or-doubt on the other. If he had made the latter transformation, he could have said that the agnostic was against the *disbeliever* because he was not for him. And once we have started down this road, we might just as well remark on the third possibility, namely, the forced option of doubt on the one hand and belief-or-disbelief on the other, in which case both theists and atheists could be described as being against the agnostic because they are not in agreement with him. Why, then, did James choose to turn the trichotomy of belief-disbelief-doubt into the dichotomy of belief and non-belief, and then equate non-belief with disbelief? Because he was more inclined to adopt the attitude of a believer than he was to adopt any of the other alternatives. Therefore, he saw all other thinkers in a uniform blur. He saw non-believers as disbelievers, and it did not make any difference that some of these non-believers were disbelievers and others doubters. A man who adored the color violet might be similarly inclined to divide the spectrum into a violet and non-violet part and not see differences among the other five colors.

After James pointed out that the options for the person who is facing the religious question are live and forced, he added one other characteristic, namely, that they are momentous,[55] by which he meant that great practical consequences are at stake when a man decides which alternative he would choose: belief or non-belief. Once James explained what he meant by a live, forced, and momentous option—in short, a genuine option—he could state the moral maxim that he wished to pit against Clifford's. It was that a person who is faced with a genuine option between believing and not believing a proposition which cannot be established by logical or empirical means, has the right to believe that proposition if not believing it will run him the risk of "losing" the valuable truth it may express and not gain him very much by way of compensation for running that risk. To illustrate his view of the option involved, James imagines that a man has been invited by Nansen, the Arctic explorer, to go on an expedition to the North Pole, and so we may think of the man as presented with the genuine option of believing that he should go with Nansen or not believing that he should go.[56] These alternatives are analogous to believing in God or not. James supposes that the man does not have a logically coercive reason for believing that he *should* go along with Nansen and that he does not have one for not believing that he should go. James also supposes that in all likelihood the man will never have another chance of attaining such "North Pole immortality", and, of course, that he *wants* to attain such immortality. So, James says, if the man adopts the belief that he should go, he stands the chance of attaining some great good that he will probably never attain again, whereas if he suspends judgment and "goes without" that belief he almost certainly loses that chance. James does not, however, make much of the fact that if the man believes that he *should* go, he also stands a good chance of getting killed. This, as we have seen, is typical of the way in which James describes his genuine options. They are usually described as options between believing and not believing a proposition where the advantages of believing truly are very great and the disadvantages of believing falsely are very small. That is why he says in the spirit of Pascal's wager that the individual who adopts a belief in God stands a chance of gaining an enormous lot if that belief is in fact true, but risks no great loss if it is in fact false. This would certainly be the case if the god in whom one believes favors those who believe in him and punishes those who don't. If he does exist and one believes in him, one is in for great happiness; but if he does *not* exist and one believes in him, one is not going to be punished for *that* mistake.[57]

However, even without regard to the special dividends issued by such a god to those who believe in him, James seemed to think that the more religious or spiritual of the contradictory beliefs involved in a genuine option is always the one that we should think of ourselves as having the right to adopt. In the abstract, of course, James need not have maintained this, since his right to believe was in principle a double-edged sword.[58] We have seen that if he had been more sympathetic to atheism, he might well have spoken of our right to adopt atheism in the absence of logically coercive evidence. Then James could have regarded the agnostics and the theists as against atheism by not being for it, and he could have pled eloquently for the right to believe that God does *not* exist. Yet it never occurred to James to advertise his Will To Believe as a device that could be used under certain circumstances to justify faith in the *non*-existence of God, because James was on the side of the angels. It was almost inconceivable to him that a man should see any practical advantage in believing that God does not exist.

On the basis of James' discussion of the status of metaphysical and religious belief we can see that by the time he had published his *Principles of Psychology* and his *Will To Believe,* he had come a long way from the doctrines of Locke. Even though he still clung to the Lockeian distinction between rational and non-rational propositions, his treatment of determinism and agnosticism, and his more general characterization of the grounds on which he thought we are entitled to adopt metaphysical and religious beliefs, showed that he gave sentiment a voice in the establishment of belief that Locke might well have described as the voice of Enthusiasm. For, after all, Locke had written against Enthusiasm: "Whatsoever credit or authority we give to any proposition more than it receives from the principles and proofs it supports itself upon, is owing to our inclinations that way, and is so far a derogation from the love of truth as such: which, as it can receive no evidence from our passions or interests, so it should receive no tincture from them".[59] And James' Will To Believe was in the tradition of Enthusiasm insofar as James was willing to permit men to justify their religious—and their metaphysical —beliefs by appealing to something other than logic and experience. True, James gave an *argument* for permitting men to accept religious beliefs on faith—the argument that they might lose valuable truth if they became mired in agnosticism while reason and experience were perforce silent—but his strategy was not radically different from that of Edwards when the Calvinist added his Sense of the Heart to Locke's five. Like Edwards, James was willing to allow logic and experience to have their say in the establishment of some beliefs provided that the will or the heart had its say in the case of others. This trialism was soon to be superseded by an even more radical doctrine that was maturing in James' mind, one which broke down the trichotomy in which reason solved the problems of pure science, experience the problems of natural science, and sentiment the problems of metaphysics, religion, and morals.

Similarities Between James' Psychology
and His Pragmatism

Although James' *Principles of Psychology* and his *Will To
Believe* help us understand the doctrines to which James
came toward the end of his life, they form no more than a
foyer that leads into the most important room of his intellectual edifice, *Pragmatism,* published in 1907. In my opinion,
there are places in *Pragmatism* where James seems to be moving away from the idea that problems of pure science are
solved by rational comparison of concepts, problems of natural science by appealing to experience, and problems of metaphysics, religion, and morals by appealing to sentiment. In
Pragmatism there are important vestiges of this earlier view,
yet we also find in *Pragmatism* a tendency to hold that the
process of arriving at belief is one in which we test our whole
stock of opinions—logical, physical, metaphysical, religious,
and moral—for the *stock*'s capacity to satisfy us emotionally,
to satisfy our need to be consistent, to satisfy our need to
anticipate experience, and to satisfy our need to have esthetically elegant explanations. A related tendency is also evident
in *A Pluralistic Universe,* where James gives evidence of
being prepared to abandon a logical principle in order to
meet a challenge from experience. Before analyzing this last
and least Lockeian phase of James' thought, it will be useful
to call attention to certain continuities between *Pragmatism*
and James' *Psychology.*

The main continuity arises from the fact that both books
contain a distinction between beliefs that purport to copy
something and beliefs that do not, although different kinds of
beliefs are called copy-beliefs in the different books. In the
Psychology the typical example of a copy-belief is a generalization like *fire burns, water wets,* or *glass refracts;* whereas in
Pragmatism James speaks of less general beliefs about sensible

objects and of beliefs about concepts as copying realities. He says that if you shut your eyes and think of a clock on the wall, you may form a belief which copies something about its dial. He also speaks of the conceptual belief that $2+2=4$ as a copy-belief. Furthermore, he speaks in *Pragmatism* of all copy-beliefs as being "coerced". One therefore gets the impression from *Pragmatism*, as from the *Psychology*, that James holds that we are *forced* by reality to hold certain beliefs whereas we have a certain kind of freedom to accept or not to accept others. And since James distinguishes between "the coercions of the sensible order"—like the coercion which is exerted upon him to believe that the large hand of his clock is at 12—and "coercions of the ideal order"—like the coercion exerted upon him to believe that $2+2=4$—he is faced with two fundamental questions: (*1*) On what grounds do we accept *un*coerced beliefs? and (*2*) What beliefs are *un*coerced?

Now the predominant answer to the first question in the *Psychology* and in several of the essays in *The Will To Believe* is that we may appeal to *sentiment* in accepting beliefs which have been coerced neither by the sensible nor by the ideal order. And in those books the predominant answer to the second question is that because metaphysical, theological, and moral beliefs are not coerced by reality, we may accept them by appealing to sentiment. It is important to emphasize that in *The Will To Believe* James shows some tendency to deny that theoretical beliefs of science are subject to the operations of the Will To Believe, since in that work he seems to regard anything established by science as "coercing the logical intellect". By contrast, *Pragmatism* reveals a tendency to regard even scientific theories as beliefs which are not coerced, and this is why they are subject to James' pragmatic theory of truth. Therefore we may say that when called upon to answer question (*1*) above, James in *Pragmatism* says that uncoerced beliefs are accepted on *pragmatic* grounds; and when called upon to answer question (*2*), he says that not only are meta-

physical, religious, and moral beliefs uncoerced, but that theoretical beliefs of science are too. For this reason, we may say
that there are places in *Pragmatism* where James continues
the trialism of the *Psychology* and *The Will To Believe*—the
trialism of (*a*) beliefs coerced by sense-experience, (*b*) beliefs
coerced by the relations between concepts, and (*c*) beliefs established by other means—even though *Pragmatism* may
change the extensions of these categories by moving the theoretical beliefs of natural science into category (*c*). Because
there are parts of *Pragmatism* in which James continues to accept his trialism, Bertrand Russell was led to say in an early
critique of the book that for James, "it is only when we pass
beyond plain matters of fact and *a priori* truisms that the
pragmatic notion of truth comes in".[60]

The Other James

Interestingly enough, however, while criticizing James' pragmatic theory of truth, Russell outlined a conception of science
not unlike one which is present in parts of *Pragmatism* that
are very important. Russell said: "In any science, we have a
collection of facts bound together (as far as possible) by general laws. The facts appear, in the formal exposition, as deductions from the laws; this, at least, holds for the most advanced sciences, such as mathematics and physics. But in
reality the laws are inductions from the facts. We cannot say
that this or that fact proves this or that law: the whole body
of facts proves (or, rather, renders probable) the whole body
of laws. It might be thought that, in an *experimentum crucis,*
a single fact establishes a single law; but this is only the case
so long as the other laws of the science are taken for granted.
If other facts should lead us to doubt the other laws, the interpretation of our *experimentum crucis* might be wholly
changed. Thus the justification of a science is that it fits all
the known facts, and that no alternative system of hypotheses

is known which fits the facts equally well. We may therefore say truly that scientific theories are adopted simply because they *work,* i.e. because their consequences are satisfactory".[61]

Such a holistic—as it is sometimes called—conception of science is espoused by James when he abandons his trialism, as I shall now try to show. It emerges in those parts of *Pragmatism* in which he describes the establishment of belief as a process in which we do not test opinions in isolation but rather as parts of a whole stock of opinions. Such a stock of opinions, however, would be larger than that contemplated by Russell in the quotation above insofar as it would include truths of natural science, of logic, of mathematics, of metaphysics, of theology, and of morals. This point of view emerges in *Pragmatism* when James expresses agreement with the views of Dewey and Schiller.[62] From them he says he takes over the idea that the act of adopting a believing attitude toward a new opinion is always performed while holding a stock of old opinions that may be logical, religious, esthetic, metaphysical, moral, or scientific in character and that even while we are contemplating the adoption of an isolated opinion, the whole stock is by implication under consideration. This stock may be put to a strain which is described as follows by James: "Somebody contradicts them [the opinions]; or in a reflective moment he [the believer] discovers that they contradict each other; or he hears of facts with which they are incompatible; or desires arise in him which they cease to satisfy".[63] It is as important to note the diversity of the things that can, according to James, put the stock to a strain, as it is to note the diversity of the kinds of beliefs he includes within the stock itself. An unsatisfied desire may challenge the stock as much as the discovery of a logical contradiction or a recalcitrant fact, and it is James' belief in the parity of unsatisfied desire with the two other creators of strain that distinguishes his later position. Had he not maintained such parity he would not have been saying anything very novel; many philosophers hold that the uncovering of a logical contradiction or a discrepancy with fact should force a man to revise his stock of opinions. James' most unusual idea is that the failure of a system to satisfy a *desire* might lead to a revision of the system in which a logical, metaphysical, scientific, or religious belief might be altered. Moreover, James did not mean that the thinker faced with one of these three kinds of difficulties—contradiction, discrepancy with fact, or unsatisfied desire—was bound to tinker only with what may be called a "corresponding" part of the system. It would seem that on the view advanced in some parts of *Pragmatism,* a conflict with fact or a failure to satisfy desire could lead to the abandonment of a logical principle, of a physical belief, a moral belief, a psychological belief, or even a metaphysical belief.

In order to highlight this element in James' thinking about belief, I shall quote and comment on several passages that immediately follow his reference to the three kinds of events that may put the individual's stock of opinions to a strain. "The result [of this strain] is an inward trouble to which his [the individual's] mind till then had been a stranger, and from which he seeks to escape by modifying his previous mass of opinions. He saves as much of it as he can, for in this matter of belief we are all extreme conservatives. So he tries to change first this opinion, and then that (for they resist change very variously), until at last some new idea comes up which he can graft upon the ancient stock with a minimum of disturbance of the latter, some idea that mediates between the stock and the new experience and runs them into one another most felicitously and expediently." [64] The process of trying to change first this opinion and then that leads the individual to conduct a trial to which any belief may be summoned; but other things being equal, the older the belief from the human race's point of view, the more likely it is that it will not be tampered with. The new idea that is adopted, he says, "preserves the older stock of truths with a minimum of modification, stretching them just enough to make them admit the novelty, but conceiving that in ways as familiar as the case leaves possible. An *outrée* explanation, violating all our preconceptions, would never pass for a true account of a novelty. We should scratch round industriously till we found something less excentric. The most violent revolutions in an individual's beliefs leave most of his old order standing. Time and space, cause and effect, nature and history, and one's own biography remain untouched".[65] But even though he says that the older truths are usually not touched, James does not maintain that they are untouchable. Referring to Dewey and Schiller on "the most ancient parts of truth", like logical truth, James remarks that "they also once were plastic. They also were called true for human reasons. They also mediated between still earlier truths and what in those days were novel observations. Purely objective truth, truth in whose establishment the function of giving human satisfaction in marrying previous parts of experience with newer parts played no role whatever, is nowhere to be found".[66] And because he held that such truth is nowhere to be found, James seemed to hold that the truths of mathematics and logic differ from so-called empirical truths only in degree. If the former were established because they performed a happy marriage, they can be disestablished when the marriage ceases to be happy: "how plastic even the oldest truths nevertheless really are has been vividly shown in our day by the transformation of logical and mathematical ideas".[67]

This holistic point of view is quite different from the trialistic view that predominates in the *Psychology* and in *The Will To Believe*. The trialistic view, which I think is by implication abandoned by James in some parts of *Pragmatism* and in *A Pluralistic Universe,* is described as follows by Professor A. J. Ayer, who, in my opinion, underestimates the holistic tendency in James. Ayer writes: "What [James] should have made much clearer than he does is that true beliefs are not treated by him as being all of a pattern. They all work, but they work in different ways. The criteria by which we have to assess a belief which relates to a matter of empirical fact are different from those which apply to a belief which is concerned only with relations between ideas: and these are different again from the criteria which apply to beliefs whose function is to satisfy our moral and emotional requirements. These distinctions are implicit in James's writing, but he does not draw attention to them. In my view, it is his failure to set them out explicitly that has been mainly responsible for the extent to which his position has been misunderstood. In particular, the notion that a belief is to be accounted true if it gives one satisfaction to hold it is applied by him only to beliefs of the third class, and to them only with reservations. It has, however, been almost universally assumed by James's critics that he puts this forward unconditionally as a general criterion of truth".[68]

This is a fair description of the trialistic strain in James' thinking, but as soon as we begin to take account of certain parts of *Pragmatism,* we see how his trialism turns into a variety of holism. As Russell correctly pointed out, the typical Jamesian belief about a plain matter of fact was James' belief about the dial of his clock—a belief which James described as "coerced by the sensible order". Therefore, the class of beliefs which relate to matters of empirical fact—when so construed —does *not* include theoretical beliefs of science, as Russell also correctly observed. But in that case where are the latter to be put in Ayer's trichotomy? If his first category coincides with James' beliefs coerced by the sensible order, they cannot be put there. And surely Ayer would not put them in his second category of beliefs that are concerned only with relations between ideas. Therefore Ayer must put them in his third class of beliefs, which are accounted true if they are emotionally satisfying. Yet it is difficult when one reads *Pragmatism* to interpret James as holding that a scientific theory is accepted

on grounds that have *nothing* to do with empirical fact and
nothing to do with logic, and that only sentiment is involved
in accepting such a theory. That is why he is prompted to hold
that when we decide whether to accept a scientific theory, a
variety of considerations plays a part. A variety of different
kinds of claims must be satisfied, and not merely the claims of
sensory experience, when we decide to accept the theory. Consider the following passage: "We must find a theory that will
work; and that means something extremely difficult; for our
theory must mediate between all previous truths and certain
new experiences. It must derange common sense and previous
belief as little as possible, and it must lead to some sensible
terminus or other that can be verified exactly. To 'work'
means both these things; and the squeeze is so tight that there
is little loose play for any hypothesis. Our theories are wedged
and controlled as nothing else is. Yet sometimes alternative
theoretic formulas are equally compatible with all the truths
we know, and then we choose between them for subjective
reasons. We choose the kind of theory to which we are already
partial; we follow 'elegance' or 'economy.' Clerk-Maxwell
somewhere says it would be 'poor scientific taste' to choose the
more complicated of two equally well-evidenced conceptions;
and you will all agree with him". Immediately after all of this,
James says: "Truth in science is what gives us the maximum
possible sum of satisfactions, taste included, but consistency
both with previous truth and with novel fact is always the
most imperious claimant".[69] This passage certainly shows that
James does not hold that there are three sharply separated categories of beliefs: one consisting of beliefs tested by sensory
experience, a second consisting of those which are tested by
perceiving the relations between concepts, and a third consisting of beliefs which we accept if and only if they satisfy our
moral and emotional requirements. Rather he holds that a
scientific theory is subject to considerations which are referred
to in the descriptions of all three of Ayer's categories. It must

derange previous belief as little as possible, including logical belief; it must have consequences verifiable by the senses;
it may have to pass muster before extra-logical and extra-
empirical considerations like those of elegance and economy;
and, I think we can add on the basis of other passages previously quoted, it may sometimes be surrendered if the stock
of which it forms a part runs counter to desire. All of this
shows that it is very hard to interpret James as holding that
there are three different cubbyholes for three different kinds
of beliefs which work in radically different ways. In the passage I have just quoted, James says explicitly that a scientific
theory works in at least two senses of the word, a statement
which is very much in accord with the holism I have been at-
tributing to him. In other words, he holds that *one* belief may
be subjected to three standards which Ayer—and, I admit,
the James of the *Psychology* and *The Will To Believe*—
associates with three different, mutually exclusive cubbyholes:
with standards set by sensory experience; by mathematico-
logical principles; and by taste, desire, or sentiment.

In spite of James' statement in 1904 that his pragmatism
was compatible with the view that he held about necessary
truth in the last chapter of the *Psychology*,[70] I think that the
passages I have just quoted from *Pragmatism* suggest that
there he was moving away from the view advocated in his
Psychology. In *Pragmatism* there is at least some tendency to
maintain that the distinction between so-called *a priori* beliefs
and *a posteriori* beliefs is not a sharp one. By 1906 James was
taking a long step away from the Lockeian dualism between
immutable and contingent truth, as well as from the Kantian
dualism between *a priori* and *a posteriori* truth. As a matter of
fact there are stirrings of this kind even in the *Psychology*
when James comes to discuss the Kantian distinction between
analytic and synthetic statements in a footnote. He says there:
"Some readers may expect me to plunge into the old debate as
to whether the *a priori* truths are 'analytic' or 'synthetic.' It

seems to me that the distinction is one of Kant's most unhappy legacies, for the reason that it is impossible to make it
sharp. No one will say that such analytic judgments as 'equi-
distant lines can nowhere meet' are *pure* tautologies. The
predicate is a somewhat new way of conceiving as well as of
naming the subject. There is *something* 'ampliative' in our
greatest truisms, our state of mind is richer after than before
we have uttered them. This being the case, the question 'at
what point does the new state of mind cease to be *implicit* in
the old?' is too vague to be answered. The only sharp way of
defining synthetic propositions would be to say that they express a relation between *two data* at least. But it is hard to
find any proposition which cannot be construed as doing this.
Even verbal definitions do it. Such painstaking attempts as
that latest one by Mr. D. G. Thompson to prove all necessary
judgments to be analytic (System of Psychology, II, pp. 232ff.)
seem accordingly but *nugae difficiles,* and little better than
wastes of ink and paper. All philosophic interest vanishes
from the question, the moment one ceases to ascribe to *any a
priori* truths (whether analytic or synthetic) that 'legislative
character for all possible experience' which Kant believed in.
We ourselves have denied such legislative character, and con-
tended that it was for experience itself to prove whether its
data can or cannot be assimilated to those ideal terms between
which *a priori* relations obtain. The analytic-synthetic debate
is thus for us devoid of all significance".[71]

Although it is difficult to square this statement with other
statements that James makes in his *Psychology,* it is also difficult to square it with an interpretation that links James too
closely to twentieth-century positivism, which depends so
heavily on something like the distinction between analytic
and synthetic. Still, the statement anticipates the view in *Pragmatism* which I have associated with James' inclination to
break down a sharp distinction between logical principles and
those of natural science. This same tendency is also present in

A Pluralistic Universe. That book brought to a grand climax James' constant inclination to favor what he called an anti-intellectualistic philosophy, an inclination which was very much encouraged by his admiration for the work of Henri Bergson.

Without entering the details of what in my opinion is James' least clear book, I think it is safe to say that that book contains statements which are very hard to square with the idea that logic and mathematics are not subject to the demands of experience. Bergson, James tells us, had led him "to renounce the intellectualistic method and the current notion that logic is an adequate measure of what can or cannot be".[72] Bergson, he says, holds that logic must stand or fall with the so-called conceptual method because its truths are established merely by the examination of concepts. "But," James continues in his redaction of Bergson, "the conceptual method is a transformation which the flux of life undergoes at our hands in the interests of practice essentially and only subordinately in the interests of theory. We live forward, we understand backward, said a danish writer; and to understand life by concepts is to arrest its movement, cutting it up into bits as if with scissors, and immobilizing these in our logical herbarium where, comparing them as dried specimens, we can ascertain which of them statically includes or excludes which other".[73] Then there is James' radical Bergsonian remark: "For my own part, I have finally found myself compelled to *give up the logic,* fairly, squarely, and irrevocably. . . . Reality, life, experience, concreteness, immediacy, use what word you will, exceeds our logic, overflows and surrounds it".[74] This, I suggest, is not the positivistic-sounding doctrine put forth in the last chapter of the *Psychology,* where James treated formal logic and mathematics as composed of beliefs which are not at the mercy of life and concrete experience. It is a doctrine more consonant with those parts of *Pragmatism* where he speaks of logic as composed of old, but nevertheless plastic, truths that may be overturned by something besides conceptual analysis. Moreover, Appendix C of *A Pluralistic Universe* explicitly diverges from the doctrine defended in the *Psychology*. For these reasons, I believe that James' enthusiastic reception of Bergson's ideas was in accord with what may be called the anti-Humeian tendency in *Pragmatism,* and with James' notion that logical beliefs fall into the stock of beliefs that must square with something besides what we perceive "at a glance" to be the relations between concepts. I believe, moreover, that this anti-Humeian strain in James is not only in keeping with some of the views of Dewey—as we shall see later—but also prefigures the views of Professor W. V. Quine, who writes: "The totality of our so-called knowledge or beliefs, from the most casual matters of geography and history to the profoundest laws of atomic physics or even of pure mathematics and logic, is a man-made fabric which impinges on experience only along the edges", and that it is "folly to seek a boundary between synthetic statements, which hold contingently on experience, and analytic statements, which hold come what may. Any statement can be held true come what may, if we make drastic enough adjustments elsewhere in the system. Even a statement very close to the periphery can be held true in the face of recalcitrant experience by pleading hallucination or by amending certain statements of the kind called logical laws. Conversely, by the same token, no statement is immune to revision. Revision even of the logical law of the excluded middle has been proposed as a means of simplifying quantum mechanics; and what difference is there in principle between such a shift and the shift whereby Kepler superseded Ptolemy, or Einstein Newton, or Darwin Aristotle?".[75] I should add that Quine, unlike James, does not hold that feeling or sentiment enters into the testing of what he calls the totality of our beliefs, but when Quine suggests that a conflict with experience may occasion a surrender even of a logical principle, he is expressing a view much like that which I find in some of James' later writings.

The main contribution of the later James was his idea that

whole men test whole, variegated stocks of opinions by appealing to a variety of considerations. By the time he came to defend this view he had abandoned—whether or not he was clearly aware that he had—not only the rationalism that appears *between* the lines of his *Psychology* but also the positivistic dualism that appears *in* some lines of that work. In advocating or adumbrating such a view, he administered the sharpest of American blows to the Lockeian conception of strict knowledge. Edwards had thought it necessary to allow a religious room for the Sense of the Heart to operate in while Lockeian business went on as usual in science and mathematics; James Wilson had let the heart have its say only in morals and law; Emerson used his sentimental Reason primarily in morals, religion, and poetry; and even in *The Will To Believe* and the *Principles of Psychology* James kept sentiment within certain limits. But in his *Pragmatism* and *A Pluralistic Universe,* a development of 150 years came to a climax. The claims of the heart were enterable in testing any claim to knowledge of any kind, and by that time the rationalistic Lockeian model had been thoroughly dismantled. No longer could James consistently hold that some truths are eternal, immutable, necessary, and *a priori* while he maintained that all truth was at some time or other plastic. Sentiment and immediate experience were never given more importance in American philosophy, and therefore it has been well said that James represented the triumph of Romanticism in American thought. It should not be surprising, therefore, to find that A. O. Lovejoy—the same Lovejoy who so carefully studied and criticized Romantic thought in so many of its manifestations—should have been shocked when he read *A Pluralistic Universe* and detected the older James' departure from the younger James' views. Lovejoy wrote to James: "In some places it seems to me that, after fetching a long compass, you have come out, via Bergson, at just those enormities which you began by most tellingly castigating in Hegel. As I always admired that castigation, and have always thought you our most resolute apostle of loyalty to the plain old Eighteenth Century Understanding—of the manful acceptance of its *entweder-oder* and its unresolved oppositions, I am now and then a good deal shocked and disappointed at this part of the new book . . .".[76]

Before concluding this chapter, I would once again emphasize that James was a divided mind on many of the subjects I have taken up. Even after *A Pluralistic Universe* appeared, he wobbled about how far the claims of sensory experience could be used in evaluating logic and mathematics; and this is well illustrated in an exchange between him and Charles Peirce which followed the writing of *A Pluralistic Universe*. As I have indicated, Appendix C of that book does seem to take back a good deal of what James had said in the *Psychology* about logic and mathematics; so much, in fact, that when Charles Peirce read it in galleys (without having been shown the rest of the book), he wrote James in a tone that was characteristic: " 'T was that acute but shallow fellow, Chauncey Wright, whom I only availed myself of as a whetstone of wits, but whom you looked up to far too much, who probably entrapped you in his notion that in some part of the universe one and one perhaps do not make two".[77] In reply, James was not in my opinion very bold, and wrote: "I don't deserve as elaborate and instructive a letter as you have written, nor do I fully deserve all your censure, even though I was conceived and born in philosophic sin, for I expressly *do* believe with you that in the universe of possibles, of merely mental truth, as Locke calls it, relations *are* exact". James then went on to say: "But wait till you see my forthcoming book!",[78] as if that would assuage Peirce. Yet anyone who reads the main body of *A Pluralistic Universe* will find it hard to believe that Peirce would have concluded that James was *not* subject to the criticism implied in Peirce's remark about the influence of Chauncey Wright. True, James grants that insofar as logic and mathematics deal with concepts, they can arrive at exact truth, but the whole thrust of his argument is that such exactness is "fake", as Whitehead might have put it later, simply because the concepts have been made or devised in such a way as not to be adequate to "reality, life, experience, concreteness, and immediacy". One cannot avoid the conclusion that James *did* think that experience could conceivably overturn the beliefs of logic and mathematics, and it was this Wrightian (and, of course, Millian) view that he did *not* bravely defend to Peirce in the letter I have just quoted.

I should add, however, that on this issue Peirce was the pot calling the kettle black, for he too held incoherent views on this enormously difficult philosophical question, as Professor Justus Buchler has pointed out. Peirce also wobbled between a view that was congenial to twentieth-century positivists, namely, that logic is independent of fact, and the view that it is not. Understandably, Professor Buchler wrote after concluding his careful study of Peirce's views on this question: "In both logic and mathematics we have found disturbing inconsistencies in Peirce. Logical principles of inference sometimes appear to be validated by empirical testing, at other times to be formal rules with a linguistic character".[79] And in the chapter below on Dewey, we shall see that he, in some parts of his writing on this subject, was inclined to accept the former view of Peirce; and in others, the latter view. Pragmatism, we can safely say, presented no unified front to the world on this vital issue. Its chief representatives, notably James, could not make up their minds on the nature and scope of natural science; [80] but it is fair to say that in some of the writings of James we find the view that in the formation of *all* opinions, the whole man within us is at work, that in that process "intellect, will, taste, and passion co-operate just as they do in practical affairs".[81] When he came to this view, James completed a rebellion against Locke which had been going on in America since Edwards.

9 · Josiah Royce: Science, Christianity, and Absolute Idealism

In dividing a history into chapters that deal with individual philosophers, one is often faced by a difficulty which arises from the fact that after one has brought the development of, say, James' thought to the end of his life, one must, if one is going to discuss the development of his successor in the story —in this case, Royce—turn back to a time earlier than that where one has left off in discussing James. The situation would be different if Royce had been born the day after James had died, or if Royce's writing had begun after James' had ceased. The fact is, however, that James was only a dozen years older than Royce, their most important writing was done during about the same period, and, to make matters even more complicated for the historian of American philosophy, Royce defended philosophical doctrines which, in the general history of philosophy, antedate the ideas for which James became famous. By comparison to James, therefore, Royce was an intellectual throwback or conservative. We shall see later that as a consequence James seemed much younger than Royce to the generation younger than both of them. Moreover, while an Absolute Idealism like that of Royce was being abandoned by younger philosophers like Dewey, James was hailed by them as a leader who was guiding them out of the idealistic jungle and into the fresh philosophical air of the twentieth century.

Now that I have explained why we are about to roll back time in order to visit that jungle again, I turn to the subject of this chapter. After Peirce and James, Royce was the next philosophical star to appear in the American sky. Through James' efforts—and James, it must be said, knew that Royce was of another philosophical persuasion but was a big enough man to welcome an opponent whose intellect he respected— Royce was invited to come to Harvard in 1882 from a teaching post at his alma mater, the University of California at Berkeley. Soon after his arrival in Cambridge, Royce made plain that of all the distinguished American philosophers of his time he was best able to manage his doubts about the implications of science for religion and metaphysics. Peirce was permanently riven by his attachments to science, scholasticism, and Schelling; and James was concerned about whether pragmatism had succeeded as a "happy harmonizer" of science and religion; but Royce was confident almost from the beginning of his professional career that a correct analysis of religious doubt and scientific belief would not only be compatible with, but also lead logically to, Absolute Idealism in metaphysics and Christianity in religion.

Born in a California mining camp in 1855, Royce came to Harvard as a sort of frontier Lochinvar to rescue the genteel tradition from the clutches of agnosticism. This task he tried to carry out by stalwartly defending the idea that everything is part of a great Spirit called the Absolute, which Royce unhesitatingly identified with the personal God of the New Testament. Before Royce, of course, Emerson had made the American public aware of post-Kantian idealism by telling them that they all lay in the lap of an immense intelligence; but, unlike Royce, Emerson did not use mathematical works as bed-books and therefore carried less weight in the post-bellum academic world. Unlike the Concord Transcendentalists, Royce was a fully equipped professional idealist and a persuasive writer and teacher. He not only read logic, mathematics, and physics, but he was full of religious enthusiasm, learned in the history of philosophy and literature, and, as one of his students observed, found lecturing the easiest form of breathing. The versatile Royce, who had taught rhetoric as well as logic at Berkeley, tried his hand at social history when in 1886 he published his book *California;* in 1887 he produced a novel called *The Feud of Oakfield Creek;* and in 1908 he addressed himself to social problems in his *Philosophy of Loyalty* and his *Race Questions, Provincialism, and Other American Problems.* He was therefore a very formidable and wide-ranging advocate of idealism, one who could meet Herbert Spencer, W. K. Clifford, and T. H. Huxley on almost all of the grounds on which they chose to do battle. In spite of his literary skill, however, he was determined to deal with agnosticism in a logical manner. He was eager to avoid "the greatest danger of idealism, namely, fantastic speculation with noble purposes, but with merely poetical methods". His method, he insisted, would "be coldly theoretical, however deeply [his] religious philosophy [was] concerned in the outcome" of the struggle against atheists and agnostics.[1] Against them Royce deployed more powerful dialectical weapons than any American since Jonathan Edwards in defense of the Pauline view that we live, move, and have our being in God.

According to Royce, Absolute Idealism expressed the very core of Christian faith. It formulated in metaphysics what Paul meant when he said to the faithful, "Ye are dead, and your life is hid with Christ in God", and what the fourth Gospel meant when it made the Logos say, "I am the vine, ye are the branches". In a succession of books, Royce gave philosophical meaning to this religious metaphor by appealing to logic and to the methodology of the sciences. This is evident in his first book, *The Religious Aspect of Philosophy* (1885), in *The Spirit of Modern Philosophy* (1892), in his contribution to the collection, *The Conception of God* (1897), and in his long-winded masterwork of over a thousand pages, *The World and the Individual,* delivered as the Gifford Lectures in 1899 and 1900. By the time that work appeared, he had been stimulated by Charles Peirce to read mathematicians like Cantor and Dedekind; and, like Whitehead in a later generation, Royce was determined to beat atheists and agnostics at their own mathematical, logical, and scientific game, to turn their own weapons against them. This gave him great influence in the philosophical world and put him in a position that none of his elders had occupied. Not only was Emerson too literary, too intuitive, and too unargumentative to be taken seriously by philosophers who were becoming more technically minded, but even James was thought to be too unprofessional and free-wheeling by those who liked their theism expounded *in more geometrico.* And since Peirce was denied the right to teach his logic or his metaphysics at Harvard because his philosophical mores were too geometrical and his personal mores too irregular, Royce emerged as *the* great academic among American philosophers of his time, the father figure against whom a later generation of American realists and naturalists would rebel.

The Absolute

In defending his Absolute Idealism, Royce offered several different, though closely related, arguments. One took its point of departure from an analysis of scientific concepts and another from an analysis of the meaning of meaning; and if we approach Royce's philosophy by way of these two analyses, we can see how he was distinguished from other idealists by his desire to rest his metaphysics and epistemology upon a scientific and logical base.

The Absolute and Science. It will be recalled that according to Peirce any statement in which we attribute an objective property to a thing is logically equivalent to a statement which says that if a normal person were to perform a certain operation on that thing, he would have a certain sensory experience. In the same spirit—the spirit of Berkeley and Kant as well as that of Peirce [2]—Royce called attention to the difference between statements about how things seem to us and statements about how they really are: "In case of an ordinary illusion of the senses we often say: This object seems thus or so; but in reality it is *thus*". Royce went on to say in a crucial passage that "the seeming is opposed to the reality only in so far as the chance experience of one point of view gets contrasted with what would be, or might be, experienced from some larger, more rationally permanent, or more inclusive and uniting point of view". Royce illustrates this by remarking that to a fevered patient the temperature of the room will seem to change even while the temperature really remains constant and that although the seeming is the content of the patient's momentary experience, "the real temperature is a fact that either is, or conceivably might be, present to a larger, a more organised and scientific and united experience, such as his physician may come nearer than himself to possessing".[3] In a similar vein, Peirce held that "to say that a Jacqueminot rose is red means, and can mean, nothing but that if such a rose is put before a normal eye, in the daylight, it will look red".[4] Yet there is a difference between Peirce's view of what it means to say that something really has a certain property and Royce's view, because where Peirce refers to a normal eye, Royce refers to a larger, more organized and united experience; and thereby hangs a tale that leads to Royce's Absolute. Royce holds that observers of the temperature of a room vary in their degree of organization or in their width from the fevered patient to the doctor; and as another example of such variation in width he cites the differ-

ence between a narrow sort of human experience to which it
appears that the sun is moving around the earth and "a wider
experience, say an experience defined from an extra-terrestrial
point of view", which "would have presented to it the earth's
rotation as immediately as we now can get the sunrise presented to us".[5] Royce then asks us in mathematical language
to "pass to the limit" in this direction and to say that "by the
absolute reality we can only mean either that which is present
to an absolutely organised experience inclusive of all possible
experience, or that which would be presented as the content
of such an experience if there were one".[6]

This passing to the limit, this belief in the existence of an
all-knowing standard mind, arises, according to Royce, from
man's social nature. Man living in society early comes to recognize that his fellow-men also have experiences as genuine as
his own, that they also have an experience of red while they
look at a Jacqueminot rose. This permits a sociable man to
think that he is not dreaming or deluded, and hence not conceiving a "mere possibility" when he asserts that the rose is
really red. When he comes to think that his companions also
have an experience of red in the presence of the rose, he
comes to regard his own statement that the rose is *really* red
as "a concrete truth, and not a merely conceived possibility,
precisely so far as he believes that his fellow or some other
concrete mind does verify it".[7] Soon, however, this appeal to a
consensus of the different experiences of his fellow men suggests to him an ideal which transcends even their experiences,
because he observes that all of them may be deluded just as he
may be deluded. At this point, Royce's socially minded man
begins to form an idea of the Absolute Mind. In philosophy
this idea was anticipated by Bishop Berkeley's conception of
the divine mind, but it was never as fully developed by him as
it was by post-Kantian idealists. According to Royce, to be
objectively red is *not* to be perceived as red by *me* or by my
equally finite friends, but rather by a super-mind; and this

super-mind, Royce stoutly maintains, is constantly appealed to "by anyone who talks of the 'verdict of science' ".[8]

Having reached this stage in the process of socialization, the philosophically minded scientist must now ask himself whether the super-mind is a "merely ideal" entity, postulated by him to give backing to his desire for objectivity, or whether it really exists.[9] In an early stage he may believe that "This rose is really red" means the same as "Tom, Dick, Harry, and I all experience the idea of red when we look at this rose"; but in the course of more thoughtful mental growth, he will "come to appeal from what the various men do experience to what they all ought to experience, or would experience if their experiences were in unity; that is, if all their moments were linked expressions of one universal meaning which was present to one Universal Subject, of whose insight their own experiences were but fragments".[10] It is when he reaches this moment in the process of socialization that Royce's philosophically minded scientist begins to wonder whether the unity to which he now appeals is more than a "bare possibility". If he could regard the statement "This rose is really red" as synonymous simply with "Tom, Dick, Harry, and I all experience the idea of red when we look at this rose", he would not have the problem he is now faced with; for these statements, Royce says, are neither of them "tainted with possiblity". But once he contends that "This rose is really red" means the same as "If there be a Universal Subject, he would experience this rose as red", while admitting that it may at best be *possible* that the Universal Subject exists, he is in a predicament. Royce's point is that so long as we cannot say categorically that the Universal Subject does exist, and hence regard "This rose is really red" as meaning the same as "The Universal Subject experiences this rose as red", we are in difficulty. We cannot regard the statement "This rose is really red", when so construed, as reporting an actual fact. It is subject to a "taint of possibility" just so long as and insofar as the statement that the Universal Subject exists is also subject to a taint of possibility. As an idealist, Royce held that reality is what is present to some subject so that, if the subject is at best only a possible entity, then reality itself becomes only possible.

How, then, will Royce deal with the problem created by the sociable man's most recently described effort to analyze what it means to say that this rose is really red? How will Royce remove the taint of possibility created by the view that it is at best possible that the Universal Subject exists? Obviously, Royce must do something to show that the Universal Subject does actually exist, and his effort is worth examining in some detail because it is so typical of his philosophizing. His first move is to call attention to the fact that when we take our private, momentary experience of the redness of the rose to indicate that if a super-mind exists, he will see it as red—in other words, when we say our perceptions could be those of an objective mind—we show that we *want* it to be the case that there is a standard objective mind who has presented to it experiences like those that we have, and in this way vindicate our own inference from appearance to reality. Royce's next move is to introduce an objector who issues a protest that Royce is always eager to pounce on. He makes the objector say: "This aim, this will, is all. As a fact, you and I aim at the absolute experience; that is what we mean by wanting to know absolute truth; but the absolute experience . . . is just a mere ideal. There need be no such experience as a concrete actuality. The aim, the intent, is the known fact. The rest is silence,—perhaps error. Perhaps there is no absolute truth, no ideally united and unfragmentary experience".[11] This kind of doubt Royce is always anxious to state and to meet, since his typical response to it is to try to show, in a manner reminiscent of Descartes, that such doubt may be turned into a victory for the believer. In the Preface to his first book, *The Religious Aspect of Philosophy,* he says:

"What is here dwelt upon over and over again [And was he right!] is . . . the consideration that the doubts of our time are not to be apologetically 'refuted,' in the old fashioned sense, but that taken just as they are, fully and cordially received, they are upon analysis found to contain and imply a positive and important religious creed, bearing both upon conduct and upon reality".[12] Further on in the same book he says that in philosophy doubt "is to be accepted as it comes, and then to be developed in all its fullness and in all its intensity. *For the truth of the matter is concealed in that doubt,* as the fire is concealed in the stony coal. You can no more reject the doubt and keep the innermost truth, than you can toss away the coal and hope to retain its fire".[13]

In keeping with this strategy, Royce launches a campaign to turn the hostile witnesses of doubt and error into friendly ones. Let us grant for purposes of argument, he says, that we are in error and that as a matter of fact there is no super-mind called the Absolute. It follows, Royce says, as he appeals to what has been called the cardinal principle of idealism,[14] that the very fact that there is no super-mind must be experienced or known by someone. For just as the idealist claims that it cannot be a fact that a rose is red unless someone experiences the fact that it is, so the idealist claims that it cannot be a fact that there is no super-mind unless someone experiences the fact that there is no super-mind. And since the statement that there is no super-mind is equivalent to the statement that all minds are non-super, i.e. finite, the question arises: Who is there to experience the fact that all minds are finite? It is either a finite mind or a super-mind, but Royce insists that it cannot be a finite mind, and therefore it must be a super-mind.

Why does Royce say that a finite mind cannot experience the fact that all minds are finite? He grants that a finite mind can know itself to be finite but denies that it can know the truth of the stronger assertion that all minds are. To know

this, Royce seems to hold, it must know that its own experience is identical with *all* experience; so that, if *it* does not experience a non-finite mind, then there is no such thing. In
short, to know what it here claims to know, a finite mind
would have to know that it embraces *the whole* of experience
and hence experience a fact that only a non-finite mind could
experience. In this way Royce supposes himself to have
shown the self-contradictoriness of the supposition that a
finite mind experiences the fact that all minds are finite, from
which it follows that only an infinite mind knows this fact.
He concludes that the hypothesis that all minds are finite has
been reduced to absurdity, and therefore that there must be
an Absolute: "The very effort hypothetically to assert that the
whole world of experience is a world of fragmentary and
finite experience is an effort involving a contradiction. Experience must constitute, in its entirety, one self-determined and
consequently absolute and organised whole".[15] Once he has
reached this point, Royce can reaffirm his analysis of scientific
belief and announce as he did in *The Spirit of Modern Philosophy*: "If the standard mind knows now that its ideal fire
has the quality of burning those who touch it, and if I in my
finitude am bound to conform in my experiences to the
thoughts of this standard mind, then in case I touch that fire I
shall surely get the idea of a burn".[16] Royce thinks he can also
say, as he does in almost all of his discussions of this subject,
that when I am *not* in error, when I find the truth, "my success is real only in so far as some conscious life, which includes my ideas and my efforts, and which also includes the
very facts of the world whereof I am thinking, actually observes my success, in the form of a conspectus of the world's
facts, and of my own efforts to find and to define them".[17]
This conscious life is the Absolute.

The Absolute, Error, and Meaning. It is worth observing that
Royce argued for the existence of the Absolute in a way that

is somewhat different from the one we have just examined. In *The Religious Aspect of Philosophy* he presented his best-known argument for Absolute Idealism by analyzing, not what we mean when we attribute an objective property like redness or hardness to an individual, but, rather, what we mean when we say that a judgment is false or erroneous. Royce points out that he "could have reached the same result had [he] set out from the problem, *What is Truth?*", but that he chose to analyze error only because the skeptics whom he wished to answer acknowledged the existence of error, but not that of truth.[18] In Royce's view we can call only a *judgment* false or erroneous. A judgment, as he conceives it, is composed of a subject-idea and a predicate-idea, and he insists that the subject-idea purports to refer to some object beyond itself; for example, if someone judges that the cat is on the mat, his idea of the cat must purport to refer to the so-called real cat. In other words, a sincerely made judgment is fundamentally different from the pseudo-judgment of a man in a trance or a dream in this respect; a judgment is properly called erroneous but these other things may not be called erroneous. It is Royce's contention, however, that if the person who judges that the cat is on the mat has only the *idea* of the cat in mind, we are faced with a paradox. For how can the man who judges that the cat is on the mat make an error when all he has in mind is his idea of the cat? Common sense will say that he can make an error by comparing his idea of the cat with the real cat to see whether the real cat is on the mat, but Royce maintains that the person judging can have in his mind only an *idea* of the cat, "for unless one talks nonsense, it should seem as if one could mean only what one has in mind"; [19] hence he cannot get to the real cat. How, then, can we analyze error or false judgment, asks Royce, so long as we accept the common-sense view of the situation? How can we avoid the paradoxical conclusion that we can never make errors?

Stated briefly, Royce's answer is that one who makes a judgment always has some feeling, however inchoate, that the sub-ject-idea of his sincerely made judgment refers to *something* external even if he cannot have it definitely in mind; that everyone who judges must therefore postulate the existence of an Absolute mind which can, by developing the judge's vague intention further, see more clearly than the judge what the idea does refer to; that such an Absolute mind can make the required comparison between idea and reality which the finite judge cannot himself make; and that the finite judge can therefore be accused, so to speak, of error by the Absolute. As in *The Conception of God,* however, Royce regards this argument as showing merely that in attributions of error we tacitly postulate the existence of an Absolute mind. What Royce then produces in *The Religious Aspect of Philosophy* is an argument which allegedly demonstrates the existence of the Absolute we postulate, but this is enough like his argu-ment in *The Conception of God* to make it unnecessary for us to state it here.

However, before leaving the Absolute as conceived in Royce's first book, it is well to remark on one of the features that remain with it throughout Royce's many accounts of it— its capacity to see in one moment all truth, whether about the past, present, or future. This emerges in Royce's special dis-cussion of our erroneous beliefs about the future. When I assert that the cat will be on the mat at 9 p.m. tonight, "I postulate certain realities not now given to my consciousness" [20] but I cannot *now* make a comparison be-tween my judgment and the future state of the world to which I refer. Still, it may be said *now* that some of my state-ments about the future are in error. Furthermore, when the future time in question comes, I cannot make a comparison between the predicted state of the world and the judgment made earlier because that judgment, a state of my mind in the past, is no longer present to be a term in the comparison. Nevertheless, Royce argues, I need to locate the two terms of the comparison—the predictive judgment and the predicted state of the world in some one consciousness, and that consciousness is the Absolute. We must "declare time once for all present in all its moments to an universal all-inclusive thought", for the "Absolute *possesses a perfect knowledge at one glance of the whole of the temporal order, present, past, and future*".[21] No wonder, then, that Royce said in words that I have already quoted: "My success is real only in so far as some conscious life, which includes my ideas and my efforts, and which also includes the very facts of the world whereof I am thinking, actually observes my success, in the form of a conspectus of the world's facts, and of my own efforts to find and to define them".[22] When Royce reaches this point in his analysis, he makes clear what he thought his relationship to more poetic idealists was. For he says: "Truly the words that some people have thought so fantastic ought henceforth to be put in the text-books as commonplaces of logical analysis". And what are those words? They are the words of Emerson's *Brahma:*

> They reckon ill that leave me out;
> When me they fly, I am the wings,
> I am the doubter and the doubt.[23]

Just after Emerson's death, then, the logician of the oversoul had succeeded the poet of the oversoul in the history of American idealism.

Idealism, History, and Evolution

Royce not only felt obliged to show that idealism should not be identified with poetic fantasy but also felt compelled to establish its manliness—a favorite word of his—by showing that, far from being an enemy of the doctrine of evolution, it smoothed the way for it in the history of Western thought.

Like Chauncey Wright and William James, Royce did not admire the evolutionary philosophy of Herbert Spencer, thinking it to be a poor version of Hobbes' materialism;[24] but Royce greatly admired Darwin, the popularity of whose work, he thought, had been made possible by the earlier vogue of post-Kantian idealism. Royce meant that idealism had encouraged great respect for historical or dynamic analysis. If the great Spirit is anywhere manifest to us, it is in the growth of humanity, he said, and modern historical research, under the influence of idealism, had tried to depict this growth. In earlier periods of modern thought, the history of things had been neglected so that external nature, "not as it grows, but as it eternally is", was the main concern of the seventeenth century; and the eighteenth century, in spite of turning to the inner life, "still studied an ideally permanent thing called human nature, which savage life illustrated in its primitive innocence, civilized life in its artificial disguises, but which nothing in heaven or earth, except the will of its creator, could essentially change".[25] By contrast, the nineteenth century regarded change and the flow of things as the most interesting feature of the universe. Karl Marx himself was not more insistent about this than Royce. Royce not only criticized pre-nineteenth-century metaphysics but also pre-nineteenth-century "old-fashioned science", which "used to go about classifying things" and which missed the importance of the evolution that Darwin tried to explain by his dynamic theory of natural selection.[26]

In trying to describe the link between idealism and evolution, Royce acknowledged that the romantic idealists reveled unscientifically in emotion and mystery. If you were a romantic poet, he admitted, "you felt, you experienced, you sang, you grew constantly more sentimental, you gloried in the wealth of your feelings, you wept in public with your numberless lyrics, and then you felt and experienced and sang again with endless ardor and garrulity". Moreover, when you studied nature, "you loved above all things mere mysteries, divining rods, magic, the night-side of nature generally".[27] But soon—and this was Royce's most interesting point—a poetic preoccupation with the remote and mysterious was transformed into scholarship and science. The Orient and the Middle Ages were carefully examined by learned researchers who made Mohammedanism, Buddhism, Hindu pantheism, and Persian Sufism objects of serious study. "Men like the Schlegels forgot the romantic irony, to learn Sanskrit; a Wilhelm von Humboldt expounded the Bhagavat-gita. Thus began the scholarship that has produced the science of modern comparative philology, and our whole knowledge of the true life of the far East." The operative word here was "life". Instead of viewing these ancient languages as merely providing "a series of crabbed linguistic puzzles",[28] the nineteenth-century scholar, who worked under the aegis of idealism, saw them as keys to the inner spirit, to the heart of by-gone civilizations. In showing how these civilizations were related to our own, he made "linguistic study a handmaid of truly humane scholarship"; and he treated "classical history, not as a mere collection of examples for moral or for literary edification, but as an evolution".[29] Here, Royce announced, "lies the continuity of thought which connects us, in all the so-called realism of our prosaic modern research, with the dreamers who dreamed, with the fantastic poets who failed, in the first decades of our century".[30] The ferment of romantic poetry ultimately led, he argued, to the view that history had meaning and that even the saddest episodes were manifestations of a Self with a capital "S". In short, "the new history"—a phrase that Royce seems to have used before James Harvey Robinson, who made it popular [31]—looked at society's development and saw the truth of the Hindu saying that Schopenhauer was so fond of quoting: "The life of all these things,—*That art thou*".

It must be borne in mind that Royce's conception of the

Absolute Spirit and of God precluded any use of the Argument from Design.[32] His Absolute did not stand to the universe as efficient cause but rather as all-knower and therefore was very different from the Divine Artificer of Paley, whose views Darwin also deplored. That is one reason why Royce did not view idealistic theism as an obstacle to the spread of Darwinism and why he thought that the former had paved the way for the latter. Royce was highly critical of those who "too frequently regard the doctrine of evolution as having for the first time flashed upon the world after the appearance of Darwin's 'Origin of Species' ".[33] He was quick to add that nobody could value the splendid achievement of Darwin more than he did, yet he insisted that it became popular mainly "because the age was ripe for the extension of the historical conception far beyond the boundaries of humanity proper. . . . It was coming into an historical age that made Darwin's book so great a prize".[34] Moreover, Royce held that idealism was the only philosophy that could extract the underlying significance of Darwin's discoveries. Royce emphasized that Darwin's principle of natural selection was only a scientific generalization that left deeper questions unsettled because it did not satisfactorily connect its own conclusions with the conclusions of metaphysics. Metaphysical "synthesis", Royce asserted, ". . . is the one undertaking of our century",[35] and synthesis was certainly needed in this case, if only because so many followers of Darwin attacked Absolute Idealism and did not regard it as an intellectual ally. In Royce's time, Herbert Spencer was *the* synthetic philosopher of the English-speaking world, but Royce had grave reservations about Spencer. Royce admired him for undertaking "to be a reconciler, an unifier, one who harmonizes through synthesis, and who brings to light oppositions only to enrich thought by suggesting their organic unity"; but Royce did not like the fact that "over every statement of Mr. Spencer's about the outer world broods that dim and shadowy Unknowable of his, whose mys-

tery gives to every assertion about the unity of its own processes an air of doubt and of unintelligibility".[36]

How, then, did Royce propose to reunite the idealistic parent and the rebellious evolutionary child who had fled its
home for agnosticism? Essentially, by emphasizing that every
statement of natural science implies the existence of the Absolute Self. According to Royce, if Darwin had looked more
deeply into his tangled bank and if he had logically analyzed
his conclusions about it, he would have said to his reader as
he pointed to the course of evolution by natural selection:
"That art thou". But the task of logically uniting evolutionary
science with post-Kantian idealism became less and less popular as the nineteenth century drew to a close, primarily because the end of the nineteenth century saw a widespread conviction that one could use evolutionary method while denying
that all of history is a manifestation of the World Spirit. This
conviction was shared by a group of influential American
thinkers I have elsewhere treated at length.[37] Dewey the philosopher, Oliver Wendell Holmes, Jr., the jurist, Thorstein
Veblen the economist, Charles Beard the political scientist,
and James Harvey Robinson the historian all agreed with
Royce that the social studies should employ the historical
method and regard society as an organic unity. They all
greatly admired the contribution of Darwin, but they could
not accept the view that the use of historical method rested on
a belief in, or implied the truth of, Absolute Idealism or
Christianity. By the end of the nineteenth century, therefore,
Royce seemed more and more like a man who rested good
methodology on bad metaphysics. Like Hegel before him he
may have been a force for good because he stressed the value
of history and the idea of cultural unity, but his historicism
and cultural organicism were so intimately linked with his
dubious idealism that he could not play the part that Dewey
came to play as the philosophical leader of American social
thinkers in revolt against formalism.

Alienation, Provincialism, and Loyalty

Some of Royce's views on social matters might also have become more popular were it not for his desire to link them with idealism in an era when idealism was on the defensive throughout the Anglo-American world. In a touching letter of 1908, Royce expressed his feeling of being prematurely out of things in the first decade of the twentieth century. "As for me", he wrote at the age of fifty-two, "I am now an oldish professor, who stoops a little, and carries too many books about, and plans many books that I do not write. I am already supposed by younger colleagues to be an old fogey. The 'Pragmatists' wag their heads and mock when I pass by. My colleague James, who although so much my senior, is eternally young, has all the interest on his side,—even although he is now an *emeritus* professor. I am rapidly passing into an early but a well earned obscurity of professorial old age. —Meanwhile, as a sort of last expression of ideals, I put forth my book on *Loyalty*".[38] Royce's *The Philosophy of Loyalty* appeared in 1908, the same year in which Royce published a volume of essays called *Race Questions, Provincialism, and Other American Problems;* and both books illustrate Royce's penchant for treating his social and moral philosophies as logically yoked to his idealistic metaphysics.

Royce's views on American life at the turn of the century were part of a long-standing American tradition of intellectual concern about the effects of urban society.[39] He was much upset by the social malaise he observed, much preoccupied with the problems posed by the new immigrants and by the decline of community and social solidarity in America. Royce felt that twentieth-century Americans should deal with some of their social and political problems by increasing their loyalty to their section rather than to their religious sect, their labor union, or their political party, because he felt that provincial loyalty would best serve as a mediator between the individual and the increasingly distant economic and political powers that seemed so menacing to thinkers of the Progressive Era.[40] Royce thought that there were three main evils at work in American life at the turn of the century: an excess of wandering strangers and unassimilated newcomers, an increasing tendency toward uniformity and mediocrity, and an increase of mob spirit. These three evils he saw as parts of a more general phenomenon which Hegel had described as "the self-estrangement of the Spirit". Individuals felt more and more distant from one another and from their government and hence ceased to view their society as homelike. In the time of the thirteen colonies this was not true of America, Royce said, for "in the province the social mind is naturally aware of itself as at home with its own"; but at the time he was writing, he thought, the curse of bigness had fallen upon the nation. The individual confronted vast impersonal powers of government and business which threatened him, and he had lost contact with other individuals who viewed these powers in the same frightened way. The distant and overwhelming national government might guarantee the individual's safety, but it did not lead him to be as loyal to his society as his "distinctly provincial fathers" had been to theirs.[41] The forces of government, industry and business, Royce complained, "excite our loyalty as little as do the trade-winds or the blizzard. They leave our patriotic sentiments cold. The smoke of our civilization hides the very heavens that used to be so near, and the stars to which we were once loyal".[42]

In the face of this, Royce maintained that the great task before America was to inculcate what he called a wise provincialism. He did not think of provincialism as a revival of that older sectionalism which had led the country to a civil war; but just as the historian Frederick J. Turner thought that the midwestern state universities might encourage a wise sectionalism, so Royce remarked on the beneficial effect of such universities, of public libraries, of local historical associations, and of genealogical associations, which illustrated, he thought, "the sort of provincialism which makes people want to idealize, to adorn, to ennoble, to educate, their own province; to hold sacred its traditions, to honor its worthy dead, to support and to multiply its public possessions".[43] This kind of provincialism he found in the English love of country life, in the Scotsman's love for his own native province, and in the provincial loyalties of Germany. Here he would have sympathized with the younger Henry James, who was so shocked by New York City at the beginning of the twentieth century as to dream "of the luxury of some such close and sweet and *whole* national consciousness as that of the Switzer and the Scot".[44] Royce also showed a typically American distrust of Paris when he said that "one of the historical weaknesses of France has been such a centralization of power and of social influence about Paris as has held in check the full development of the dignity of provincial consciousness in that country"; [45] and, more generally, he was falling in line with an established tradition of anti-urbanism among American intellectuals from Jefferson onward. Insofar as Royce served as a critic of American alienation and insofar as he argued for the value of encouraging loyalty to communities which were smaller than the nation, even in order to achieve national loyalty, he won the support of many other American thinkers who were alarmed by the breakdown of what the Germans called *Gemeinschaft*. But in resting his regionalism on an ethics which rested on his idealistic metaphysics, Royce lost allies in social philosophy as he had lost them in the philosophy of history. American social thought at the turn of the century was breaking away from the rigidities of absolutistic metaphysics and was much more sympathetic to the pluralism of James and the relativism of Dewey. Not only did Royce's teacher James seem younger than he but John Dewey, who was born only four years after Royce, was also in spirit the member of a later generation.

Royce's distance from the newer intellectual tendencies of his time is measured by his desire to connect his provincialism with an ethic that rested on his idealistic metaphysics. He thought *The Philosophy of Loyalty* "ought to help at least some readers to see that such philosophical idealism as I have long maintained is not a doctrine remote from life, but is in close touch with the most practical issues; and that religion, as well as daily life, has much to gain from the right union of ethics with a philosophical theory of the real world".[46] We need not enter the details of his moral philosophy to see what he had in mind. Stated briefly, his basic contention was that loyalty to a spiritual cause which unites one with a group of people—like a family, a province, or a nation—is the fundamental concept of ethics; and that loyalty to loyalty, by which he meant perseverance in the effort to maximize the amount of loyalty in society, is the basic precept of ethics. Royce held that all ethical notions, like those representing the duties and the virtues, are definable in terms of loyalty and that all ethical principles are derivable from his basic precept of loyalty to loyalty. But Royce was not content with maintaining this thesis; he also had to defend a characteristic thesis about "the right union of ethics with a philosophical theory of the real world".

The first step in his defense was to argue that loyalty, as devotion to a cause which unifies many human lives, is profoundly religious in spirit because men, viewed merely as natural phenomena, are creatures in conflict, and therefore the unification of them at which loyalty aims "has its supernatural meaning". "Loyally to serve causes is to aim to give human life a supernatural,—an essentially divine meaning." [47] "Loyalty . . . is . . . a communion with invisible aspects of our social existence",[48] and that is why loyalty to lost causes, to causes whose worldly fortunes seem lost, often forms the basis of great religious movements.[49] Royce's next step was to argue that a loyal man must not only *believe* that his cause is a reality which transcends his individual life and his personal experience but also believe so truly, "for any or all loyalties may be founded in illusion, and then it would be an illusion that the fostering of loyalty amongst men is a finally worthy undertaking".[50] Just as Royce had held in his first book, *The Religious Aspect of Philosophy,* that one who posits or postulates physical objects in order to organize sense-data must ground his postulate in reality, so a quarter of a century later Royce argued that we must show the reality of the spiritual causes we postulate when we are loyal.[51] In seeking "to know what truth is behind and beneath the moral life",[52] Royce was led from his "wise provincialism" to loyalty as the basic concept of ethics, and from there to the restatement of his idealistic metaphysics. In brief, his path from social philosophy to metaphysics via ethics is as follows: provincialism is a good thing; provincialism is a form of loyalty; loyalty is devotion to a spiritual cause; spiritual causes are supernatural entities; the knowledge that such entities exist and are good can be attained by no one man or collection of men; therefore it can only be attained by the Absolute. If the loyal man's belief in the existence and goodness of his causes is not to be a "convenient illusion", their existence and goodness must be "experienced upon some higher level of consciousness than any one human being ever reaches".[53] By the time Royce had reached this point in his intellectual development, he had stated and restated several times, though with modifications of course, the basic thesis of his first book: that science and ethics require first the postulation and then the proof of the existence of the Absolute. And the proof of the existence of the Absolute, no matter how restated, was always the same in form: he who denies its existence is somehow involved in reasserting it. About that we have already said enough.

Royce's philosophy was one against which many social thinkers and philosophers rebelled at the turn of the twentieth century, but it did not go down without a struggle. It was encased in thick-plated armor since it was formidably protected by the use of mathematical logic, a philosophy of science, a theory of meaning, and modern biology; [54] it lived in the mighty fortress of Christianity; it had its links with the American tradition; it was formulated in the rolling periods of a powerful preacher. But, as the saying goes, the bigger they are, the harder they fall; and when the mighty Royce fell, it was as if the temple of American philosophy itself had collapsed.

10 · George Santayana: Sage of Materialism

Few thinkers shook the pillars of idealism more vigorously than George Santayana, the first American philosopher of great influence to have been born on foreign soil. He was born in Madrid in 1863 of Spanish parents, but at a very young age he began a complicated relationship with America. His mother, before marrying Santayana's father, had been married to a Bostonian, Robert Sturgis, who had died in 1857. With Sturgis she had had three children whom she promised to bring up in America after his death; and she brought them to Boston from Spain in 1869 after she had become the mother of George by her second husband, a Spaniard. In three years George followed her to America. In due course he became a student at Boston Latin School and at Harvard College, which he entered in 1882. After graduate study there, he was appointed in 1889 to the Harvard Department of Philosophy, where he became the colleague of James and Royce. The youngest of that triumvirate, he was also the least happy in America, which he left for good in 1912 after forty years of spiritual estrangement in this country. For the remaining forty years of his life he stayed in England and on the Continent until he died in Rome, a very distinguished philosopher and man of letters.

Santayana's special role in American intellectual life was to be a poet and philosophical materialist in a time and place when that seemed like a contradiction in terms. He was the most cultivated and literate American philosopher of his time but he boldly spurned belief in God, in immortality, or in final causes; he thought that all causal explanation is physical in nature; and he held with David Hume that there are only two kinds of truths, those established by experience and those established by the analysis of intent or meaning. Although he occasionally made exceedingly penetrating forays into technical philosophy, his accomplishments in that area leave much to be desired. Late in his life he became more and more preoccupied with espousing and defending his rather elaborate doctrine of essences, but in my opinion that is not a very important contribution to the history of American philosophy. Santayana would not have been altogether flattered to hear himself likened to Emerson—we have seen that he believed that Emerson was "not primarily a philosopher but a Puritan mystic with a poetic fancy and a gift for observation and epigram"[1]—but it is Emerson who comes to my mind when I try to summarize Santayana's position in American philosophy.[2] If Emerson was the sage of American idealism who had a poetic fancy and a gift for observation and epigram, then Santayana was the similarly endowed sage of American materialism.

Santayana on the Genteel Tradition

In 1911 this sage of materialism delivered a famous lecture on the sage of idealism and kindred spirits, and found them wanting. In that year Santayana sharply disassociated himself from the idealistic tradition of Edwards, Emerson, and Royce by delivering a sharp attack on Calvinism and Transcendentalism. Just before he was to resign his Harvard professorship, he tried to settle accounts with what he called "The Genteel Tradition in American Philosophy". Using that as his title, Santayana gave a lecture which, like Royce's "Conception of God" and James' "Philosophical Conceptions and Practical Results", was delivered at the University of California at Berkeley; but unlike his senior colleagues he did not mount that distant rostrum in order to defend a positive philosophical thesis so much as to deliver a discourse in the history of ideas and to get a few things off his chest. In doing so, he struck a note that the intellectual world was waiting to hear, for his phrase "the genteel tradition" quickly took its place in textbooks beside Edwards' "Sinners in the Hands of an Angry God", Emerson's "American Scholar", and "Pragmatism". Santayana did not take kindly to what he had been forced to live with in philosophical New England, since he disliked Edwards' Calvinism and Emerson's Transcendentalism; but he used his California valedictory more as an occasion for history and diagnosis than for criticism or condescension, though criticism and condescension had a way of breaking in. The basic historical idea in Santayana's lecture was a distinction between the antiquated mentality of America and its youthful social relations. He claimed that in all the higher things of the mind a sleepy hereditary spirit prevailed, whereas American technology and society were dominated by an entirely different and more vital outlook. While philosophy, religion, and literature floated gently in a backwater, practical America was leaping down a sort of Niagara rapids. Using another, more striking figure, he said that the division between the two American minds was symbolized in architecture: "a neat reproduction of the colonial mansion—with some modern comforts introduced surreptitiously—stands beside the skyscraper". Then he went on to say: "The American Will inhabits the skyscraper; the American Intellect inhabits the colonial mansion. The one is the sphere of the American man;

the other, at least predominantly, of the American woman. The one is all aggressive enterprise; the other is all genteel tradition".[3]

According to Santayana, the genteel tradition began with Calvinism, the religion and philosophy of an agonized conscience. Its idea that it is beautiful for sin to exist and to be punished could easily take hold, Santayana reflected, in a small, isolated nation living under pressure and constant trial. Through an irony of history, however, observance of the Calvinist ethic helped America to a prosperity that allowed it to give up that ethic; and the Calvinists' belief in total depravity was replaced by Transcendentalist optimism and subjectivism, which constituted the second phase of the genteel tradition. But whatever the differences between these two phases of the tradition, they were both out of touch with the main forces of American life, said Santayana, and so he remarked: "To keep them alive they required, one an agonised conscience, and the other a radical subjective criticism of knowledge. When these rare metaphysical preoccupations disappeared—and the American atmosphere is not favourable to either of them—the two systems ceased to be inwardly understood; they subsisted as sacred mysteries only. . . ". Yet, Santayana continued, "natural science, history, the beliefs implied in labour and invention, could not be disregarded altogether; so that the transcendental philosopher was condemned to a double allegiance, and to not letting his left hand know the bluff that his right hand was making. Nevertheless, the difficulty in bringing practical inarticulate convictions to expression is very great, and the genteel tradition has subsisted in the academic mind for want of anything equally academic to take its place".[4]

In speaking of academic gentility, Santayana was very probably referring to the idealism of his teacher Royce; and Royce's use of mathematics, science, and logic may well have been in Santayana's mind when he said that the genteel tradi-

tion was a colonial mansion into which modern comforts had
been surreptitiously introduced. In any case, Santayana drew
a devastating portrait of Royce and his philosophy in *Character and Opinion in the United States* (1920). Though he paid
him a few compliments, he regarded Royce as essentially an
"overworked, standardised, academic engine, creaking and
thumping on at the call of duty or of habit, with no thought
of sparing itself or any one else" [5] as it tried to show that "all
lives were parts of a single divine life in which all problems
were solved and all evils justified".[6] By contrast, Santayana regarded James as the first great American philosopher to break
with the genteel tradition; and although he never became
very friendly with James,[7] he admired him partly because he
saw him as essentially an unacademic person, a man of wide
sympathies, and a professor in spite of himself. In Santayana's
mind, James was something like Hegel's hero, a man with "a
prophetic sympathy with the dawning sentiments of the age,
with the moods of the dumb majority", and one whose "way
of thinking and feeling represented the true America, and
represented in a measure the whole ultra-modern, radical
world".[8] Because James' ideas came to him from the depths,
he sang in tune with what Santayana called "the normal practical masculine American",[9] for even when James defended
the theism of the genteel tradition, his pragmatic way of defending it was certainly not genteel. Santayana pointed out
that James held, under the influence of Darwin, that intelligence is merely a help toward survival; that ideas are not mir-
rors but weapons; that "all creeds and theories and all formal
precepts sink in the estimation of the pragmatist to a local
and temporary grammar of action; a grammar that must be
changed slowly by time, and may be changed quickly by
genius"; [10] that omniscience is impossible; that time is real;
and many other propositions that were neither Calvinistic nor
transcendental.[11] "I am not concerned with the rights and
wrongs . . .", Santayana the historian paused to say of his for-

mer teacher and colleague who had just died, "my point is only that William James, in [his] genial evolutionary view of the world, has given a rude shock to the genteel tradition",[12] primarily because his philosophy was an "impassioned empiricism, welcoming popular religious witnesses to the unseen, reducing science to an instrument of success in action, and declaring the universe to be wild and young, and not to be harnessed by the logic of any school".[13]

Santayana's admiration of James' unprofessorial approach was in keeping with Santayana's view of himself, since he had always hated being a professor and gave up his professorship as soon as he was in a financial position to do so.[14] Santayana's anti-academicism was also in keeping with the entire history that we have been studying, since, with the possible exception of Royce and Dewey, America's most distinguished philosophers have been either non-professors or professors who wanted to be non-professors and, in one way or another, estranged from the academic world. Edwards had taught for only a short time at Yale and died after serving as president of Princeton for only about five weeks. Emerson's lectures at Harvard were unsuccessful, as were Chauncey Wright's teaching efforts there. Peirce, who wanted so much to be a Harvard professor, failed to become one. And although outwardly James was a great academic success, Santayana depicted James' attitude toward teaching as follows: "Perhaps in the first years of his teaching he felt a little in the professor's chair as a military man might feel when obliged to read the prayers at a funeral. He probably conceived what he said more deeply than a more scholastic mind might have conceived it; yet he would have been more comfortable if some one else had said it for him. He liked to open the window, and look out for a moment. I think he was glad when the bell rang, and he could be himself again until the next day. But in the midst of this routine of the class-room the spirit would sometimes come upon him, and, leaning his head on his hand, he would let

fall golden words, picturesque, fresh from the heart, full of
the knowledge of good and evil. Incidentally there would
crop up some humorous characterisation, some candid confession of doubt or of instinctive preference, some pungent scrap
of learning; radicalisms plunging sometimes into the sub-soil
of all human philosophies; and, on occasion, thoughts of simple wisdom and wistful piety, the most unfeigned and manly
that anybody ever had".[15]

Santayana: Naturalistic Philosopher of Religion

As a humane and incisive analyst of the American intellectual
past, Santayana had no peers among his contemporaries. In
order to find his equal, one must go back to Emerson in "Historic Notes of Life and Letters in New England". Santayana
was detached enough to see a hundred and fifty years of
American society in perspective, close enough to that society
to understand and describe the human beings who composed
it, and conversant enough with its leading ideas to analyze
them brilliantly. His discussion of American ideas is almost
always illuminating and shows him at his best as a thinker. In
works of the genre represented by "The Genteel Tradition"
—a genre he had mastered more successfully than any other
American writer—he could combine incisive historical commentary and moving "thoughts of simple wisdom". It is not
surprising, then, that he believed that only the history of philosophy should be taught in a university, and that he disap-
proved of professors who expounded their own systems of
metaphysics and epistemology in the hope of founding sects
among captive students.[16] It is also not surprising that when
he himself felt called upon to teach systematic courses at Harvard, he gravitated to such fields as esthetics and the philosophy of history, where he could spend much of his time in the
kind of critical and historical analysis illustrated by his lecture on the genteel tradition. He was absorbed, he tells us of

his early days, in "the historical spirit of the nineteenth century, and to that splendid panorama of nations and religions, literatures and arts, which it unrolled before the imagination"; [17] but, unlike Hegel and Royce, who saw that panorama as a manifestation of the Absolute, Santayana viewed it mainly as a subject for description and moral review.

In the five volumes of *The Life of Reason* (1905–6)— *Reason in Common Sense, Reason in Society, Reason in Religion, Reason in Art,* and *Reason in Science*—Santayana converted his Harvard lectures on the philosophy of history into a dissection and estimate of the chief accomplishments of Western civilization. That work was dominated by a naturalistic outlook that leaned heavily on the Greeks, and in it Santayana made one of his most impressive contributions to American philosophy. Although he later advanced views on more staple philosophical topics—as in his *Scepticism and Animal Faith* (1923) and his *Realms of Being* (1927–40), where he put forward a theory of knowledge and a metaphysics—and although he was capable of acute observations in analytical ethics—as in his critique of what he called the hypostatic ethics of Moore and the early Russell [18]—in the long run I think Santayana will be remembered for the kind of philosophical writing that one finds in *The Life of Reason,* and in collections of essays like *Interpretations of Poetry and Religion* (1900), and *Winds of Doctrine* (1913). When he came to write a new preface to *The Life of Reason* in 1922, he shrewdly observed that in his later writing "nature has come forward, and the life of reason . . . has receded". He also observed that "the vicissitudes of human belief" had come to absorb him less. Yet I think that he reached his heights in *The Life of Reason,* where he had shown a remarkable power to serve as a critic of those vicissitudes.

Santayana's conception of his enterprise in *The Life of Reason* is made clear in his distinction of various kinds of writing associated with history. There is, he says, investigation of the past which results in a bare statement of what happened, a chronicle; there is the effort to discern historical causes which he thought should be left to what he called physical theory; and finally there is the effort to identify and assess things of the past that one values, the "phases of human progress", as he calls them in the subtitle of *The Life of Reason*. In Santayana's mind this third type of effort, represented by *The Life of Reason* itself, does not seek laws of history but is an enterprise in which the philosopher scrutinizes events in order to "abstract from them whatever tended to illustrate his own ideals, as he might look over a crowd to find his friends".[19] Therefore, it is essentially a part of substantive moral philosophy, an attempt to evaluate institutions like science, religion, and art, to say why it was good that they should have arisen in the course of history. Yet the moral critic or evaluator of these phases of human progress must know what they are if he is to evaluate them. The man who looks over a crowd to find his friends must say something about who they are before he tells us why he likes them; and for this reason a considerable portion of *The Life of Reason* is devoted to analyzing the nature of science, religion, and art.

In his philosophy of religion Santayana brought together his views on science, religion, and art. One of the main themes of *The Life of Reason* is that a religious man need not fear the results of science nor those of materialistic philosophy, primarily because religious language may be construed as poetically expressing moral truth which is not in conflict with science or materialism. Santayana warns in the Preface to his *Interpretations of Poetry and Religion* that "religious doctrines would do well to withdraw their pretension to be dealing with matters of fact. That pretension is not only the source of the conflicts of religion with science and of the vain and bitter controversies of sects; it is also the cause of the impurity and incoherence of religion in the soul, when it seeks its sanctions in the sphere of reality, and forgets that its proper concern is to express the ideal".[20] Yet Santayana's way of resolving the conflict between science and religion involves at least two complications which must be explained in order to gain a clearer idea of his intent.

First of all, he did not wish to deny that many sincere Christians have construed and do now construe their dogmas literally. He warned that "in saying that a given religion was the poetic transformation of an experience, we must not imagine that it was thought to be such—for it is evident that every sincere Christian believed in the literal and empirical reality of all that the Christian epic contained".[21] It is one of the greatest possible illusions in these matters, he insisted, to suppose that the meaning which we see in parables was the meaning they had in the beginning for religious devotees.[22] His main point was that although many sincere believers construed Christian dogmas as expressing theological propositions in conflict with scientific truths, that very conflict showed the theological propositions to be false and hence not to be taken as the meaning of the Christian dogmas in a sympathetic interpretation of them. Santayana asks us not to saddle religions with damaging literal interpretations which place them in conflict with science but rather to interpret them as expressing true moral propositions in a poetically affecting way. In trying to clarify his view, Santayana appealed to the distinction between origin and value. He said that the effort to convey moral truth is not the origin of any religion. Such truth comes to be seen after the religion has been founded, and it is what gives religion value in the life of reason. Using Darwinian language, Santayana said that "moral significance has been a spontaneous variation of superstition, and this variation has insured its survival as a religion".[23] Although the prophets may not have thought of themselves as speaking allegorically, their words were read by others as expressing moral insight which recommended itself to some human interest.

Religion, Santayana concluded, "differs from superstition not psychologically but morally, not in its origin but in its worth. This worth, when actually felt and appreciated, becomes of course a dynamic factor and contributes like other psychological elements to the evolution of events; but being a logical harmony, a rational beauty, this worth is only appreciable by a few minds, and those the least primitive and the least capable of guiding popular movements. Reason is powerless to found religions, although it is alone competent to judge them. Good religions are therefore the product of unconscious rationality, of imaginative impulses fortunately moral".[24]

I spoke earlier of two complications in Santayana's view of the relationship between science and religion, and I now come to the second. It is exceedingly important to bear in mind that although Santayana insisted that religions are not to be taken as expressing scientific truths, but rather moral truths, his view is somewhat complicated by the fact that he regards moral truth as a species of scientific truth. In other words, he is what is called an ethical naturalist, and holds that when we say that something is good or bad we are asserting propositions which are true or false. Consequently, he holds that the propositions of ethics are identifiable with propositions of psychology or social science. Therefore, when he says that "religions will thus be better or worse, never true or false",[25] he gives his reader an opportunity to misunderstand. Strictly speaking, a religion *will* be true or false in his view in the degree to which it may be construed as expressing true or false *moral* propositions; but Santayana's assumption is that such moral propositions, though in the broadest sense propositions of natural science, will not be false physical propositions like those which literally assert the creation of the world in six days, the resurrection, or immortality. When Santayana says religions are better or worse, he means they metaphorically express true or false scientific *moral* propositions and that they express those propositions in ways that are esthetically appealing or repelling. Therefore, the test of a religion's value *is* in one sense scientific.

Santayana's Ethical Theory

Having referred to Santayana's ethical views, I want now to examine in greater detail that important part of his philosophy. The moral truths that religions express metaphorically may also be expressed literally, and the task of so expressing them falls to what Santayana sometimes calls "the science of values".[26] His conception of this science, however, is not without ambiguity, as we shall see presently. Although he subscribed to the Humeian view that there are two kinds of scientific truths, those established by experience and those established by the analysis of intent or meaning, he was not always definite about how to classify the truths of morality.

One dominant strain in his thinking leads him to ethical naturalism, as we have already seen. In one part of his writing he asserts that moral statements are empirical in character, and therefore he decisively rejects the view of G. E. Moore in *Principia Ethica* that goodness is a non-natural quality which is attributed to things in statements that are not empirical in character. This emerges in Santayana's criticism of what he calls the hypostatic ethics of Russell when Russell followed Moore; and it is even more evident in *The Life of Reason,* where he says that the general test of progress is whether a harmony and cooperation of impulses has been achieved, "leading to the maximum satisfaction possible in the whole community of spirits affected by our action".[27] According to Santayana, when we assert that an action is right, in the last analysis we appeal to the *fact* that it leads to satisfaction. "Satisfaction," he maintains, "is the touchstone of value; without reference to it all talk about good and evil, progress or decay, is merely confused verbiage, pure sophistry in which the juggler adroitly withdraws attention from what works the won-

der. . . . A good, absolute in the sense of being divorced from
all natural demand and all possible satisfaction, would be as
remote as possible from goodness: to call it good is mere dis-
loyalty to morals, brought about by some fantastic or dialectical passion".[28] And while Santayana voices certain criticisms of
hedonism, he says that "in spite of all logical and psychological scruples, conduct that should not justify itself somehow by
the satisfactions secured and the pains avoided would not
justify itself at all".[29]

While linking value, or what he also called the moral ideal,
with satisfaction, Santayana said that "the ideal has the same
relation to given demands that the reality has to given perceptions", and then added that "in the face of the ideal, particular demands forfeit their authority and the goods to which a
particular being may aspire cease to be absolute; nay, the satisfaction of desire comes to appear an indifferent or unholy
thing when compared or opposed to the ideal to be realised.
So, precisely, in perception, flying impressions come to be regarded as illusory when contrasted with a stable conception of
reality. Yet of course flying impressions are the only material
out of which that conception can be formed".[30] This suggests
that Santayana may have subscribed to Peirce's view that "X
is really red" means the same as "X will appear red to a person with normal vision who looks at it in white light". Such a
view permits us to say that an object may be really red even
though it appears green on some occasions, since a red object
may appear green to a person who is color-blind or who looks
at it in light which is not white. Santayana also seemed to
hold that statements like "X is desirable" may be analogously
analyzed, because he said that just as we form our conception
of being really or objectively red out of sensory impressions,
so "in the same way present demands are the only materials
and occasions for any ideal". Furthermore, he said, "if the
ideal can confront particular desires and put them to shame,
that happens only because the ideal is the object of a more

profound and voluminous desire and embodies the good which they blindly and perhaps deviously pursue".[31] But what is a more profound and voluminous desire? Royce might have said that it is one experienced by the Absolute, but Santayana was not entitled to "solve" the problem of value in this way. What, then, did he mean by the phrase? And was his notion of a profound and voluminous desire naturalistic? We may discover by the use of natural science whether a person has normal vision and whether an object is being seen in white light, so that when we translate "X is really red" into "X will appear red to a person with normal vision who looks at it in white light", we are presumably translating it into a statement of natural science. But is it obvious that when we translate "X is desirable" into "X is desired by a person whose desire for X is profound and voluminous" we are translating it into a naturalistic statement? Is there not some danger that the notions of profundity and voluminousness are themselves value-notions, so that Santayana's definition of "desirable" contains a non-naturalistic value-word? Santayana never faced up to such difficulties and dangers, and therefore we must regard his ethical naturalism in *The Life of Reason* as a program rather than an accomplishment, a statement that moral ideal and desire are connected somehow, but not a statement of exactly how they are connected.

So far I have merely called attention to a lack in Santayana's ethical theory, but now I wish to turn to a possible inconsistency in it. Although Santayana, as an ethical naturalist, seems to maintain that ethical statements are scientific and empirical, he also says that ethics is a dialectical science whose practitioners engage in an analysis of intent.[32] But in that case it would seem that the conclusions of ethics are not empirical and therefore very different from the conclusions of a naturalistic science. How does Santayana arrive at this apparent inconsistency; and is it merely apparent?

We may get a clearer idea of what Santayana is driving at

by considering some illustrations. What is an example of a conclusion which is arrived at by one of Santayana's dialectical analysts of intent? At some places in *The Life of Reason* it is typically a definition or an analysis of something like courage or piety. But here we may say exactly what Hume and Reid said more than a century earlier about Locke's statement that wherever there is no property there is no injustice. Any statement which is merely the consequence of a definition of courage is not a *moral statement,* and therefore Santayana does not abandon his naturalism merely by saying that the analysis of a virtue like courage is dialectical or non-empirical. So far so good. At other places, Santayana seems to say that one who defines goodness is also engaged in dialectic and that his conclusions are also non-empirical. But once again it may be argued that even the consequence of a definition of goodness is not a *moral statement;* and once again we may say that Santayana is not involved in serious inconsistency.

Now, however, we come to a part of Santayana's discussion which makes it harder to defend him. At one place in *The Life of Reason* Santayana says: "This method, the Socratic method, consists in accepting any estimation which any man may sincerely make, and in applying dialectic to it, so as to let the man see what he really esteems. What he really esteems is what ought to guide his conduct . . .".[33] Let us assume therefore that Socrates has used his dialectic on an unphilosophical friend and has led him to realize that he really esteems courage. And let us also assume that when Santayana says that what the friend really esteems is what ought to guide his conduct, Santayana means that the friend's conclusion, "I really esteem courage", is a moral statement. Does it follow that such a moral statement is not naturalistic because it has been arrived at dialectically? Does Santayana wish to maintain that a first-person statement like "I really esteem courage", which he sometimes treats as though it were equivalent to the statement "Courage is good", is established by dialectic and not by

what he calls natural science? If he does, then he has contra-
dicted his ethical naturalism in a way that is hard to account
for. Necessarily, if ethical statements like "Courage is good"
are dialectical in Santayana's sense, they are very different
from truths about nature; and there are *many* passages in *The
Life of Reason* where Santayana asserts that there is a discipline called "rational ethics" composed of moral truths like
"Courage is good" which have the same logical status as mathematics and which therefore transcend psychology and history. In such passages he seems to think that rational ethics is
composed of propositions about essences, and that the truth of
such propositions may be perceived without appealing to experience. His inconsistency, I think, was intimately related to
his confusion about the nature of science.

Like William James—not to mention the inevitable John
Locke—Santayana never fully escaped the grip of classical rationalism. For after making a sharp distinction between eternal, dialectical, mathematical truths and the contingent truths
of physics, he goes on to say that "it is the evident ideal of
physics, in every department, to attain such an insight into
causes that the effects actually given may be thence *deduced*
[Santayana's emphasis]; and deduction is another name for
dialectic. . . . [T] he hope of science, a hope which is supported
by every success it scores, is that a simpler law than has yet
been discovered will be found to connect units subtler than
those yet known; and that in these finer terms the universal
mechanism may be exhaustively rendered. Mechanism is the
ideal of physics, because it is the infusion of a maximum of
mathematical necessity into the flux of real things. It is the as-
piration of natural science to be as dialectical as possible, and
thus, in their ideal, both branches of science [physics and dia-
lectic] are brought together".[34] In short, Santayana seems to
maintain that the aim of the physicist is to arrive at truths
which are established merely by examining the relationships
between meanings or essences and that from these truths the

physicist can derive the lesser empirical discoveries of experi-
mentalists. A similar conception leads Santayana to suppose
that the discovery of a rational ethics by observing meanings
will permit us to derive concrete moral judgments via moral
principles like the ten commandments. It is a conception
which shows Santayana cracking under the logical strain of
being both a naturalist and a Platonist. Like Locke before
him, he was a half-hearted empiricist whose belief in essences
brought him to a rationalistic dead-end in ethics.

Santayana: Sage and Cultural Critic

In spite of his obscurities and ambiguities on technical matters, Santayana occupies a very important position in the history of American philosophy as a wise man and critic of
American civilization. I think, therefore, that G. E. Moore
was excessively harsh when he began his review of *The Life of
Reason* by writing: "This book is so wanting in clearness of
thought that I doubt whether it can be of much use to
anyone" [35] and that John Dewey came closer to the truth
when he said in his review of the same book: "We are grateful
to Mr. Santayana for what he has given us; the most adequate
contribution America has yet made, always excepting Emerson, to moral philosophy".[36] In agreeing with Dewey about
Santayana, however, we must construe moral philosophy not
as the analysis of moral concepts but as substantive moral criticism and psychology; and this makes clear what likening Santayana to Emerson means. Emerson was a moral seer, and Santayana was that too. He was often deep and wise in his observations of human beings, no matter how lacking he was in the
kind of analytic power that G. E. Moore valued. No reader of
his work can fail to see that Santayana, like Emerson, had "a
poetic fancy and a gift for observation and epigram".

To show this, I shall quote some remarks that clearly reveal
this talent. Speaking of Christian philosophy, he says: "The in-

stinct to regard poetic fictions as revelations of supernatural
facts is as old as the soul's primitive incapacity to distinguish
dreams from waking perceptions, sign from thing signified,
and inner emotions from external powers".[37] Speaking of ancient Hebrew thought, he says: "Fanaticism consists in redou-
bling your effort when you have forgotten your aim".[38]
"Mechanism," he insists, "is not one principle of explanation
among others. In natural philosophy, where to explain means
to discover origins, transmutations, and laws, mechanism is
explanation itself".[39] "Philosophers," he remarks, "have sometimes said that all ideas come from experience; they never
could have been poets and must have forgotten that they were
ever children".[40] And he says with profundity: "The first
principles of logic are like the senses, few but arbitrary".[41]
With equal profundity, he declares that "thought is a form of
life, and should be conceived on the analogy of nutrition, generation, and art"; [42] yet he is wise enough not to press the
analogy too far, since he adds: "Knowledge is not eating, and
we cannot expect to devour and possess *what we mean.*
Knowledge is recognition of something absent; it is a saluta-
tion, not an embrace".[43]

Dealing shrewdly with Kant, he asks: "What possible objects are there for faith except objects of a possible
experience?" [44] and maintains that "the 'practical' proofs of
freedom, immortality, and Providence—of which all evidence
in reason or experience had previously been denied—exceed
in perfunctory sophistry anything that can be imagined".[45]
According to Santayana, Berkeley was "a party man in philosophy, where partisanship is treason".[46] Perhaps echoing
Chauncey Wright through some intermediary, Santayana
writes on indeterminism: "Men's thoughts, like the weather,
are not so arbitrary as they seem and the true master in observation, the man guided by a steadfast and superior purpose,
will see them revolving about their centres in obedience to
quite calculable instincts, and the principle of all their flutter-

ings will not be hidden from his eyes. Belief in indeterminism is a sign of indetermination".[47] And of belief in Cartesian dualism he declares: "The world, instead of being a living body, a natural system with moral functions, has seemed to be a bisectible hybrid, half material and half mental, the clumsy conjunction of an automaton with a ghost".[48] Of all ignorant men, philosophers included, he says: "Those who cannot remember the past are condemned to repeat it".[49]

I turn now to some of Santayana's penetrating remarks about social life. Speaking of the family, he says: "A child, half mystery and half plaything, comes to show us what we have done and to make its consequences perpetual. We see that by indulging our inclinations we have woven about us a net from which we cannot escape: our choices, bearing fruit, begin to manifest our destiny. That life which once seemed to spread out infinitely before us is narrowed to one mortal career. We learn that in morals the infinite is a chimera, and that in accomplishing anything definite a man renounces everything else. He sails henceforth for one point of the compass".[50] About the family which extends into a tribe, Santayana is quite shrewd: "There is no real instinct", he contends, "to protect those who can already protect themselves; nor have they any profit in obeying nor, in the end, any duty to do so. A *patria potestas* much prolonged or extended is therefore an abuse and prolific in abuses".[51] This attitude of Santayana rests in part on his conviction that "individualism is in one sense the only possible ideal; for whatever social order may be most valuable can be valuable only for its effect on conscious individuals. . . . It would be a gross and pedantic superstition to venerate any form of society in itself, apart from the safety, breadth, or sweetness which it lent to individual happiness".[52] Santayana's individualism is also associated with his hatred of militarism, about which he issues one of his profound sociological generalizations: "A military class is . . . always recalling, foretelling, and meditating war; it fosters artificial and senseless jealousies toward other governments that possess armies; and finally, as often as not, it precipitates disaster by bringing about the objectless struggle on which it has set its heart".[53] Well before 1914 he attacked what he called barrack-room philosophy: "Since barbarism has its pleasures it naturally has its apologists. There are panegyrists of war who say that without a periodical bleeding a race decays and loses its manhood. Experience is directly opposed to this shameless assertion. It is war that wastes a nation's wealth, chokes its industries, kills its flower, narrows its sympathies, condemns it to be governed by adventurers, and leaves the puny, deformed, and unmanly to breed the next generation. . . . To call war the soil of courage and virtue is like calling debauchery the soil of love".[54]

Santayana's observation of individual behavior is often as acute as his observation of philosophers and forms of social life. Discussing vanity, he observes: "What others think of us would be of little moment did it not, when known, so deeply tinge what we think of ourselves. Nothing could better prove the mythical character of self-consciousness than this extreme sensitiveness to alien opinions; for if a man really knew himself he would utterly despise the ignorant notions others might form on a subject in which he had such matchless opportunities for observation. Indeed, those opinions would hardly seem to him directed upon the reality at all, and he would laugh at them as he might at the stock fortune-telling of some itinerant gypsy. As it is, however, the least breath of irresponsible and anonymous censure lashes our self-esteem and sometimes quite transforms our plans and affections. The passions grafted on wounded pride are the most inveterate; they are green and vigorous in old age. We crave support in vanity, as we do in religion, and never forgive contradictions in that sphere; for however persistent and passionate such prejudices may be, we know too well that they are woven of thin air. A hostile word, by starting a contrary imaginative current, buffets them rudely and threatens to dissolve their being".[55]

Santayana's writing on religion also contains its share of well-phrased wisdom, like: "Every superstition is a little science, inspired by the desire to understand, to foresee, or to control the real world".[56] Then there is the passage in which he says that prayer's "essence is poetical, expressive, contemplative, and it grows more and more nonsensical the more people insist on making it a prosaic, commercial exchange of views between two interlocutors",[57] as well as the following comment on mythical thinking: "Mythical thinking has its roots in reality, but, like a plant, touches the ground only at one end. It stands unmoved and flowers wantonly into the air, transmuting into unexpected and richer forms the substances it sucks from the soil. It is therefore a fruit of experience, an ornament, a proof of animal vitality; but it is no *vehicle* for experience; it cannot serve the purposes of transitive thought or action".[58] And since I have been quoting these passages in part to point up a quality of mind that Santayana shares with Emerson, it is appropriate to quote at length Santayana's remarks on the distinction between what he calls primary and secondary religion. He is speaking of the difference between those in whom religion is spontaneous and those in whom it is imitative and says: "To the former, divine things are inward values, projected by chance into images furnished by poetic tradition or by external nature, while to the latter, divine things are in the first instance objective factors of nature or of social tradition, although they have come, perhaps, to possess some point of contact with the interests of the inner life on account of the supposed physical influence which those superhuman entities have over human fortunes. In a word, theology, for those whose religion is secondary, is simply a false physics, a doctrine about eventual experience not founded on the experience of the past. Such a false physics, however, is soon discredited by events; it does not require much experience or much shrewdness to discover that supernatural beings and laws are without the empirical efficacy which was attributed to them. True physics and true history must always tend, in enlightened minds, to supplant those misinterpreted religious traditions. Therefore, those whose reflection or sentiment does not furnish them with a key to the moral symbolism and poetic validity underlying theological ideas, if they apply their intelligence to the subject at all, and care to be sincere, will very soon come to regard religion as a delusion. Where religion is primary, however, all that worldly dread of fraud and illusion becomes irrelevant, as it is irrelevant to an artist's pleasure to be warned that the beauty he expresses has no objective existence, or as it would be irrelevant to a mathematician's reasoning to suspect that Pythagoras was a myth and his supposed philosophy an abracadabra. To the religious man religion is inwardly justified. God has no need of natural or logical witnesses, but speaks himself within the heart, being indeed that ineffable attraction which dwells in whatever is good and beautiful, and that persuasive visitation of the soul by the eternal and incorruptible by which she feels herself purified, rescued from mortality, and given an inheritance in the truth. . . . Proofs of the existence of God are therefore not needed, since his existence is in one sense obvious and in another of no religious interest. It is obvious in the sense that the ideal is a term of moral experience, and that truth, goodness, and beauty are inevitably envisaged by any one whose life has in some measure a rational quality".[59]

What could be more Emersonian than this rejection of traditional theology, this identification of religious insight with moral insight, and this spurning of theological disputation and argument by a man who once wrote, "I detest disputation and distrust proofs and disproofs"?[60] True, Santayana was a materialist and Emerson an idealist; but Santayana said of Emerson that "philosophy for him was rather a moral energy flowering into sprightliness of thought than a body of serious and defensible doctrines" and that "a literal belief in Christian doctrines repelled him as unspiritual, as manifesting no understanding of the meaning which, as allegories, those doctrines might have to a philosophic and poetical spirit".[61] This shows how closely united these two poet-moralists were on religion, a subject that may have been the greatest concern of each of them. Even though Santayana, unlike Emerson, put forward a body of doctrines in philosophy, I do not think that he will be read a century from now as the author of those doctrines but rather as a discerning moral critic and observer of what he called the vicissitudes of human belief. He was therefore more like Emerson than he may have realized.[62]

In fact, Santayana is like Emerson in a respect which is rarely noted even by those who perceive major similarities between them. I have in mind Santayana's antipathy to modern urban life. There is an understandable tendency to think that Emerson is the romantic, Protestant, subjective, nature-loving hater of civilization and cities, whereas Santayana is the cool, classical, Catholic, realistic, civilized, indeed urbane, lover of urban life.[63] Yet, when Santayana remarked on the great shift in emphasis in his work at about the age of fifty—the one that led him to be more concerned with nature and less concerned with the vicissitudes of human belief—he said that he came at that time to feel himself "nearer than ever before to rural nature and to the perennial animal roots of human society".[64] As he developed this feeling, a latent animus against the big modern city seems to have become more prominent in his thinking. Of commercial cities he came to say: "Civilisations and towns created by commerce may grow indefinitely, since they feed on a toll levied on everything transportable; yet they are secondary. However much they may collect and exhibit the riches of the world they will not breed anything original".[65] He hated "the monstrous growth of cities, made possible by the concentration of trade and the multiplication of industries, mechanised, and swelling into monopolies"; [66]

and an objectionable tone entered his voice when he discussed Judaism, positivism, liberalism, and New York critics, many of whom were great admirers of his philosophy.[67]

If historians of American thought find it surprising that Santayana should have converged with the romantic Emerson on the city, they should recall that he also converged with his idealistic colleague Royce on the same subject.[68] And while remarking on paradoxical alliances, they might observe that one of Santayana's great admirers was V. L. Parrington. Parrington was a Populist, a Jeffersonian democrat, an ally of F. J. Turner and Charles Beard, and very unlike the suave, detached, and aristocratic Santayana. Yet Parrington was delighted with Santayana's concept of the genteel tradition and used it as a stick against all those who had what he called "an exaggerated regard for esthetic values". "Our literary historians", said Parrington in the Introduction to his *Main Currents in American Thought,* "have labored under too heavy a handicap of the genteel tradition—to borrow Professor Santayana's happy phrase—to enter sympathetically into a world of masculine intellects and material struggles. They have sought daintier fare than polemics, and in consequence mediocre verse has obscured political speculation, and poetasters have shouldered aside vigorous creative thinkers." [69] Following Santayana, Parrington attacked the paleness and gentility of Emerson and Hawthorne,[70] and went so far as to assert that "the spirit of Henry James marks the last refinement of the genteel tradition",[71] even though Santayana himself had explicitly said that the great brother of William James had overcome the tradition by understanding it and analyzing it.[72]

We see, then, that Santayana's thought leads us in different and unexpected directions: back to Emerson and forward to Parrington and other American liberals. But why was he admired by Jewish intellectuals when he could be so nasty not only about ancient but also about modern Jewish habits of thought? And how could the anti-belletristic, Populistic Par-

rington rest so heavily on a thinker with whom he shared little more than a phrase? I cannot give anything like a complete answer to such questions, but I shall venture a few
observations that ought to figure in an adequate explanation.
In the first quarter of this century intellectual America was, I
suggest, especially hospitable to naturalism, to materialism, to
realism, to the notion that only physics yields real causal explanations, to the idea that ethics may be reduced to a natural
science, to the view that Calvinism and Transcendentalism
were antiquated because they were out of touch with the dynamic forces of science and technology, and to the idea that
religion allegorically communicated only moral truth. So,
when all of these ideas were expressed in prose as persuasive
and respectable as Santayana's, they could not help inspiring
the young, the radical, and the liberal of the early twentieth
century, no matter how much the master himself may have despised some of those who followed him. The followers were
right, however, in what they carried away from his writing.
They were right to admire his naturalism and his attack on
gentility; and to disregard the technical and more other-
worldly doctrine of essences that began with skepticism and
terminated in faith. Understandably, American thinkers
listened more to the early, American Santayana than to the
later, transatlantic Santayana.

If, in conclusion, one asks: Did Santayana originate a very
important idea in logic, the philosophy of science, metaphysics, epistemology, or ethics? I think the answer must be
no. If one asks: Did Santayana say something of importance
about literature, society, history, religion, or politics? Here I
think the answer must be yes, and his distinction in the philosophy of civilization rests on the total effect of a long and
rich intellectual life. His range of interests was remarkably
wide. He was a poet, he wrote a well-received novel, and he
was an influential literary critic. He attended to philosophical
matters of general concern while he worked hard on narrower

questions. He was a stalwart advocate of materialism who respected things of the spirit. He was a humanist and philosopher of civilization. He was, therefore, the sage of American materialism.

11 · John Dewey: Rebel Against Dualism

One of the more noteworthy facts about our story is that whereas Edwards, the first American treated in this volume, was a Yale man who became president of Princeton and Dewey, the subject of this chapter, was a Vermonter who spent most of his intellectual life in New York City after a brief stay in Chicago, the middle of our story has been virtually glued to Boston and its environs. One of the things this reflects, of course, is the philosophical pre-eminence of New England in the period between Edwards and Dewey, as well as the pre-eminence of Concord-cum-Cambridge in nineteenth-century philosophy. But it is also worth noting that when in the second decade of this century Dewey assumed James' mantle as *the* American philosopher, New York replaced Cambridge as the point from which philosophical pronouncements about American life were issued. Dewey developed a mode of operating which was in keeping with his urban situation. His prose failed to sparkle as James' and Santayana's did, and he rarely managed as ministerial a tone as Royce. He cared less than all of them did about the manner in which he communicated his message, and he was as much

at home with labor leaders, schoolteachers, and politicians as
he was with professors—if not more so. James, Royce, and
Santayana also wanted to reach an audience beyond that of
the classroom and the American Philosophical Association,
but by comparison with Dewey's efforts in that direction
theirs were primarily literary in character. Unlike Dewey,
they did not lead third-party political movements, they did
not create and run laboratory schools, and they did not rub
elbows with the urban immigrants who worried Royce so
much and who hastened Santayana's flight from America in
1912. It is true that like Peirce before him Dewey was a pragmatist, but this merely makes the point in another way; for
New York pragmatism as represented by Dewey was very different in ambition from the pragmatism of Peirce. Peirce's
pragmatism was almost entirely technical and theoretical, a
logical pragmatism which was devoted to analyzing the nature
of science, but Dewey's grew into a philosophy of life and a
social weapon which, in Dewey's mind, would help remake
our civilization.

It was Dewey's activism that linked him with another New
Englander who had moved to a more dynamic place in order
to serve society—Supreme Court Justice Oliver Wendell
Holmes, Jr. It was Dewey's social liberalism that led him to
admire some of the ideas of the economist Thorstein Veblen.
It was Dewey's interest in industrial society and its development that linked him spiritually with historians like Robinson and Beard. All of this I have described as part of a revolt
against formalism in American social thought; and today, in
1972, it might well be called a movement in the direction of
making philosophy, law, economics, history, and political science relevant. It was Dewey's preoccupation with the social
problems of modern urban society, as well as his great intellectual curiosity and enormous capacity for work, that led him
to become the last distinguished American philosopher to operate in the grand manner. He worked in every branch of the

subject as professionally conceived—in metaphysics, ethics, and epistemology; he wrote in the philosophy of education, esthetics, the philosophy of science, the philosophy of religion, political philosophy and the history of philosophy; and until the very end of his life in his nineties he was a symbol of philosophical participation in public affairs.

Dewey was born in 1859 in Burlington, Vermont, but he once said that he left that "God-forsaken country" as soon as he could.[1] After being graduated from the University of Vermont, he took his doctor's degree at Johns Hopkins, and after that went to teach at the University of Michigan. Soon after the University of Chicago opened in 1893, he joined its staff; after about ten years there, he moved to Columbia, where he taught until his retirement from teaching in 1929. Since Dewey's mature work was done in Chicago and New York, the two most bustling and vital cities of his time, he was further removed from the influence of the genteel tradition than any philosopher of his generation. None of his far-ranging contemporaries—James, Peirce, Royce, or Santayana—equalled him in concern for the needs and travails of the new technological America, nor in the breadth of his accomplishment within philosophy itself; and it is extremely unlikely that any future American philosopher will match his accomplishment in those respects unless there is a radical shift from prevailing tendencies within the discipline. After the death of Dewey in 1952, no American philosopher who attained professional eminence as a technical thinker was able to command anything like his influence on the general public nor on intellectuals or scholars in other fields. After his death a great change came over the face of American philosophy as it used more and more refined logical techniques, squinted its eyes, and peered into smaller and smaller places.

Philosophy's Past Failures

Dewey's intellectual range was in part a legacy of his nine-teenth-century philosophical education, which subjected him to the influence of such world-spanning minds as Comte, Hegel, and Darwin. Reading Comte, he tells us, awakened his interest in the interaction of social conditions with scientific and philosophical thought; [2] Hegel's idea of cultural institutions as an " 'objective mind' upon which individuals were dependent in the formation of their mental life" supplemented that influence of Comte; [3] and the influence of Darwin was so great that Dewey tried in the 1890's to interpret even Hegel's logic in terms of Darwinian notions.[4] Hegel and Darwin, who in their different ways emphasized the importance of the concept of continuity, greatly influenced Dewey's criticism of those who divided the universe into sharply separated kinds of entities—like Platonic forms and concrete particulars, or material bodies and immaterial minds—and his criticism of those who were given to distinguishing between radically different kinds of knowledge and truth. From Hegel he derived an abiding antipathy to the idea that there is a gulf between the mind and its objects, and Darwin led him to see that man is not sharply separated from the rest of nature. Dewey argued that one of the most distinctive features of Western philosophy was its propensity to dualistic thinking, and he vigorously attacked this in virtually everything he wrote.[5] He regarded it as an intellectual legacy of the pre-technological, pre-scientific, pre-democratic origins of philosophy. He held that the Greek distinction between master and slave was reflected in the tendency of Greek philosophers to distinguish between knowledge as a form of passive contemplation and the lowly practical activity of those who were forced to use their hands in order to live. This Greek bias was perpetuated, he argued, by Christian thought and then bequeathed to modern philosophy, which failed—as in the case of Locke—to articulate or to apply the method implicit in modern scientific technology and democracy. That task was therefore essayed by Dewey himself, and to it he devoted his life.

Dewey's condemnation of all previous philosophy was reminiscent of Santayana's attack on the genteel tradition in America. Both held that a philosophy which had arisen under one set of conditions could lose touch with social life upon the emergence of new conditions and become a spiritual drag on society. Dewey, however, was much more insistent than Santayana about the political and social importance of creating a philosophy that would more adequately express the newly emerged social and intellectual conditions. It was Karl Marx, therefore, whom Dewey most resembled in his conception of the relationship between philosophy and society, for Marx held that an outmoded ideology can be an illusion or a nightmare that paralyzes the society in which it persists.

Among the dualisms that Dewey renounced and denounced, this split between knowledge and practice was the most fundamental, since he held that it was the most direct intellectual expression of the social chasm between those who had leisure and those who labored with their hands. The notion that theory was utterly divorced from practice, said Dewey, was paralleled by an ontological separation between two realms that were cut off from each other. One consisted of eternal, immaterial things like essences, forms, ideas, or universals, and the other of changeable material things. According to tradition, Dewey said, the objects contemplated by theory had to be fundamentally different from the objects upon which the artisan worked his changes: the doer dealt with chancy, dangerous things whereas the theorist dealt with immutable objects and their unchanging relationships. Because the theorist was preoccupied with so etherial a realm, he hoped he would escape—in imagination at least—the peril inherently present in the world of action; and because the theorist's mind was traditionally thought to be immaterial by contrast to his body, another unDeweyan dualism between "inner" mind and "outer" body was created. When such an inner, immaterial mind contemplated external, eternal objects, it supposedly came to know necessary, *a priori,* certain truths, whereas the best that could be achieved in this line by a doer was to arrive at mere opinion, which was contingent, *a posteriori,* and probable.

Dewey's condemnation of dualism was the central feature of his philosophy; and most of his distinctive opinions may be subsumed under it, notably his views in ethics. From the Greeks onward, he said, the philosophical tradition tried to support moral values by appealing to supposed contrasts between knowledge and opinion, between eternal and changeable objects, and between *a priori* and empirical truth. Moral values were thought to be too exalted to be supported by the lowly methods of the artisan, so they had to be defended by knowledge of what Dewey disparaged as "antecedent reality" and "ultimate Being". If one could show that moral truth is established merely by gazing up at Platonic ideas, one could show that it had the requisite stability and permanency by raising it to the level of metaphysical, mathematical, and logical truth, high above mere opinion, mere practice, and mere sensation. In this way, moral truth became a species of scientific truth as conceived by the tradition—a body of necessary, *a priori,* immutable, absolutely certain propositions.

When modern science emerged, said Dewey, it upset this ancient philosophical picture, because it used a refined version of the despised artisan's method in arriving at those modern exemplars of knowledge, the beliefs of the new astronomy and mechanics. Cinderella was discovered by the Prince, as it were, invited to come out of the kitchen and to become the star of the new theory of scientific knowledge. According to that theory, knowledge and action are intrinsically connected, said Dewey, and once this was recognized, however dimly, the

old way of supporting values was undermined. Once it was
fully recognized that the authority of science as conceived by
the Greeks and their medieval followers could no longer be
used as a basis for immutable moral values, only religion and
metaphysics remained as supports for those values. It could no
longer be said that immutable scientific principles underlay
moral thought and practice, and therefore those who wanted
their ethics immutable were forced to seek dubious aid from
Locke, Kant, the Scottish philosophers, or other moderns in
quest of certainty. The American genteel tradition, with its
contrast between the head of science and the heart of morals,
represented a variety of dualism against which Dewey rebelled when he abandoned his early idealism under the influence of evolutionary doctrine. He said of the latter: "The philosophic significance of the doctrine of evolution lies precisely
in its emphasis upon continuity of simpler and more complex
organic forms until we reach man. The development of organic forms begins with structures where the adjustment of
environment and organism is obvious, and where anything
which can be called mind is at a minimum. As activity becomes more complex, coordinating a greater number of factors in space and time, intelligence plays a more and more
marked role, for it has a larger span of the future to forecast
and plan for. The effect upon the theory of knowing is to dis-
place the notion that it is the activity of a mere onlooker or
spectator of the world, the notion which goes with the idea of
knowing as something complete in itself. For the doctrine of
organic development means that the living creature is a part
of the world, sharing its vicissitudes and fortunes, and making
itself secure in its precarious dependence only as it intellectually identifies itself with the things about it, and, forecast-
ing the future consequences of what is going on, shapes its
own activities accordingly. If the living, experiencing being is
an intimate participant in the activities of the world to which
it belongs, then knowledge is a mode of participation, valu-

able in the degree in which it is effective. It cannot be the idle view of an unconcerned spectator".[6]

When Dewey abandoned his youthful idealism, he abandoned what he called the quest for certainty, the search for transcendental truth on which morals was to be rested; and he declared that the only way in which ethical judgments could be confirmed was by the use of scientific method in the modern as opposed to the ancient sense. When he became an ethical naturalist, he warned that the failure of his philosophical contemporaries to apply the method of modern science to ethics would mean their isolation as uninfluential pedants, and he announced in Jeremiah-like tones that the failure of society to do so was responsible for its most dire ills. *The* great problem for modern man, said Dewey, was to heal the breach between morals and science which had opened up after the medieval synthesis had broken down. This, he said, could be accomplished only by resting moral knowledge on science properly conceived. Armed with such knowledge, philosophers could participate in a great effort to make society over by applying science to individual conduct and to social institutions.

Dewey was not content to argue that ethics was closely tied to natural science. He also challenged a more fundamental part of traditional philosophy by arguing that logic, that bastion of Platonism, should free itself from subservience to metaphysics and recognize that it too was not radically different from natural science. Therefore Dewey's struggle against dualism was composed of the following major strands: his view of the connection between scientific knowledge and action; his effort to show that moral and logical beliefs are different only in degree from the pragmatically analyzable beliefs of natural science; and his attempt to apply his pragmatic or instrumentalist theory of scientific knowledge and ethical judgment to the concrete problems of man, chiefly in education and politics. In order to describe in more detail Dewey's revolt against dualism, I shall begin with his philosophy of science, then turn to his ethics and his logical theory, and finally to his philosophies of education and politics. In the course of my discussion I shall not only present what I think Dewey's main aims in these areas were, but also express some doubts about his success in achieving the demolition of dualism. Though he tried mightily in some of his writings to demolish it, in others his effort was seriously weakened by a variety of crypto-dualism which I shall describe below.

Dewey's Theory of Knowledge: In Peirce's Steps

Dewey thought that much of modern epistemology was preoccupied with asking how we, with our ideas "in here", can know about objects "out there"; and therefore he regarded it as a misguided effort to put together what should not have been sundered by Descartes in the first place. In opposition to traditional theories of perception, he identified his own theory of knowledge with what he called logic, or inquiry into the publicly observable processes of scientific inquiry. At its clearest, his theory of knowledge closely resembled Peirce's at *its* clearest. Dewey agreed with Peirce that all scientific knowledge rests on objective statements of fact, like "This piece of sugar is sweet", which may be analyzed as asserting that if an operation were performed, a certain experience would be had. In this spirit, Dewey said: "To judge that this object is sweet, that is, to refer the idea or meaning 'sweet' to it without actually experiencing sweetness, is to predict that when it is tasted—that is, subjected to a specified operation—a certain consequence will ensue".[7] If Dewey had said no more on this subject, his doctrine would have been virtually identical with Peirce's theory of meaning. But Dewey added a philosophical comment on the consequences of this theory of meaning which he associated with his adverse reflections on the quest for certainty. The prag-

matic theory of meaning, he said, showed how absurd it was
to view scientific knowledge as a purely spectatorial insight
into immutable "antecedent reality". His suggestion that the
object of our knowledge that a piece of sugar is sweet, is not
the piece of sugar "as it really is" prior to inquiry, seems an-
tithetical to what Peirce himself had said about the implications of pragmatism. Peirce, it will be recalled, held that pragmatism entailed a variety of scholastic realism according to
which a piece of sugar that tastes sweet when put into the
mouth has a disposition or a potentiality which is a universal.
However, Peirce recognized that the lump of sugar itself was
concrete, sensible, and mutable. The very fact that it has a
disposition like sweetness which it manifests only *sometimes*
shows that it is not an eternal, changeless object like the disposition itself. Therefore, it would seem that according to
Peirce our knowledge that the piece of sugar is sweet is
knowledge that a concrete "antecedent reality" possesses a
property which is also an "antecedent reality". Yet, in the
name of pragmatism, Dewey constantly inveighed against the
notion that the object of knowledge is an "antecedent reality",
and so one is prompted to look with special care at his doctrine on this matter.

Dewey held that to know that a piece of sugar is sweet is
not to record, in what he calls a photographic way, a feature
of the piece of sugar as it is *prior* to tasting. To gain such
knowledge, he says, one must perform an operation on the
sugar and *then* have an experience as a consequence. This is
all that Dewey seems to mean when he says that *the object of
knowledge* is the piece of sugar *after* it has been transformed
by the performance of an operation. "The object of knowledge," he says, "is eventual; that is, it is an outcome of directed experimental operations, instead of something in sufficient existence before the act of knowing." [8] Dewey does *not*
say that a piece of sugar that no one has tasted does not exist
prior to our discovering that it is sweet; Dewey does *not* hold

that the experimenter calls the piece of sugar into existence when he tastes it. All he means is that the experimenter cannot establish his claim to *know* that the piece of sugar is sweet without performing an operation. Furthermore, it is the experimentally tested piece of sugar which Dewey calls "the object of knowledge" because our experience of it in that state constitutes what he calls the final and decisive stage of our inquiry. On the other hand, he holds, the piece of sugar as it exists prior to our tasting it furnishes stimuli or challenges to our inquiry into its sweetness. Inquiry itself, Dewey sometimes says, constructs its own object, but he does not mean by this that the piece of sugar did not exist before someone tried to find out whether it was sweet.[9]

One more explanation may be offered in order to dispel another misunderstanding of Dewey. When he says that scientific knowledge is achieved through inquiry and that all inquiry involves transformation of its object, does he believe that we transform the rose by looking at it under different conditions? The answer is that he *does* believe this, primarily because he construes the notion of transformation very broadly as the alteration of the experimenter's relationship with the rose. He says, for example: "In astronomy . . . we cannot introduce variation into remote heavenly bodies. [He was writing in 1929.] But we can deliberately alter the conditions under which we observe them, *which is the same thing* . . .".[10] And elsewhere he says: "While the astronomer cannot change the remote stars, even he no longer merely gazes. If he cannot change the stars themselves, he can at least by lens and prism change their light as it reaches the earth; he can lay traps for discovering changes which would otherwise escape notice. Instead of taking an antagonistic attitude toward change and denying it to the stars because of their divinity and perfection, he is on constant and alert watch to find some change through which he can form an inference as to the formation of stars and systems of stars".[11] We see now why even looking at or attending to the rose is a case of experiment or transformation for Dewey: it alters our relationship with the rose.

Before leaving this part of Dewey's thought, it would be well to remark that he held that the mere having of an experience of redness which ensues upon looking at a rose, is not to be confused with knowledge about the rose. When I am having an experience which I report with words like "It seems to me exactly as if I were seeing a red thing now", I am merely recording an experience I have had. If the experience is one that I have had under normal conditions and my vision is normal, then I may say that I *know* that an object like a rose is really red. But this knowledge, which is expressible in a conditional statement connecting the performance of an operation with the having of an experience, must not be confused with the having of the experience.[12] My knowledge that the rose is red is distinct from the rose's looking red to me now; my knowledge records a disposition of the rose but its looking red to me is an episodic manifestation of that disposition. Therefore, in spite of his antipathy to making what he called dualistic distinctions, Dewey had no compunction about making a very sharp distinction between scientifically knowing that something is the case and having a direct, immediate experience of the kind that one has after one tastes sugar, smells a rose, scratches a diamond, or touches velvet. In fact, this is one of the fundamental distinctions in Dewey's entire philosophy, upon which he built not only his theory of physical knowledge but also his theory of value, as we shall see.

Dewey's Ethical Naturalism

Like so many philosophers before him, Dewey approached the analysis of moral judgments with a great desire to avoid the view that moral judgment is dependent on insight into Plato's forms, on perceiving so-called non-natural qualities, or

on the use of Locke's intuitive reason, because Dewey regarded moral knowledge as a species of empirical knowledge.
But in his flight from all forms of irrationalism, he did not
wish to be forced into the view that value judgments merely
record the fact that an object has satisfied the irrational, im-
pulsive wants or desires of human beings. And because he
thought that value judgments may express knowledge, he
could not accept that version of the so-called emotive theory
of ethics which said that ethical sentences have emotive meaning but no cognitive meaning.[13] Therefore he tried, as Santayana had, to devise an analysis of statements like "That is
good" modeled on the Peircean analysis of statements like
"That is sweet", "That is hard", and "That is red". The statement "That is good", he said, is quite different in meaning
from "That satisfied my desire", but the problem is to say
how they are logically connected with each other.

Before turning to Dewey's specific efforts in this direction, I
should call attention to a problem which he is obliged to keep
his eye on in the course of his analysis. On the assumption
that "This piece of sugar is sweet" means the same as "If any
normal person were to taste this piece of sugar under normal
circumstances, he would experience sweetness", it would seem
that "This piece of sugar is good" must be analyzed as meaning the same as "If any normal person were to taste this piece
of sugar under normal circumstances, he would experience
satisfaction". But since the second statement factually reports
a disposition of the piece of sugar to affect normal people in a
certain way under normal circumstances, some philosophers
have wondered why it is equivalent—as Dewey says it is—
with a statement to the effect that it is *right* for a person to be
satisfied by the piece of sugar, or that he ought to be satisfied
by it. The problem becomes more evident when we find
Dewey saying that statements of goodness are "*de jure*" rather
than "*de facto*".[14]

Dewey was not unaware of the need for dealing with this

difficult problem, but his efforts to deal with it are not altogether satisfactory. For example, in one place he says that "escape from the defects of transcendental absolutism is not to be had by setting up as values enjoyments that happen anyhow, but in defining value by enjoyments which are the consequences of intelligent action")[15] I take this to mean that if the satisfying taste of, say, a cup of tea follows upon the kind of operation in which a professional tea-taster engages, we may conclude that the tea is *really* good; but if the satisfaction comes by a less intelligent route, so to speak, we cannot conclude that the tea is really good. Yet there are two possible ways of taking this less intelligent route. One is where the satisfaction or enjoyment "happens anyhow", a route which is hard to illustrate realistically. Presumably, for example, it is a case where the satisfying taste of tea comes to us in a completely random way, where we do not make a deliberate effort to drink but, perhaps, fall into a vat of tea, which yields satisfaction as it enters the mouth. The other route, as I interpret Dewey, is illustrated when the person deliberately does something *non-standard* which results in a satisfying experience. For example, he does something analogous to looking at an object with colored glasses, with poor vision, in the wrong light, or under the influence of drugs. Obviously, it is possible to come by a satisfactory experience in this way and yet deny that the evaluated object is good. Here the experience comes as a consequence of "intelligent" action in the sense of deliberate action, but this does not support a judgment of goodness. Therefore, the question arises: Does Dewey think that something is good if the satisfying experience comes as a consequence of *any* deliberate action, or does he think that the satisfactory experience must come as a consequence of *standard deliberate action*? If he holds the latter view, then he must face the charge that *standard deliberate action* is itself a value-notion, just as Santayana must face the charge that his notion of a profound and voluminous desire is a value-

notion.[16] If *standard deliberate action* is a value-notion for
Dewey, then it may be legitimately denied that he has defined
value in non-evaluative or scientific terms. In my opinion,
Dewey never successfully answers this charge.

Dewey's Logical Theory

The same motives that led Dewey to treat ethics as a natural
science were at work in his reflections on logic. He wished to
bring logic as well as ethics into closer connection with natural science, and in doing so participated in the general intellectual movement I have called the revolt against formalism.
But it is helpful to distinguish two different expressions of his
anti-formalism within logical theory. For one thing, there is
the simple fact that he was not interested in the systematic development of formal logic. He had no talent for it, and he
began his philosophical career as a Hegelian who thought
that formal logic was *fons et origo malorum* in philosophy.[17]
What he called logic throughout his life was close to what idealist logicians like Bradley and Bosanquet engaged in when
they tried to describe the nature of thought, and to what the
British inductive logicians, like Mill and Venn, were interested
in. This led Dewey to view logic as the theory of inquiry, as a
study of the processes of scientific thinking which was very
different from what Frege called logic and what Russell and
Whitehead systematized in their *Principia Mathematica.* This
is why Peirce preferred to call Dewey's work in this area the
"natural history of thought".[18]

The other anti-formalistic strain in Dewey's reflections on
logic emerges when he tries to depict the epistemological status of formal logic and pure mathematics. Although he was
not a practitioner of either discipline, he held very pro-
nounced views on the nature of their principles. These views
are of special interest to us because they show him once again
trying to avoid dualism by developing a pragmatic or instru-

mentalist view of those principles which have traditionally provided transcendentalists, *a priorists,* and Platonists with their most powerful ammunition. The major thrust of Dewey's effort here is to show that there is no sharp epistemological distinction between the principles of formal logic or pure mathematics and those of natural science.

In several places Dewey gives the impression that he denies that there are necessary truths which are independent of experience and that he regards this doctrine as a part of philosophy's fruitless quest for certainty. In these places he seems to reject the quest for certainty both in its Greek form and in its modern form as defended by David Hume, and in consequence seems to deny that pure mathematics and pure logic are composed of beliefs which express relations between abstract ideas.[19] The following passage typifies this tendency in Dewey's thinking: "Mathematics is often cited as an example of purely normative thinking dependent upon *a priori* canons and supra-empirical material. But it is hard to see how the student who approaches the matter historically can avoid the conclusion that the status of mathematics is as empirical as that of metallurgy. Men began with counting and measuring things just as they began with pounding and burning them. One thing, as common speech profoundly has it, led to another. Certain ways were successful—not merely in the immediately practical sense, but in the sense of being interesting, of arousing attention, of exciting attempts at improvement. The present-day mathematical logician may present the structure of mathematics as if it had sprung all at once from the brain of a Zeus whose anatomy is that of pure logic. But, nevertheless, this very structure is a product of long historic growth, in which all kinds of experiments have been tried, in which some men have struck out in this direction and some in that, and in which some exercises and operations have resulted in confusion and others in triumphant clarifications and fruitful growths; a history in which matter and methods have been constantly selected and worked over on the basis of empirical success and failure. The structure of alleged normative *a priori* mathematics is in truth the crowned result of ages of toilsome experience. The metallurgist who should write on the most highly developed method of dealing with ores would not, in truth, proceed any differently. He too selects, refines, and organizes the methods which in the past have been found to yield the maximum of achievement. Logic is a matter of profound human importance precisely because it is empirically founded and experimentally applied."[20]

We should note that Dewey is here talking about pure mathematics and explicitly disagreeing with certain mathematical logicians about its epistemological status. He is not commenting on *applied* mathematics, which many philosophers of a Platonic or a Humeian persuasion might also regard as empirical, but he is saying that *pure* mathematics is empirically founded and experimentally applied. And this of course brings him into conflict not only with Greek thinkers and David Hume but also with Bertrand Russell and twentieth-century positivists, who think that there are necessary truths which are independent of experience and which are therefore different *in kind* from the truths of natural science. The same anti-dualistic tendency is evident in parts of Dewey's *Logic,* where he follows the lead of Charles Peirce in distinguishing leading principles which are counterparts of laws of logic merely on the basis of what Peirce called width.[21] In physics, for example, there is a leading principle that allows the inference of "This rotating copper disk will come to rest" from "This rotating copper disk has been placed between magnets", whereas in logic there is a leading principle which allows us to infer "Callias is mortal" from "All men are mortal and Callias is a man" and which is more widely applicable. Dewey does not say that the physical leading principle is based on experience whereas the logical one is not and that therefore the latter is to be tested merely by an examination of meanings, universals, forms, or Platonic ideas. That is what philosophers who quest for certainty say, but Dewey wishes to separate himself from them by distinguishing these two kinds of leading principles merely in terms of their width—which is of course a matter of degree. Both principles articulate or formulate habits of inference which may be observed by the logician of scientific inquiry. These are habits which may at first be implicitly manifested by scientific inquirers without their being aware of them as their own habits, and may later be articulated in a more explicit way as habits which they can depend on to take them from acceptable premises to acceptable conclusions. The same *kind* of dependability may therefore characterize both the inference from "This rotating copper disk has been placed between magnets" to "This rotating copper disk will come to rest" and the inference from "All men are mortal and Callias is a man" to "Callias is mortal" This means, in effect, that the laws of nature and laws of logic are in a very important respect on the same footing. Neither of them has come to the mind of man *ab extra* because both express modes of inference which have been successfully used in scientific inquiry. When Dewey writes in this spirit, he shows no signs of holding that logical principles are used successfully because *they* are "analytic", whereas physical principles are used successfully because *they* are based on experience—which is what a follower of Hume might say as he argued that logical principles are based on relations between *ideas,* whereas physical principles are not. It is in this spirit that Dewey calls special attention to "the principle of the continuum of inquiry", the importance of which he thinks only Peirce had previously noted. Dewey says that application of this principle enables him to give "an empirical account of logical forms" which will allow him to go beyond traditional empiricism.

Whether Dewey was successful in this is a large and very difficult question. It is important, however, to call attention to the fact that he distinguishes in his *Logic* between "existential" and "ideational" propositions, saying that existential propositions refer "to actual conditions as determined by experimental observation", whereas ideational propositions "consist" of "inter-related meanings, which are non-existential".[22] In my opinion, the mere fact that Dewey draws such a distinction in his *Logic* marks a departure from the spirit of other parts of his *Logic* and from that of Chapter II in *The Quest for Certainty,* which is called "Philosophy's Search For The Immutable". There Dewey wrote: "In this chapter we are especially concerned with the effect of the ideal of certainty as something superior to belief upon the conception of the nature and function of philosophy. Greek thinkers saw clearly—and logically—that experience cannot furnish us, as respects cognition of existence, with anything more than contingent probability. Experience cannot deliver to us necessary truths; truths completely demonstrated by reason. Its conclusions are particular, not universal. Not being 'exact' they come short of 'science.' Thus there arose the distinction between rational truths or, in modern terminology, truths relating to the relation of ideas, and 'truths' about matters of existence, empirically ascertained".[23] The general impression one gets from this and also from his *Reconstruction in Philosophy* is that Dewey holds that there are no necessary truths and no truths "relating to the relation of ideas", whereas in some parts of the *Logic* he does distinguish between "existential" and "ideational" propositions, does call the latter "necessary", and does speak of them as concerned with "meanings". All of this seems quite foreign to the tenor of Dewey's impassioned polemic against the quest for certainty.

A more serious departure from the doctrine of Dewey's *The Quest for Certainty* is to be found at those points in Dewey's *Logic* where he deals with the problem of characterizing scientific laws. We know that for a very long time philosophers have worried about how to distinguish a law from a mere summary of what has happened in the past; for example, how to distinguish a law like "All bodies not impressed by an external force maintain their velocity" from a statement like "All of the pieces of paper on my desk this morning are yellow", bearing in mind that the first expresses what is sometimes called a necessary connection, whereas the second expresses a mere accidental fact. We have seen that even Emerson worried about this under the influence of the Kantian tradition. It is therefore ironic that when Dewey, the arch-opponent of questing for certainty, comes to deal with this difficult question, he is led to maintain that Newton's first law of motion expresses a "necessary relation between abstract characters". Furthermore, it is surprising to discover that Dewey maintained that laws of science which express "necessary relations between abstract characters" are valid by definition and hence are analytic statements, or true by virtue of the meanings of their terms. It is extraordinarily interesting to the historian of American philosophy to discover that the conception of science he finds in Locke should have continued its hold on Dewey, as it did on James and Santayana, for Dewey was so dedicated to defending what he called an *experimental* empiricism, to rejecting all forms of rationalistic intuition, and to abandoning the quest for certainty. Yet how far from Locke's view that the basic principles of natural science are self-evident—seen immediately to be true by one who understands their terms—is Dewey's view that laws of science are true by definition or analytic? In the end, we are tempted to say, is the beginning of American philosophy; and we are also tempted to say that the thrust of Dewey's *Logic,* published when he was seventy-nine years old, is very different from that of *The Quest for Certainty* and *Reconstruction in Philosophy.*[24]

Dewey the Reformer

It is helpful to keep in mind that there are two main respects in which Dewey thought of himself as an opponent of dualism. On the one hand he advanced doctrines of the kind we have just considered, that is to say, criticized certain epistemological and ontological distinctions between kinds of truth and kinds of entities. On the other, he complained about philosophers who confined themselves to debating questions of this kind because he thought that philosophers should apply their conclusions (preferably Deweyan conclusions, of course) and change the world with their help. That is why Dewey was so interested in education. Indeed, his educational theories flow very naturally from his opposition to dualistic theories of knowledge and his attachment to what he called the principle of continuity. He believed that because learning is a process whereby the young come to *know* something, philosophers are bound to approach learning and hence education in a manner which is intimately connected with their theories of knowledge. Therefore Dewey says that since the philosophical tradition misconceived the nature of knowledge, it was bound to misconceive the process of education—not only education in matters commonly called scientific but also moral education. Dominated as society was by class divisions, he said, it set up its educational schemes in accordance with the philosophic dualisms it encouraged and, as a result, treated learning as something divorced from doing, as the possession of a detached leisure class. Such theories of education led to the cultivation of an abstract, pure Reason which supposedly discerned universal principles while the senses gleaned particular facts, and which would lead the child to the light of truth and away from the heat of emotion. "Literary, dialectic, and authoritative methods of forming beliefs", he complained, governed the schools of the past rather than the method of science; and in those few instances where the method of science was the model of learning, it was usually limited to use in natural science while "the forming and testing of ideas in social and moral matters" were viewed in a way that was still dominated by classical philosophy.[25]

By contrast, Dewey's philosophy of education emphasized

the centrality of learning by doing, of treating it as a habit of intelligent inquiry rather than as a process of storing up facts which led to no capacity to predict and control the future. Dewey insisted that in a democratic society which sought to break down class barriers, the classroom should be a miniature social community in which fluent, free, and democratic social intercourse was encouraged. As society progressed more and more from its undemocratic, unscientific, pre-technological ways, so education was to become more and more "progressive"—a term that became synonymous with Dewey's views. The new anti-dualistic school was oriented toward intelligent activity, centered on the child, freed from the formalism of mere drill and rote learning, and dedicated to viewing its curriculum as a pliant instrument rather than as a catechetical and canonical set of texts to be regarded as purely esthetic objects that endowed their owner with social status. If anyone doubts that Dewey's views in education were virtually theorems in his systematic attack on dualism, let him look up the index of Dewey's *Democracy and Education* under "Dualisms, educational results", where he will be directed to "see also Activity and knowledge; Activity *vs.* mind; Authority *vs.* freedom; . . . Body *vs.* soul; Capital *vs.* labor; Character *vs.* conduct; Character *vs.* intelligence; Conservativism *vs.* progressiveness; Culture *vs.* efficiency; Discipline *vs.* interest; Doing *vs.* knowing; . . . Duty *vs.* interest; Emotions *vs.* intellect; Ends *vs.* means; . . . Experience *vs.* knowledge; Habit *vs.* knowledge; Humanism *vs.* naturalism; . . . Individuality *vs.* institutionalism; Intellectual *vs.* practical studies; Inner *vs.* outer; Logical *vs.* psychological method; . . . Matter *vs.* mind; Method *vs.* subject matter; Nature *vs.* nurture; Objective *vs.* subjective knowledge; Particular *vs.* general; . . . Physical *vs.* psychical; Practice *vs.* theory; Rationalism *vs.* empiricism or sensationalism; . . . Thinking *vs.* knowledge".[26] In this garden of *versuses* we may find not only Dewey's philosophy of education, but his entire philosophy.

In fact, Dewey once said that philosophy may be defined as

the general theory of education [27] because he believed that philosophy, when serious, must influence the conduct of life. Philosophy influences conduct not by giving advice on specific personal problems but by fostering general attitudes or dispositions like open-mindedness and intelligence, and by helping resolve fundamental conflicts within society. Philosophy can, he said, encourage people to use their intelligence to resolve a clash between the interest in order and the interest in freedom, or a conflict between the religious interest and the scientific. The emergence of a new astronomy called for such readjustment in early modern times; and when the emergence of Darwinian biology called for a readjustment of attitudes in Dewey's own lifetime, he played a courageous part in fostering that readjustment. He also defended his own interest in education and in politics by warning: "Unless a philosophy is to remain symbolic—or verbal—or a sentimental indulgence for a few, or else mere arbitrary dogma, its auditing of past experience and its program of values must take effect in conduct. Public agitation, propaganda, legislative and administrative action are effective in producing the change of disposition which a philosophy indicates as desirable, but only in the degree in which they are educative—that is to say, in the degree in which they modify mental and moral attitudes".[28] That is why he said that "if we are willing to conceive education as the process of forming fundamental dispositions, intellectual and emotional, toward nature and fellow men, philosophy may even be defined *as the general theory of education*".[29]

This conception of philosophy as resolving social conflict through the educational formation of fundamental dispositions committed Dewey to the kind of political liberalism with which he was identified for most of his life. To the extent to which he viewed this process as a gradual one, he was attacked by Marxists who, although they believed as he did that philosophers must help change the world, differed with him about the means. And to the extent to which he abandoned supernaturalism and authoritarianism, he was anathema to all religious bigots and political reactionaries. Dewey was for the better part of a century the symbol of liberalism and the apostle of intelligence in social and political affairs, and he tried to carry out his conception of the philosophical life as faithfully as any philosopher ever has. It is true that he sometimes unnerved readers who tired of hearing him constantly talk about the importance of using scientific intelligence in political affairs without hearing him describe concrete political programs. The fact is, however, that Dewey was primarily a political educator, and an educator, he thought, is primarily concerned to encourage dispositions and attitudes. At the age of eighty he modestly said to a critic that, although he had done little or nothing in the direction of producing skills that would constitute a political technology, that failure did not detract from his "recognition that in the concrete the invention of such a technology is the heart of the problem of intelligent action in political matters".[30] In the same spirit, we may say that his failure to solve certain enormously difficult problems in moral philosophy and the philosophy of science did not detract from the general correctness of his vision in those fields. For most of his long life he was a profound and courageous rebel against dualism; and in the breadth of his concerns he was a worthy successor to the distinguished American philosophers who preceded him.

Epilogue: In Retrospect, In Prospect, and In Candor

In this chapter I shall summarize the main steps in the preceding narrative; underscore a few of its dominant themes; briefly compare the American philosopher's role in the period before Dewey with his role in the period after Dewey; and then make explicit some attitudes and views of my own that figure in some of my previous assessments of American philosophical ideas.

In Retrospect and Prospect

Having elected to focus on American views of the nature and scope of science, I began with a discussion of the profound impact on them of Locke's philosophy of science. To Americans who thought seriously about the intellectual foundations of religion, morals, and politics—the main concerns of philosophically minded Americans in the eighteenth century—Locke appeared as the champion of a strange pair of views. On the one hand, he was an empiricist who thought that all our ideas arise from sensation or reflection on our mental processes; on the other, he believed that the model to be followed by all disciplines aiming at knowledge is mathematics, viewed as a body of propositions composed of self-evident, necessary, immutable, axiomatic truths and of many theorems deducible from them. Locke maintained that all strict science should be cast in the demonstrative form exhibited by mathematics, even though he conceded that he was not able to develop ethics, nor what we would today call physics, in that fashion. Intuitive reason, he said, was to be used in arriving at the axioms of strict science; and discursive reason was to be used in deriving its theorems. The emotionalism of what he called religious enthusiasm was to be shunned, and every effort made to find self-evident axioms in all disciplines, including theology and morals. Because he held such views, Locke was in a very important respect just as rationalistic as those modern philosophers who are contrasted with him—Descartes, Leibniz, and Spinoza—in spite of the fact that he is usually called an empiricist.

Locke's uneasy combination of empiricism and rationalism helps us understand certain American reactions to his thought in the eighteenth century. The most important American philosopher of religion, Jonathan Edwards, diverged from Locke's empiricism primarily by maintaining that there is a mystical Sense of the Heart which gives Protestant saints non-Lockeian access to religious truth; whereas James Wilson, the ablest colonial philosopher of law, attacked Locke's rationalism by taking two big steps which Thomas Jefferson also took. First Wilson agreed with Thomas Reid that morals cannot be transformed into a demonstrative science even though there are self-evident moral principles, simply because discursive reason is unable to derive many theorems of morality; then he agreed with Shaftesbury, Hutcheson, and Hume that intuitive reason cannot perceive the fundamental truths of morals because they depend not on reason but on sentiment and affection. Edwards' appeal to the Sense of the Heart in religion and Wilson's denial that Lockeian intuitive and discursive reason play a great part in ethics gave much support to the democratic idea that all men—of whatever intellectual power—can perceive the important truths of morals, religion, and politics, since all men are capable of sentiment, even those who are not blessed in great degree with intuitive or discursive reason.

The denigration of Locke's view of reason and of science was continued in the early nineteenth century by the Transcendentalists, who thought that all men are endowed with the mystical insight that Edwards attributed to the saints alone, and that men of sentiment and passion have access to important truth which those who are merely learned and logical cannot perceive. In addition, Transcendentalists called upon continental forms of idealism and ancient varieties of mysticism in their battle against Locke, Unitarianism, and utilitarianism. In this spirit, Emerson encouraged the cultivation of what he called an original relation to the universe, celebrated nature as against artifice, harped on the value of self-reliance, attacked bookishness and argumentation, and regarded concentration on the past and its forms as a reactionary defense of the Establishment. Emerson was not gifted in technical philosophy, but he used it to great rhetorical effect in defense of his moral and literary attitudes. In his writings we find a typically Romantic combination of anti-intellectualism and anti-urbanism defended by an appeal to Coleridge's version of Kant. The most conspicuous element in Emerson's borrowed philosophical armor was Coleridge's distinction between the Reason and the Understanding. Emerson held that the Reason can see truth that the empirical Understanding cannot see; and in espousing this Transcendentalist dualism, he was perpetuating in different language the distinction between reason and sentiment already made by Edwards and Wilson in their efforts to establish theological and moral truth by non-Lockeian methods. By the time we reach Emerson's declaration that Reason is exercised in intuiting moral sentiments, we have come very far from Locke's rationalistic idea that *his* version of intuitive reason could perceive not only the axioms of Euclid but also the fundamental truths of morality and religion.

In the century of Edwards, the Declaration of Independence, and Transcendentalism—roughly from the middle of the eighteenth century to the Civil War—American philosophy was successively bound in service to religion, politics, law, and literature. It was a time when distinguished minds moved down from pure speculation—or up, depending on one's point of view—to philosophizing with a concern for the ordinary man's spiritual condition. It was a time when Americans were, according to Tocqueville, as unphilosophical as any people in the civilized world, so it is not surprising that their most popular thinkers did not confine themselves to the questions of metaphysics or epistemology. Even in his most technical philosophical work, Edwards defended the orthodox doctrine of original sin; and even after Emerson left the Unitarian ministry in early manhood, he continued to serve as an unfrocked parson to all of America, measuring out his homiletic wisdom in poems, literary essays, and lectures that made him a sort of oracle. Although George Santayana later associated Edwards and Emerson with what he called the genteel tradition and said that their philosophies were becalmed while American technology and society rushed on past them, the fact is that their concerns were as close to the concerns of their fellow Americans as were those of any American philosopher to follow them. Edwards and Emerson were deeply interested in the affairs of men even though their ideas did not please all men of affairs. And while Santayana was right to point out that they did not focus their philosophical attention on the inner workings of the scientific method that was transforming America and the world, they did try, as did some of the political theorists of the Revolution, to formulate a *philosophy of science* that would bear on American religion, law, politics, morals, and literature. Even more than Edwards' addition of a Sense of the Heart to Locke's five senses, Emerson's abandonment of Locke's view of reason was a reflection of the growth of American democracy. Emerson came to maturity in a time when faith, feeling, and mystical insight were far more respectable as avenues to truth and knowledge than they were for Locke; and the increase of their respectability was connected with the idea that faith and feeling were more likely to be possessed by ordinary people than by learned intellectuals. We have seen that when Locke rejected the doctrine of innate principles but accepted the doctrine of self-evident principles, he too thought that he was striking a blow for the people against the "dictators of principles"; but the main American philosophers in the period of the Enlightenment and Transcendentalism thought they were even more democratic than Locke when they replaced his Euclidean intuition by one which was more emotional. We have seen that Edwards' determinism and his Lockeian methods of logical analysis were shelved by Transcendentalists who preferred to remember his Pauline view that a saintly ignoramus can see truths with his heart that cannot penetrate the head of a learned intellectual. We have also seen that one of the most articulate revolutionary philosophers of Natural Law, James Wilson, abandoned Locke's notion that first moral principles have the same logical status as first mathematical principles, as well as his notion that morality is a demonstrative science. In the same vein, Emerson maintained under the influence of Coleridge that young, innocent, rural, and poetic hearts use an exalted emotion-laden Reason while their opposite numbers lumber along with a lowly prosaic empirical Understanding.

In this way, Edwards and Emerson transformed intuitionism and mysticism from what was thought by some philosophers to be conservative or reactionary theories of knowledge into democratic ones. Whereas George Ripley rested his socialist beliefs on Scottish "consciousness", John Stuart Mill

took it upon himself to attack the use of Scottish consciousness and Germano-Coleridgian Reason while launching his
own crusade for democracy. Mill declared: "The notion that
truths external to the mind may be known by intuition or
consciousness, independently of observation and experience,
is, I am persuaded, in these times, the great intellectual support of false doctrines and bad institutions. By the aid of this
theory, every inveterate belief and every intense feeling, of
which the origin is not remembered, is enabled to dispense
with the obligation of justifying itself by reason, and is
erected into its own all-sufficient voucher and justification.
There never was such an instrument devised for consecrating
all deep-seated prejudices".[1] And yet in democratic America,
one finds admirers of Edwards celebrating the Sense of the
Heart, Emerson celebrating Jacobi's Reason and the Moral
Sense, the Brook Farmer George Ripley appealing to Scottish
consciousness, and James Walker and Orestes Brownson *feeling* the truth of dark propositions—all in the interest of
showing, not that the rich and the powerful have a special
road to truth, but rather that children, poets, farmers, and ignorant men do. A form of populist anti-intellectualism is
what Edwards and Emerson espoused when they endowed infant saints and poetic farmers with power to see the truth
with their hearts. Thus the tendency to think that there is a
royal road to higher truth is not the only form of anti-intellectualism in Western thought. There is also a tendency to think
that there is a people's road, and it was this second tendency
that Edwards encouraged in his *Religious Affections* and that
Emerson encouraged throughout his life. This populistic
anti-intellectualism may help explain the dearth of memorable technical philosophy in America between Edwards' *Freedom of the Will* of 1754 and the mature work of Chauncey
Wright, who was born in 1830. For the atmosphere in which
Edwards' Sense of the Heart and Emerson's Reason were celebrated was not one in which technical philosophy and logic

could easily flourish. The scientific, mathematical, Millian Chauncey Wright entered the American philosophical scene like one of those Darwinian variations about which he wrote so knowledgeably; and when he did, he started a new species of American philosopher.

Wright opposed Lockeian rationalism but certainly not in the manner of Emerson. Because Wright was a follower of John Stuart Mill, Wright declined to postulate such faculties as Locke's Reason, Edwards' Sense of the Heart, Emerson's Reason, Shaftesbury's and Hutcheson's Moral Sense, or Scottish Common Sense. And because he followed Darwin, Wright's idea that there are no radically different methods for establishing different kinds of knowledge was accompanied by his equally anti-dualistic idea that men are separated from the brutes only in degree. Wright was also led to a low opinion of metaphysics and theology conceived as sciences. Having concluded that they do not supply us with knowledge as he understood it, he turned, in a typically Comteian and Darwinian way, to a genetic investigation of the motives that led men to engage in such activities; and here his most interesting conclusion—sketchily developed by comparison to Santayana's similar conclusion a generation later—was that metaphysics and theology do not conflict with science because they stand in a relationship to it analogous to that in which poetry stands to it. Accordingly, Wright was one of the first American philosophers after Emerson to hold that the sage of Concord was a prose-poet and that his Pauline faith was a form of acceptable sentiment but not a way of justifying claims to knowledge. Understandably, however, Wright could not see much poetic value in the writings of Herbert Spencer; and since Wright could see little scientific value in them either, he wrote Spencer off in a manner that was imitated by younger American philosophers. In agreement with Wright, philosophers like James, Royce, and Dewey expressed great admiration for Darwin's evolutionary *biology* but something close to contempt for the evolutionary *philosophy* of Spencer.

Yet, in spite of commanding a good deal of respect from Darwin and from influential Harvard thinkers who knew him personally, Chauncey Wright is a minor figure in the history of American philosophy. When we survey the general drift of that history, we form the impression that his Millian empiricism had very little immediate effect in opposing the persistent view that scientific method is only one method of establishing *knowledge* and *truth*. For soon after Wright died in 1875, his younger Cambridge friends, Peirce and James, plainly showed that they subscribed to variants of the view that passion can justify claims to a kind of knowledge which is distinct from, yet coordinate with, scientific knowledge. Even after the decline of Transcendentalism and the rise of pragmatism, then, we find a tendency to regard something like religious enthusiasm as an avenue to knowledge. So logical and scientific a thinker as Charles Peirce spoke of the heart as a "perceptive organ" through which we may see God, and William James became famous for advocating the right to believe —on what he called "passional" grounds—in a realm beyond nature. That is why I have argued that a strong dualistic tendency is deeply ingrained in American philosophy of the period I have treated. In spite of the profound differences among Edwards, James Wilson, Emerson, Peirce, and the younger James, all of them subscribed to the idea that there are methods of establishing *knowledge* which are fundamentally different from that used by the sciences; and all of them appealed to some form of emotion, sentiment, or passion as centrally involved in the use of these non-scientific methods.

In the case of Peirce and James, however, the perpetuation of the dualistic tradition was accompanied by more anxiety, confusion, and inconsistency than that which prevailed earlier. As men trained in science, they were more aware than Edwards or Emerson was of its power; and as men who came of age in the 1860's, they were obliged to confront forms of empiricism, nominalism, and agnosticism more persuasive than those that had prevailed a century earlier. They were the first really original American philosophers but they were also ambivalent revolutionaries. That is why it should not be surprising that Peirce, who played such a distinguished role in the founding of modern logic and philosophy of language, was also enthralled by metaphysical and theological ideas that many of his twentieth-century admirers find embarrassing. Not only does his notion that the heart is an organ through which we can perceive God link him to Jonathan Edwards and much earlier mystical philosophers, but so does his penchant for cosmological speculation, which distinguishes him, of course, from many of his twentieth-century admirers. Unlike the more positivistic among them, he hoped to build a vast philosophical edifice which would rival that of Aristotle; he severely criticized the varieties of positivism and nominalism with which he was familiar; he opposed determinism; and he even expressed sympathy with Schelling's idealism and with that of Royce. For all of these reasons, Peirce was a divided philosophical self by comparison to the Transcendentalist Emerson and the empiricist Wright. On the one hand Peirce was the founder of a very deflationary, scientific, and anti-metaphysical pragmatism, but on the other he kept insisting that his main contribution to philosophy—his pragmatic maxim—entailed a belief in universals which are very similar to the occult qualities that early modern thinkers regarded as stumbling blocks in the way of science. Peirce's view that a statement like "This diamond is hard" must, to be meaningful, be equivalent to a statement of what sensible results would follow the performance of an operation on the diamond, was used by him as a device whereby he hoped to show the reality not only of universals but even of God, thereby confounding nominalists, agnostics, and atheists alike.

As a scientific mind who refused to dismiss metaphysics and theology as nonsense, Peirce is properly linked with his great

friend, William James. Even more self-consciously than Peirce
—and with much more popular success—James sought to defend God, freedom, and immortality. He showed less sympathy than Peirce showed for scholastic philosophy and for German idealism, but he certainly resembled Peirce in being
concerned lest the truculent agnostics and determinists of his
day frighten people out of their religious beliefs. At first,
James' response to agnostics and determinists was to argue
that whereas some beliefs are established by conceptual analysis and others by sensory experience, still others—notably
those of religion and metaphysics—may be defended by an
appeal to sentiment; and this trialistic response, as I have
labeled it, linked him to his dualistic predecessors in the
history of American thought. But toward the end of his life
he began to sketch the outlines of a philosophy which sought
to avoid the multiplication of methods for establishing beliefs; and here he joined forces with his admirer Dewey.
Moreover, James shared with the pragmatic Dewey a healthy
contempt for the pretensions of idealistic metaphysics and
epistemology, even as they were represented by Josiah Royce,
James' protégé, colleague, and friend.

Royce was probably the most scholastic of all idealists, em-
ploying with dubious success several high-powered logical and
scientific techniques of his day as he tried to establish the existence of the Absolute, which he regarded as necessary for defending the core of Christian faith. He aimed to be the most
monumental of all American philosophers, using logic, biology, and history in his multi-volumed effort to defend a metaphysics which Emerson was content to convey in the epigram
that we all lie in the lap of an immense intelligence. As an
easily visible intellectual obelisk, Royce became the target of
younger American philosophers who, like Russell and Moore
in England, were fatigued with the pretentiousness and the
casuistry of Absolute Idealism. No wonder Royce seemed—as
he himself ruefully observed—like a philosophical old fogey

at the age of fifty-two in 1908; and when the great conciliator, James, died in 1910, no one of stature could persuade the philosophical world that there was much truth in Royce's absolutism. Young realists—whom I hope to treat in a sequel to this volume—cooperated with young pragmatists in chipping away at the shaky foundations of his system, and it soon became evident after Royce's death in 1916 that some form of naturalism would become the next dominant movement in American philosophy.

The two most distinguished leaders of naturalism were Santayana and Dewey; and from the point of view of our narrative, the most interesting thing about them is the manner in which they tried—with varying degrees of success—to oppose the dualism that gripped all of their predecessors who reflected on the impact of science. Santayana's major effort in this direction was to argue that religion should be interpreted as a poetic way of expressing moral truth rather than as a "false physics". Dewey concentrated his energies on showing that moral truth is a species of natural science, and even essayed the more difficult task of showing that logic is. In his attack on the quest for certainty and his defense of naturalism, he launched the first full-scale criticism of the dualism which had dominated American philosophy from the days of Edwards. One may at times question the effectiveness of his criticism, but there can be no doubt about his intentions. Dewey called upon philosophers to abandon the quest for certainty, and the classical dualism between mind and body; Dewey postulated nothing like Edwards' Sense of the Heart, Emerson's Reason, James' Will To Believe, and Peirce's perceiving heart; and, for Dewey, all knowledge was to be attained by the methods used in the sciences.

In linking Santayana and Dewey as naturalists, I do not wish to underestimate the very great differences between them. In his best work, *The Life of Reason,* Santayana concentrated on what he called the vicissitudes of human belief, serving as a profound analyst of civilization; whereas Dewey distinguished himself mainly as a theorist of knowledge and as a political and educational reformer. Yet in spite of the differences between Dewey and Santayana and in spite of their disagreements with the American philosophers before them, they both practiced philosophy in essentially the same manner as it had been practiced by their predecessors: they continued to operate in the grand manner. Even though they were concerned with the method of science, their concern with it was part of their wider interest in the philosophy of all of civilization. They moved with ease from metaphysics to esthetics, making significant stops at epistemology, logic, and ethics; they were also interested in the history of philosophy, political philosophy, and the philosophy of education; and while Dewey concentrated on the concrete social and political problems of America, Santayana was an acute, though Olympian, observer of its ways.

Anyone familiar with American philosophy after the days of Dewey knows that it abandoned the grand manner. The ablest American philosophers continued to be interested in the nature and scope of science; but their motivation ceased to be as obviously religious, political, legal, or educational as it had been for their predecessors. They did not invest the problem of knowledge with the significance it had for Dewey, who felt—as Locke and Mill and James had—that the fate of a whole society might depend on the correct analysis of scientific method. This narrowing of philosophical vision was accompanied by a predictable decline of philosophical influence in American society. From Edwards to Dewey, American philosophers were the most respected commentators of their times just because they were interested in such things as religion, politics, and education. But their successors, for the most part, did not keep in touch with the wider world. As a consequence, the next generation in American philosophy tended to concentrate on the logic of science and left philosophical problems about the foundations of law, education, history, politics, and religion to philosophasters. How and why this came about is a story that needs a volume as large as this one.

In Candor

While I think that I may with justice postpone a history of post-Deweyan philosophy, I think that I cannot ask the reader to wait for a brief expression of those views that have played a part in my evaluations of some of the thinkers treated earlier. Of all such views, the one I might articulate most usefully is my general view of the anti-intellectualism rampant today and the connection between that view and my assessments of some of the figures treated in this book. I believe that the current wave of anti-intellectualism in American thinking has certain affinities with tendencies that have dominated American philosophy from Edwards onwards; and I admit that many of my comments on earlier manifestations of anti-intellectualism were made while I also had my eye on recent manifestations. I shall divide my remarks into two parts. First I shall try to say—briefly—what I mean by philosophical anti-intellectualism, or the anti-intellectualism of intellectuals, and then I shall try to say why I think that this variety of anti-intellectualism has been very closely connected with more widespread social attitudes toward the life of the mind in America. I realize, however, that some readers who approve of my earlier historical judgments may disapprove of what I am about to say.

Philosophical Anti-intellectualism. By philosophical anti-intellectualism I mean the rejection of the view that logic and experience must play their parts in the establishment of reliable belief, and the espousal of the view that raw emotion, passion, or sentiment can *by itself* establish reliable belief. This is an untenable philosophical doctrine which is not made acceptable by the fact that it has been attacked in our times by unscrupulous demagogues. That fact makes me uncomfortable but it is not daunting. When I confront it, I take courage in recalling what Jonathan Edwards said when he confronted those who accused him of coming to the same conclusion on necessity as Thomas Hobbes—a very serious accusation to be leveled against any churchman: "Let his opinion be what it will, we need not reject all truth which is demonstrated by clear evidence, merely because it was once held by some bad man. This great truth, that Jesus is the Son of God, was not spoiled because it was once and again proclaimed with a loud voice by the devil".[2]

Although anti-intellectualism as I have defined it is a philosophical doctrine, we do not find it only in philosophical works. We find it espoused by quasi-philosophers who would rather be dead than well read in epistemology. We meet it in a quietistic form when we are urged to give up discourse for vision or television, or to drug ourselves into a dreamworld, or to seek refuge in Indian trances, or to take seriously the maxim that one flower speaks louder than a thousand words. And we meet it in an activistic form when we are urged to abandon all efforts at scientifically studying society as so much collaboration with the class enemy. To quietists who give up arguing I have little to say, since they are not interested in discourse; but I would point out that once they start to *argue* the merits of anti-intellectualism, they concede a great deal to their philosophical opponents. To activists who spurn due process of thought I would say that it is one thing to *feel* the horror of today's world, but it is another to think that we can evaluate it or change it by appealing to moral sentiment alone. The activist who hopes to liberate society without studying its ways is as powerless as the bridge-builder who knows no mechanics. No one can transform anything effectively without knowing its ways, and knowing its ways requires more than "feeling the truth" in the manner of the Transcendentalists. So far I have mentioned only a comparatively inarticulate level of anti-intellectualism, yet everyone knows writers who think they have what D. H. Lawrence called "blood-knowledge", and historians who think we can express truth about the past only by using imprecise, evocative, nonscientific rhetoric. Like those who say it with flowers and those who seek to save the world without studying it, such deep thinkers also rest on a philosophy with which readers of this book are now very familiar. In short, on all of the lower floors of philosophical anti-intellectualism we can hear the noise of philosophers who live at the top. Those Americans who have lived at the very top of our high culture have thumped their messages down to lower floors for two hundred years. Edwards, Emerson, and James—in his earlier writings —have all held that there is a way of feeling our way to knowledge. Therefore, if our previous story teaches anything, it is that intellectual anti-intellectualism is as American as apple pie, indeed, as American as apple pie in the sky; the doctrine has been formulated and defended by three of the most widely read philosophers treated in this book.

However, I do not wish to be misunderstood. I do not disapprove of feeling, or of men of feeling; and I do not deny the existence of feeling. But I do contend that it does not *of itself* establish claims to knowledge of any kind—not even those made in ethics and religion. This is a good time to repeat that although I do not agree with what I called James' earlier *trialistic* view in the chapter on him, I am very sympathetic to his later view that we test, not individual opinions, but a whole stock of opinions by appealing to the stock's capacity to satisfy the claims of time-tested logic, of experience, and of feeling simultaneously. I therefore think that we must abandon contemporary views which are essentially holdovers of faculty psychology. We should not say—as so many philosophers do—that one method is used to establish claims to mathematico-logical knowledge, another to establish claims to physical knowledge, another to establish claims to moral knowledge, and so on through metaphysical and theological knowledge. We must think of ourselves rather as facing the world with a totality of beliefs of *all* kinds; and we should emphasize that this totality must harmonize with our experience, with logical beliefs that have stood the test of time, *and* with our feelings. A discrepancy with our feelings will typically lead us to abandon a moral belief, but in principle it could lead to an abandonment of *any* kind of belief. This view is an extension of one that has been defended by Pierre Duhem, by Russell, by James, and in recent times by W. V. Quine. I call it an *extension* because in the version I defend, ethical beliefs are also included in the totality of beliefs, and because feelings or emotions are included among those things which the totality of beliefs must reckon with. Such an extension is obviously necessary if one is any kind of an ethical naturalist, and I do not think that anyone has ever successfully refuted ethical naturalism except by relying on the very distinction between analytic and synthetic statements which the view I accept undermines.

In the light of what I have just said, it should be evident that my disagreement with anti-intellectualism is a special case of my disagreement with any doctrine which focuses on one element—like sensory experience, or feeling, or an attachment to long-standing principles of logic—and which says either (*1*) that by appealing to *experience alone* we can establish or reject beliefs of natural science; or (*2*) that by appealing to *sentiment alone* we can establish or reject moral, metaphysical, or religious beliefs; or (*3*) that by appealing to *intuition alone* or to linguistic usage alone we can establish or reject beliefs of logic and mathematics. The anti-intellectualist, as I have called him, does think we can establish some beliefs by appealing to sentiment alone, and perhaps he is better called a sentimentalist; a philosopher who says we establish scientific beliefs by experience alone may be called an empiricist; and one who appeals only to intuition or only to a sense of linguistic propriety in the case of logic may be called an intuitionist. It is worth adding that for some reason the anti-intellectualist or sentimentalist (e.g. the early James) usually advertises his philosophy as the only one which defends the interests of the "whole man", whereas it should be obvious that if any doctrine can be defended in the name of the whole man, it is the doctrine (of the later James) that the claims of experience, of feeling, and of our attachment to time-honored beliefs must all be balanced against each other when we justify the stock of our opinions.[3]

Philosophical and Social Anti-intellectualism

Now that I have all too briefly explained my philosophical views on anti-intellectualism, I wish to offer some historical reflections about its impact on American life. It has sometimes been said [4] that anti-intellectualism is not a philosophical doctrine but rather a social attitude, a resentment and suspicion of the life of the mind. But what is the life of the mind? Presumably it may be lived by a scientist, a poet, a painter, a philosopher, a musician, a historian, or an economist; and I am not disposed to challenge this view. Yet we must recognize that under different historical and social circumstances, different occupations on the above list are visited with more social hostility than others. Sometimes it may be the poet and sometimes the philosopher who is singled out for public attack; sometimes that attack may be made in the interest of the few and sometimes in the interest of the many. In my opinion, however, anti-intellectualism as a social attitude in America has been predominantly populistic or democratic in animus. For that reason it has expressed the people's understandable preference for the values of the hand and the heart over those of the head. In the period we have been studying, anti-intellectualists typically singled out for attack intellectuals whose work was associated with Reason as conceived by Locke. Intellectuals whose work was associated with practical skill and emotion came under less fire. The populace thought of itself—whether correctly or not is beside the point —as better with its hands and heart than with its head, and ideologists who spoke for the populace reflected that thought. We have seen how James Wilson and George Ripley regarded their elevation of sentiment as democratic; and James said of pragmatism to a popular audience: "You see . . . how democratic she is. Her manners are as various and flexible, her resources as rich and endless, and her conclusions as friendly as those of mother nature".[5]

America has never been hospitable to philosophies which celebrate powers rarer than those possessed by pure mathematicians. Even mystics like Edwards and Emerson adopt the Pauline idea that God may be more easily seen by a baby or an ignorant farmer than by a mind which goes beyond even mathematics in its powers to see abstract truth. The absence of a feudal tradition made it difficult for Americans to espouse aristocratic forms of anti-intellectualism such as Locke supposed the doctrine of innate ideas to be; and I have pointed out that even though Locke thought that his own theory of rationally perceived self-evident principles was more democratic than the doctrine of innate principles, American thinkers were quick to see anti-democratic implications in the former. With such considerations in mind, I suggest that the most aggressive social resentment and suspicion of intellectuals in America has been directed against those "mental workers" whom the public identifies with a respect for logic and scientific method. The result has been a tendency to elevate above logic and systematic experiment the use of practical skill and the expression of emotion. The anti-intellectualist in the street has understandably admired those skills and talents which he thinks of himself as having in abundance, while he has understandably feared those who have skills and talents that he thinks of himself as lacking. He has been especially fearful of the application of logic and systematic experiment to matters that are closest to his heart and his fundamental values.

If we examine the attitudes of the anti-intellectual in the American street, we can distinguish four areas in which his attitudes and ideas have flourished: in religion, in politics, in business, and in education.[6] And what forms did anti-intellectualism take in these areas? In religion it led to evangelicalism and revivalism—"the religion of the heart"—which subscribed to the Edwardsean and Emersonian view that the emotions provide a more reliable source of religious truth than natural religion. In politics the victory of Andrew Jackson over John Quincy Adams, we are told, represented a victory of the common man over the expert, since the Jacksonians held that government required no science or scholarship but only the intuitions of folk wisdom. In the field of business, the importance of theory was minimized and the school of hard knocks took precedence over the school of Athens. In education the training of pupils in lifemanship was put way above training in arithmetic.

If these be the ways in which ordinary Americans have minimized the life of the mind, it is plain that popular anti-intellectualism is virtually a corollary of what I have called philosophical anti-intellectualism. Moses Coit Tyler once declared: "In its inception New England was not an agricultural community, nor a manufacturing community, nor a trading community: it was a thinking community; an arena and mart for ideas; its characteristic organ being not the hand, nor the heart, nor the pocket, but the brain . . . ".[7] And the fall from this high estate came about when the heart, the hand, the pocket and other things that are distinguishable from the brain—like the character—came to take precedence over the brain. In short, the attack on the intellect in American life was primarily an attack on what Tyler called the brain as distinct from the heart and the hand. And that, I submit, is the attack that Edwards, Emerson, and James encouraged by some of their philosophical reflections though I believe that in some of his writings James pointed the way to a more acceptable view of these matters.

Although I disagree profoundly with Emerson's anti-intellectualism, I think that it reflects certain admirable attitudes which he shares with some anti-intellectuals of today. When Emerson looked at the uses to which logic and experience were put in his time, he was rightly revolted. The snobbish, misguided scientism of Andrews Norton's theology, the grasping appeals to empirical expediency on State Street, the bogus natural religion of Paley—these were the forces that Emerson, Ripley, Thoreau, and Parker identified with logic and experience in their time. So it is not surprising that they thought that the Reason of Jacobi and Coleridge was the only faculty whereby persons of good will and purity—children, Brook Farmers, ordinary farmers, orators, and poets—could perceive the moral principles that had been forgotten or subverted by the bankers and brokers of Boston before the Civil War. And I cannot help thinking as I listen to some young people today that they share Emerson's feelings when they contemplate some of the representatives of the logico-empirical intellect around them. They see callousness, heartlessness, and moral indifference; and they say that if this is what the intellect is, they will drop out, sit in, stand up, and be counted. Yet, while my heart goes out to them, my whole being tells me that they are repeating Emerson's philosophical mistake. They fail to see that moral truth can be reached only by a whole man who uses his powers to arrive at a whole stock of opinions which will satisfy all of his needs as a thinking, sensing, feeling, active being. In 1837 Emerson was worried lest the American scholar become a bookworm and a valetudinarian, and so he tried to imbue him merely with Transcendentalist feeling by saying: "Whatsoever oracles the human heart, in all emergencies, in all solemn hours, has uttered as its commentary on the world of actions,—these he shall receive and impart".[8] In the nineteen-seventies, however, the oracles of the heart are not enough. In our emergencies, in our solemn hours, the American scholar should be uniting logic, learning, experience, and sentiment in behalf of a world which needs their union more desperately than ever. Sentiment is not enough, logic is not enough, and experience is not enough, if we wish to know and to know what to do. Each should be given its due by the intelligent man as he tests his stock of beliefs and his actions.

Notes

Chapter 1—The Legacy of Locke

1. Sereno E. Dwight, *The Life of President Edwards*, in *The Works of President Edwards* (New York, 1830), Volume I, p. 30. Edwards reports that when he read Locke while an undergraduate at Yale, he derived more pleasure "than the most greedy miser finds, when gathering up handfuls of silver and gold from some newly discovered treasure".

2. Jefferson reports that Richard Henry Lee charged that the Declaration of Independence was "copied from Locke's treatise on Government". Quoted in Carl Becker, *The Declaration of Independence* (New York, 1922), p. 25.

3. "Locke is as surely the influx of decomposition and of prose, as Bacon and the Platonists of growth. . . . 'Tis quite certain that Spenser, Burns, Byron and Wordsworth will be Platonists, and that the dull men will be Lockists." *The Complete Works of R. W. Emerson* (Boston, 1903–4), Volume V (*English Traits*), p. 239.

4. Merle Curti, "The Great Mr. Locke: America's Philosopher, 1783–1861", *Huntington Library Quarterly*, Number XI (April 1937).

5. See R. I. Aaron, *John Locke* (Second Edition, Oxford, 1955), pp. 88–94. Aaron says that Descartes for one may have defended the doctrine of innate ideas attacked by Locke.

6. John Locke, *An Essay Concerning Human Understanding*, Book IV, Chapter XV, Section 1. Hereafter referred to as *"Essay"*.

7. *Ibid.*, Book IV, Chapter III, Section 25. On Locke's atomism, see M. Mandelbaum, *Philosophy, Science, and Sense Perception* (Baltimore, 1964), pp. 1–60. On Locke's view of science, see D. J. O'Connor, *John Locke* (London, 1952), pp. 153–65. I regret that J. W. Yolton's *Locke*

and the Compass of the Understanding (Cambridge, England, 1970) came to my attention when it was too late to make use of it here.

8. *Essay*, Book IV, Chapter III, Section 29.

9. *Ibid.*, Book IV, Chapter III, Section 25.

10. *Ibid.*, Book III, Chapter XI, Section 16.

11. John Locke, *The Second Treatise of Government*, Chapter II, Section 4.

12. *Ibid.*, Chapter II, Section 5.

13. Locke, *Essay*, Book IV, Chapter III, Section 18.

14. *Ibid.*, Book I, Chapter II, Section 1.

15. I have developed the foregoing criticism of Locke at length in the Epilogue to a paperback reprint of my *Social Thought in America*, published by Beacon Press, Boston, 1957. The Epilogue is entitled "Original Sin, Natural Law, and Politics". When I say that Locke cannot avoid supposing that there are self-evident principles of morality because he says that there are certain theorems of morality, I assume, of course, that he did not contemplate the possibility of deriving moral theorems from non-moral axioms. At any rate, I find no clear indication of his contemplating such a possibility.

16. *Essay*, Book I, Chapter II, Section 13.

17. *Ibid.*, Book IV, Chapter XVII, Section 14.

18. *Ibid.*, Book I, Chapter III, Section 25.

19. *Ibid.*, Book IV, Chapter X.

20. *Ibid.*, Book IV, Chapter XVIII, Section 2.

21. *Ibid.*, Book IV, Chapter XVIII, Section 3.

22. *Ibid.*, Book IV, Chapter XVIII, Section 4.

23. *Ibid.*, Book IV, Chapter XIX, *passim.*

24. *Ibid.*, Book IV, Chapter XIX, Section 3.

25. *Ibid.*, Book IV, Chapter XIX, Section 5.

26. *Ibid.*, Book IV, Chapter XIX, Section 7.

27. *Ibid.*, Book IV, Chapter XIX, Section 15.

28. *Ibid.*

29. *Ibid.*, Book IV, Chapter XIX, Section 16.

30. *Ibid.*, Book IV, Chapter II, Section 1.

31. *Ibid.*, Book IV, Chapter XIX, Section 8.

32. *Ibid.*, Book IV, Chapter XIX, Section 13.

33. *Ibid.*, Book IV, Chapter XIX, Section 1.

Chapter 2—Jonathan Edwards

1. Dugald Stewart, *Collected Works*, ed. W. Hamilton (Edinburgh, 1854), Volume I, p. 424.

2. C. H. Faust and T. H. Johnson, eds., *Jonathan Edwards: Representative Selections* (New York, 1935), p. 167.

3. *Ibid.*, p. 162.

4. *Ibid.*, p. 155.

5. *Ibid.*, p. 156.

6. Jonathan Edwards, *Religious Affections,* ed. J. E. Smith (New Haven, 1959), p. 96. See also Jonathan Edwards, *Freedom of the Will,* ed. Paul Ramsey (New Haven, 1957), p. 137. I shall use these editions in references below.

7. *Freedom of the Will,* p. 133.

8. T. H. Johnson, "Jonathan Edwards' Background of Reading", *Publications of the Colonial Society of Massachusetts,* Volume XXVIII (Transactions, 1930–33), p. 210. See also E. C. Smyth, "Some Early Writings of Jonathan Edwards", *Proceedings of the American Antiquarian Society,* New Series, Volume X (1895), p. 235.

9. Among more recent discussions of the extent to which Locke and Newton influenced Edwards, see L. Howard, *"The Mind" of Jonathan Edwards: A Reconstructed Text* (Berkeley and Los Angeles, 1963), especially Chapter III, on the impact of Locke; see P. Miller, *Jonathan Edwards* (New York, 1949), especially pp. 71–99, and C. Cherry, *The Theology of Jonathan Edwards* (New York, 1966), pp. 98–99, for a discussion of Newton's influence.

10. See S. E. Dwight, *The Life of President Edwards,* p. 54, where it is said that had Edwards' life been devoted to science "in a country where he could at once have availed himself of the discoveries of others, and, the necessary instruments, he would have met with no ordinary success, in extending the bounds of human knowledge, in the most important and interesting fields of Physical Science". For a different view of Edwards' scientific powers, see C. H. Faust, "Jonathan Edwards as a Scientist", *American Literature,* Volume I (January 1930), pp. 393–404. Faust refers to a number of other opinions on this issue.

11. *Essay,* Book II, Chapter IX, Section 1.

12. *Ibid.,* Book II, Chapter XXI.

13. Faust and Johnson, *op. cit.,* pp. xxxix–xliii; Ramsey's Introduction to Edwards' *Freedom of the Will,* pp. 2–7.

14. *Freedom of the Will,* p. 171.

15. Locke, *Essay,* Book II, Chapter XXI, Sections 6–21.

16. *Freedom of the Will,* pp. 171–72.

17. *Ibid.,* p. 174.

18. *Ibid.,* p. 179.

19. *Ibid.*

20. *Ibid.,* p. 181.

21. *Ibid.*, pp. 184–85.

22. *Ibid.*, p. 195.

23. *Ibid.*, p. 197.

24. *Ibid.*, p. 148.

25. *Ibid.*, p. 164.

26. *Ibid.*, p. 144; pp. 196ff. For further discussion of Edwards' views on these matters and others discussed in the next section, see pp. 34–47 of the Introduction by Paul Ramsey to the edition of *Freedom of the Will* that I have been citing and the Introduction by A. S. Kaufman and W. K. Frankena to their abbreviated edition of *Freedom of the Will* (New York, 1969, paperback edition).

27. See especially *Freedom of the Will*, pp. 149–62.

28. Sometimes it is said that whereas Edwards held that sometimes a man may *do* as he pleases, Edwards denied that a man can *please* as he pleases. This, however, is not in accord with Edwards' granting that a man may successfully resolve on Monday to refuse to drink on Tuesday. Such a man has chosen to choose in a certain way, but without supplying a counter-example to Edwards' argument. The crucial point in Edwards' argument is that it makes no sense to say of a man who made a certain choice that if he had chosen—at the very moment when he made his choice—not to make that choice, he would not have made that choice. The simultaneity is what bothers Edwards; and that is why he would not have responded favorably to certain statements by G. E. Moore in his *Ethics* (New York, 1949), pp. 135–36.

29. *Essay*, Book II, Chapter II, Section 3.

30. See W. K. Frankena's Introduction to his edition of *The Nature of True Virtue* (Ann Arbor, 1960); also Faust and Johnson, *op. cit.*, pp. xxiv–xxxix; pp. lxxv–xciii.

31. Edwards held that in the minds of such beings "there is some new sensation or perception of the mind, which is entirely of a new sort, and which could be produced by no exalting, varying or compounding of that kind of perceptions or sensations which the mind had before". In an obvious allusion to Locke, Edwards said that in the minds of such beings "there is what some metaphysicians call a new simple idea", *Religious Affections*, p. 205. Incidentally, W. K. Frankena says that, so far as he knows, Hutcheson was the first British writer to speak of "simple ideas" in ethics, "Hutcheson's Moral Sense Theory", *Journal of the History of Ideas*, Volume XVI (1955), p. 361.

32. *Religious Affections*, p. 274.

33. Faust and Johnson, *op. cit.*, p. 107.

34. *Religious Affections*, p. 278.

35. *Ibid.*, p. 303.
36. *Ibid.*
37. *Freedom of the Will*, p. 424.
38. *Essay*, Book IV, Chapter XVIII, Section 3.

Chapter 3–"We Hold These Truths To Be Self-Evident"

1. See A. C. Fraser's edition of Locke's *Essay* (Oxford, 1894), Volume I, p. 65, n. 2.
2. Thomas Reid, *Essays on the Intellectual Powers of Man* (Edinburgh, 1785), p. 555. (Essay VI, Chapter IV.)
3. *Ibid.*
4. *Ibid.*, p. 566.
5. Locke, *Essay*, Book IV, Chapter III, Section 18.
6. Reid, *op. cit.*, p. 682.
7. David Hume, *An Enquiry Concerning Human Understanding*, in *Enquiries*, ed. L. A. Selby-Bigge (Oxford, 1902), p. 163.
8. Reid, *op. cit.*, pp. 675–76.
9. R. G. McCloskey, Introduction to his edition of *The Works of James Wilson* (Cambridge, Mass., 1967), Volume I, p. 2.
10. *Ibid.*, Volume II, p. 723.
11. Reid, *op. cit.*, pp. 683–84.
12. Wilson, *op. cit.*, Volume I, p. 136.
13. *Ibid.*, p. 124.
14. *Ibid.*, p. 136.
15. *Ibid.*
16. *Ibid.*, pp. 132–33.
17. *Ibid.*, p. 142.
18. Hume, *An Enquiry Concerning the Principles of Morals*, in *Enquiries*, ed. Selby-Bigge, Appendix I, p. 293.
19. Wilson, *op. cit.*, p. 143; Hume, *ibid.*, p. 294.
20. Reid, *Essays on the Active Powers of Man* (Edinburgh, 1788), pp. 236 ff.; *Essays on the Intellectual Powers of Man*, p. 611. It is worth noting that Wilson vigorously attacked Hume's (and Locke's) theory of perception in the manner of Reid; that is to say, Wilson attacked the view that we do not directly perceive external objects but Lockeian ideas. However, certain commentators on Wilson have failed to point out that in spite of attacking Hume's theory of perception, Wilson shared some of Hume's views in moral theory. R. G. McCloskey in his Introduction to Wilson's *Lectures on Law* fails to emphasize this agreement with Hume in ethics, perhaps because Wilson failed to acknowledge it him-

self. A similar neglect of Hume's influence on Wilson is evident in A. B. Leavelle's article, "James Wilson and the Relation of the Scottish Metaphysics to American Political Thought", *Political Science Quarterly*, Volume 57 (September 1942), pp. 394–410. For a useful discussion of the Scottish philosophy as a whole, see S. A. Grave, *The Scottish Philosophy of Common Sense* (Oxford, 1960); Chapter VII contains an especially helpful discussion of Reid's moral philosophy and its relationship to that of Hume.

21. *The Papers of Thomas Jefferson*, ed. J. P. Boyd (Princeton, N.J., 1955), Volume 12, pp. 14–15.

It may be of some interest to observe that at one place where he considers questions of this kind, Alexander Hamilton does not reveal the influence of what has been called sentimentalism in moral theory. In *Federalist Number 31*, Hamilton begins by making the Lockeian distinction between axioms and theorems, but adds that where supposedly self-evident axioms do not command the assent of the mind, it must be because the mind is suffering from "some defect or disorder in the organs of perception, or from the influence of some strong interest, or passion, or prejudice". Here Hamilton does not make the sort of distinction that Wilson made between the first principles of mathematics and those of morals; he does not let the former rest on reason and the latter on sentiment. Moreover, Hamilton does not say that *all* men are able to perceive the truth of first principles in morals and politics. He says that because the objects of geometrical inquiry are so remote "from those pursuits which stir up and put in motion the unruly passions of the human heart", mankind is willing to adopt even the most paradoxical mathematical conclusions; whereas "in the sciences of morals and politics, men are found far less tractable". To a certain degree, he adds, it is right and useful that this should be the case, because "caution and investigation are a necessary armor against error and imposition". But this "untractableness," he continues, "may be carried too far, and may degenerate into obstinacy, perverseness, or disingenuity. Though it cannot be pretended that the principles of moral and political knowledge have, in general, the same degree of certainty with those of the mathematics, yet they have much better claims in this respect than, to judge from the conduct of men in particular situations, we should be disposed to allow them. The obscurity is much oftener in the passions and prejudices of the reasoner than in the subject. Men, upon too many occasions, do not give their own understandings fair play; but, yielding to some untoward bias, they entangle themselves in words and confound themselves in subtleties".

The basic idea underlying Hamilton's view goes back at least as far as Aquinas, who in his *Treatise on Law* made a distinction between a principle being self-evident in itself and being self-evident in relation to us. He says that the subject of a proposition may really contain the predicate but that this may not be evident to one who does not know the definition of the subject. Hence "some propositions are self-evident only to the wise, who understand the meanings of the terms of such propositions: thus to one who understands that an angel is not a body, it is self-evident that an angel is not circumscriptively in a place: but this is not evident to the unlearned, for they cannot grasp it", Thomas Aquinas, *Summa Theologica*, First Part of the Second Part, Q.94, Art. 2. For further discussion of this, see the Epilogue to the paperback edition of my *Social Thought in America* (Boston, 1957).

Chapter 4—Transcendentalism

1. Between Edwards and Emerson there were several American philosophers who might be discussed in a survey; but in a selective study like this, we may safely neglect them. The American Samuel Johnson was a disciple of Bishop Berkeley who did not add enough to the thoughts of his master to merit our attention. Franklin and Jefferson, though they were giants on the American scene, were not primarily philosophers. The materialism of Cadwallader Colden, Thomas Cooper, and Benjamin Rush is better treated in a chapter of a history of colonial thought; and the same may be said for American deists and for most of the American philosophers who espoused the Scottish philosophy of Common Sense. American deists added little to what had originated in England and France, and American representatives of Scottish philosophy were for the most part imitators of the school of Reid, Stewart, and company. Besides, we have already touched on Scottish elements in the thought of James Wilson and will soon consider some in the thought of certain Transcendentalists. For a comparatively recent account of the impact of Scottish philosophy in America, see S. E. Ahlstrom, "The Scottish Philosophy and American Theology", *Church History*, Volume XXIV (1955), pp. 257–72.

2. On the impact of German philosophy on the Transcendentalists and Emerson, see R. Wellek, "The Minor Transcendentalists and German Philosophy", *The New England Quarterly*, Volume XV (1942), pp. 652–80, and "Emerson and German Philosophy", *ibid.*, Volume XVI (1943), pp. 41–62. It has been well said, however, that "it is manifestly impossible to select out of all the many influences which lie behind

American Transcendentalism any one author and to say that here is the chief source of transcendental idealism", E. G. Berry, *Emerson's Plutarch* (Cambridge, Mass., 1961), p. 117; and that "the literature on Transcendentalism is vast", C. Crowe, *George Ripley, Transcendentalist and Utopian Socialist* (Athens, Ga., 1967), p. 295.

3. See W. R. Hutchison, *The Transcendentalist Ministers: Church Reform in the New England Renaissance* (New Haven, 1959), especially Chapter 1.

4. W. E. Channing, "Unitarian Christianity", *The Works of William E. Channing, D.D.* (Boston, 1877), p. 371. This was Channing's famous Baltimore Discourse of 1819.

5. *Ibid.*, p. 376.

6. *Ibid.*, p. 377.

7. *Ibid.*, p. 378.

8. *Ibid.*

9. *Ibid.*, p. 368.

10. *Ibid.*, p. 381.

11. *Ibid.*, p. 406. This reference to Locke appears in Channing's essay, "Objections to Unitarian Christianity Considered".

12. George Ripley, *A Letter Addressed to the Congregational Church in Purchase Street* (Boston, 1840); quoted in C. Crowe, *op. cit.*, p. 75.

13. A. O. Lovejoy, *The Reason, The Understanding, and Time* (Baltimore, 1961), p. 4.

14. O. B. Frothingham, *Transcendentalism in New England* (New York, 1886, originally published in 1876), p. 23; p. 27. George Ripley also lists Jacobi as one of the central figures in the revolt against Locke. See Volume II, p. 239, of Ripley's anthology, *Philosophical Miscellanies, from the French of Cousin, Jouffroy, and Benjamin Constant* (2 volumes, Boston, 1838). These are the first two volumes of Ripley's *Specimens of Foreign Standard Literature* (14 volumes, Boston, 1838–42).

15. Quoted in translation by Lovejoy, *op. cit.*, pp. 8–10. The original appears in the *Berliner Monatsschrift* for May 1796 under the title "On a Certain Genteel Tone which has of late appeared in Philosophy" (*Von einem neuerdings erhobenen vornehmen Ton in der Philosophie*). Lovejoy calls this the liveliest thing Kant ever wrote. It should be added that Kant's annoyance with Jacobi's appeal to mystical Reason is similar to Locke's annoyance with the Enthusiasts. Locke spoke of the "ease and glory" of their feeling "above the common and natural ways of knowledge"; and of the fact that such a feeling "flatters many men's laziness, ignorance, and vanity", *Essay*, Book IV, Chapter XIX, Section 8.

16. *The Letters of Ralph Waldo Emerson*, ed. R. L. Rusk (New York, 1939), Volume I, pp. 412–13. The reference to Milton is related to *Paradise Lost*, V, 486–88. Incidentally, the Scottish philosopher Dugald Stewart refers to these lines of Milton in his (Stewart's) discussion of intuitive and discursive reason in *Elements of the Philosophy of the Human Mind*, which Emerson had studied in Harvard College. In the same place Stewart notes that Locke had written in Section 3 of his *Conduct of the Understanding:* "The two most different things in the world are a logical chicaner, and a man of reason". See *The Collected Works of Dugald Stewart*, ed. W. Hamilton, Volume III, pp. 7–12 and the notes there.

The editor of Emerson's *Letters*, Rusk, points out that Coleridge had discussed reason and understanding in *The Friend* for September 14, 1809, and in Chapter X of *Biographia Literaria*. Rusk opines that Emerson remembered the lines of Milton from Marsh's edition of Coleridge's *Aids to Reflection* (Burlington, Vt., 1829), where they are quoted in two places. See Emerson's *Letters*, Volume I, p. 412, n. 31.

17. Speaking of Emerson's Divinity School Address, Arthur Schlesinger, Jr., observes that Emerson said little there that Ripley or Brownson had not said before, "but he had the gift of crystallizing the impulses of the day and disclosing them with a profundity and richness of suggestion that made even those who had already voiced them wonder at facets they had overlooked and beauties they had not suspected", *Orestes A. Brownson, A Pilgrim's Progress* (New York, 1963; reprint of original edition of 1939), p. 131. See also C. L. F. Gohdes, "Some Remarks on Emerson's 'Divinity School Address'", *American Literature*, Volume 1 (1929), pp. 27–31.

18. R. V. Wells, *Three Christian Transcendentalists* (New York, 1943), p. 29, n. 37; Perry Miller, "From Edwards to Emerson", *Errand into the Wilderness* (Cambridge, Mass., 1956), Chapter VIII; John Dewey, "James Marsh and American Philosophy", *Journal of the History of Ideas*, Volume II (1941), pp. 131–50; Marjorie H. Nicolson, "James Marsh and the Vermont Transcendentalists", *Philosophical Review*, Volume XXXIV (1925), pp. 28–50.

19. A. O. Lovejoy points out in his paper, "Coleridge and Kant's Two Worlds": "In *Aids to Reflection* . . . it is above all because the Reason justifies the belief in human freedom that he [Coleridge] assures the 'youthful readers' of that work that 'The main chance of their reflecting aright, and of their attaining to a contemplation of spiritual truths at all, rests on their insight into the nature of this disparity,' i.e., between

Understanding and Reason". Lovejoy also shows how Coleridge had misunderstood some of Kant's views on related matters. See A. O. Lovejoy,
Essays in the History of Ideas (Baltimore, 1948), p. 255.

20. *The Remains of the Rev. James Marsh, D.D.*, ed. Joseph Torrey
(Second Edition, Burlington, Vt., 1845), pp. 136–37.

21. *The Transcendentalists*, ed. Perry Miller (Cambridge, Mass.,
1950), p. 168.

22. See Samuel Taylor Coleridge, *Aids to Reflection*, in which Marsh's
"Preliminary Essay" is reprinted, pp. xxviii–xxxii.

23. Frothingham, *op. cit.*, p. 108.

24. George Ripley, *"The Latest Form of Infidelity" Examined: A Letter to Mr. Andrews Norton* (Boston, 1839), pp. 87–89.

25. *Ibid.*, pp. 32–33.

26. Andrews Norton, *A Discourse on the Latest Form of Infidelity*
(Cambridge, Mass., 1839), pp. 58–59. This is the pamphlet to which Ripley was replying in the pamphlet mentioned in note 24 above. See C.
Crowe, *op. cit.*, Chapters 3–5, for a description of Ripley's thought in
his Transcendentalist period; Chapter 3 of W. R. Hutchison, *op. cit.*, for
an account of the Norton-Ripley controversy; and A. R. Schultz and H.
A. Pochmann, "George Ripley: Unitarian, Transcendentalist, or Infi-
del?", *American Literature*, Volume 14 (1942).

27. Ripley, *op. cit.*, p. 102.

28. *Ibid.*, pp. 102–3.

29. *Ibid.*, pp. 69–70. Walker's unsigned review appeared in the *Christian Examiner*, Volume XIV (New Series, Volume IX), May 1833, pp.
192–93. The words capitalized by Ripley are not capitalized in the original. Walker's views may be contrasted with those of Andrews Norton.
"Religious feeling," said Norton, "must be founded on religious belief;
and, in proportion as any one's belief is clear and firm and true, so will
his feelings be strong and permanent and operative of good. But all rational belief must be founded on reason", "Some Further Remarks on
the Characteristics of the Modern German School of Infidelity", pp.
49–50, note appended to Norton's *A Discourse on the Latest Form of
Infidelity*, pp. 39 ff.

30. See Arthur Schlesinger, Jr., *Orestes Brownson*, p. 32; pp. 46–50;
pp. 57–59; pp. 124–28.

31. *Christian Examiner*, Volume XVII (New Series, Volume XII),
September 1834, p. 70.

32. *Ibid.*, pp. 72–73.

33. *Ibid.*, p. 71.

34. *The Collected Works of Dugald Stewart*, ed. W. Hamilton, Volume III, Chapter 1, especially pp. 44–45.

35. See *ibid.*, pp. 41 ff., for a discussion of some subtle points of difference between Stewart and other Scottish thinkers on whether it is by the evidence of "consciousness" that we are assured that we ourselves exist. The same part of this work also contains extended discussions of certain differences within the Scottish school about what Stewart called the primary elements of human reason.

36. *Christian Examiner*, Volume XXI, November 1836, p. 245.

37. *Ibid.*, p. 246.

38. *Ibid.*, p. 247.

39. *Ibid.*, pp. 250–51. This attitude toward the senses was related to Ripley's praise of the views "set forth by President Marsh, in his admirable Preliminary Essay to Coleridge's *Aids to Reflection*", *ibid.*, p. 236. Also see the high praise of Marsh in Ripley's *Philosophical Miscellanies*, Volume I, pp. 39–40.

40. Walker prepared several abridged editions of the works of Scottish philosophers.

41. *Christian Examiner*, Volume XVII (New Series, Volume XII), September 1834, p. 1.

42. *Ibid.*, pp. 2–3.

43. *Ibid.*, pp. 3–4.

44. *Ibid.*, p. 4.

45. *Ibid.*, p. 2; p. 11.

46. *Ibid.*, p. 11.

47. *Ibid.*, p. 12.

48. *Christian Examiner*, Volume XIII, January 1833, pp. 311–32. This review is one of the clearer pieces of Transcendentalist writing, being utterly free of Emerson's obliqueness and weakness in argumentation. In the same journal for January 1832, Ripley had also reviewed Charles Follen's *Inaugural Address* and remarked that whereas Coleridge was "impassioned", "bold", and "excursive", Kant was "cool", "far-reaching", and "austere"; and that "the severe logic, the imperturbable patience, the mathematical precision, and the passionless exhibition of the results of pure reason, which distinguish Kant from all other writers on philosophy, are in striking contrast with the moody restlessness, the feverish irritability, the incoherent ramblings, and the bright flashes of imagination playing over the dark obscurity of his page, which, in the writings of Coleridge, mark the philosopher struggling with the poet, and finally yielding the victory", *Christian Examiner*, Volume XI, January 1832, p.

375. (Also see Ripley's less than adulatory remarks about Coleridge in *Philosophical Miscellanies*, Volume I, pp. 41–42.) In his review of Mackintosh, Ripley also departed from the typically Transcendentalist line on Hume by praising him for the variety and playfulness of his illustrations, which, Ripley said, made his style very attractive and gave him "the rank of a most entertaining as well as acute writer on subjects of abstract speculation", *Christian Examiner*, Volume XIII, January 1833, p. 312. Compare this with Emerson's view of Hume in note 19 of the next chapter.

I wish to add that I agree wholeheartedly with W. K. Frankena when he calls Ripley's review of Mackintosh "the best piece of moral philosophy by a Transcendentalist". See Frankena's article, entitled "Moral Philosophy in America", in V. Ferm, ed., *Encyclopedia of Morals* (New York, 1956).

49. *Christian Examiner*, Volume XIII, January 1833, pp. 314–15.

50. *Ibid.*, p. 315.

51. *Ibid.*, p. 319.

52. *Ibid.*, p. 320.

53. *Ibid.*

54. *Ibid.*, pp. 323–24.

55. *Ibid.*, p. 329.

56. *Ibid.*, pp. 331–32.

57. Henry David Thoreau, *Walden and Civil Disobedience*, ed. S. Paul (Boston, 1960), p. 236.

58. *Ibid.*, pp. 238–39. See E. H. Madden, *Civil Disobedience and Moral Law in Nineteenth-Century American Philosophy* (Seattle, 1968), pp. 96–98; also W. Smith, "William Paley's Theological Utilitarianism in America", *William and Mary Quarterly*, 3rd Series, Volume XI (1954), pp. 402–24.

59. Ralph Waldo Emerson, "The Transcendentalist", *Complete Works* (Boston, 1903), Volume I, p. 336.

Chapter 5—Ralph Waldo Emerson

1. *The Complete Works of Ralph Waldo Emerson* (Boston, 1903–4), Volume XI, pp. 20–21.

2. See the previous chapter, note 16.

3. See the interesting discussion of Emerson and other Transcendentalists in E. H. Madden, *Civil Disobedience and Moral Law in Nineteenth-Century American Philosophy* (Seattle, 1968), Chapter 7.

4. Emerson, *Complete Works*, Volume I, pp. 339–40.

5. See the previous chapter, note 34; M. R. Davis, "Emerson's 'Reason' and the Scottish Philosophers", *New England Quarterly*, Volume XVII (1944), pp. 209–28; H. A. Pochmann, *German Culture in America* (Madison, Wisc., 1957), p. 156; E. W. Todd, "Philosophical Ideas at Harvard College", *The New England Quarterly*, Volume XVI (1943), especially pp. 88–90. Curiously enough, because of Emerson's tendency not to make fine distinctions among different traditional conceptions of intuitive truth, his attitude conformed to a view of John Stuart Mill, who explicitly denied that there was any great difference between the Scottish philosophy and the "Germano-Coleridgian" doctrine. Mill declared in his famous essay on Coleridge that, but for "the peculiar technical terminology which [Coleridge] and his masters the Germans have introduced into philosophy . . . it would be difficult to understand how the reproach of mysticism (by which nothing is meant in common parlance but unintelligibleness) has been fixed upon Coleridge and the Germans in the minds of many, to whom doctrines substantially the same, when taught in a manner more superficial and less fenced round against objections, by Reid and Dugald Stewart, have appeared the plain dictates of 'common sense,' successfully asserted against the subtleties of metaphysics", *Dissertations and Discussions* (London, 1875), Volume I, pp. 409–10.

6. Late in life, Emerson does refer to Kant's categorical imperative but René Wellek has observed that he was then capable of presenting "an almost grotesque caricature" of Kant's thought, "Emerson and German Philosophy", *The New England Quarterly*, Volume XVI (1943), p. 46. See the effort to clarify Emerson's views on moral sentiment in J. Bishop, *Emerson on the Soul* (Cambridge, Mass., 1964), pp. 66–72; also Chapter 4 of J. Porte, *Emerson and Thoreau: Transcendentalists in Conflict* (Middletown, Conn., 1966), in which the author shows the influence of Richard Price on Emerson's moral philosophy. It may be doubted whether Price had succeeded in saving the necessity of moral principles while "practically" agreeing with Hutcheson's doctrine of moral sense, but Porte quotes some interesting passages which show that Emerson was *concerned* with this problem as early as 1822. In his *Journal* he writes that the moral "Sentiment differs from the affections of the heart and from the faculties of the mind. The affections are undiscriminating and capricious. The Moral Sense is not" (Porte, pp. 72–73).

7. Emerson never exploited in a systematic way the Kantian distinction between Pure and Practical Reason, even though his mentor Coleridge carefully distinguished between them. See, for example, Coleridge's *Aids to Reflection* (Burlington, Vt., 1829), p. 153. During

1831 Emerson showed how widely he could cast the net of Reason, without making any subtle Kantian distinctions. In his *Journal,* he records a statement which he attributes to Plotinus, "Of the Unity of God, Nothing can be predicated, neither being, nor essence, nor life, for it is above all these", and then he exclaims: "Grand it is to recognize the truth of this & of every one of that first class of truths which are *necessary*". He then gives other illustrations of what he thinks are necessary truths: "Design proves a designer", and "Like must know like", or "The same can only be known by the same". Next he says that out of this second proposition "come" certain propositions like "If you would be loved, love", "God without can only be known by God within", "The Scriptures can be explained only by that Spirit which dictated them", and a thousand other sayings. His final important comment is that "it would be well for every mind to collect with care every truth of this kind he may meet, & make a catalogue of 'necessary truths.' They are scanned & approved by the Reason far above the understanding. They are the last facts by which we approximate metaphysically to God". *The Journals of Ralph Waldo Emerson,* eds. W. H. Gilman, Alfred R. Ferguson, George P. Clark, and Merrell R. Davis (Cambridge, Mass., 1960–), Volume III (1963), pp. 235–36.

8. On Emerson's mysticism, see Wellek, *op. cit.,* p. 44; E. G. Berry, *Emerson's Plutarch* (Cambridge, Mass., 1961), p. 14; and Bliss Perry, *Emerson Today* (Princeton, 1931), Chapter 3.

9. Emerson's *Journals,* eds. E. W. Emerson and W. E. Forbes (Boston, 1909–14), Volume III (1910), pp. 235–37; p. 377. Also, the later edition of the *Journals,* eds. Gilman *et al.,* Volume IV (1964), p. 348.

10. R. W. Emerson, "The Present State of Ethical Philosophy", in *Two Unpublished Essays* (Boston, 1896), pp. 50–51. This was a Bowdoin Prize Essay at Harvard in 1821; it won second prize.

11. *Ibid.,* pp. 55–56.

12. *Ibid.,* p. 79. On Emerson's undergraduate essays see K. W. Cameron's daunting but informative *Transcendental Climate* (Hartford, 1963), Volume I, pp. 1–179.

13. Theodore Parker, "Transcendentalism", Chapter I, *The World of Matter and The Spirit of Man: Latest Discourses of Religion,* ed. G. W. Cooke (Boston, 1907), pp. 10–11.

14. *Ibid.,* p. 14.

15. Parker also held that Transcendentalism provided the best defense of traditional American rights. Parker wrote that "the great political idea of America, the idea of the Declaration of Independence, is a composite idea made up of three simple ones: 1. Each man is endowed with

certain unalienable rights. 2. In respect of these rights all men are equal. 3. A government is to protect each man in the entire and actual enjoyment of all the unalienable rights. Now the first two ideas represent ontological facts, facts of human consciousness; they are facts of necessity. The third is an idea derived from the two others, is a synthetic judgment *a priori;* it was not learned from sensational experience; there never was a government which did this, nor is there now. Each of the other ideas transcended history: every unalienable right has been alienated, still is; no two men have been actually equal in actual rights. Yet the idea is true, capable of proof by human nature, not of verification by experience; as true as the proposition that three angles of a triangle are equal to two right angles; but no more capable of a sensational proof than that", *ibid.*, pp. 26–27.

16. *Complete Works,* Volume I, p. 3.

17. *Ibid.,* pp. 66–67.

18. *Ibid.,* Volume V, p. 242.

19. *Ibid.,* p. 239. Emerson, like Coleridge, thought better of Francis Bacon than he did of Locke or Hume. "Hume's abstractions," he said, "are not deep or wise. He owes his fame to one keen observation, that no copula had been detected between any cause and effect, either in physics or in thought; that the term cause and effect was loosely or gratuitously applied to what we know only as consecutive, not at all as causal", *ibid.*, pp. 244–45.

20. Mill introduced Emerson to Carlyle at the request of Gustave d'Eichthal. In 1833 Mill wrote to Carlyle: "he appears to be a reader and professes to be an admirer of your writings; therefore you might possibly do him some good: but from one or two conversations I have had with him, I do not think him a very hopeful subject". And a little later in the same year Mill wrote: "Since you were so much pleased with Emerson I feel encouraged to try you with almost any person whatever who has any sort of good in him: I should have thought *he* was about the last person who would have interested you so much as he seems to have done". See *The Earlier Letters of John Stuart Mill: 1812–1848,* ed. F. E. Mineka (Toronto, 1963), Volume XII, p. 169; p. 171; p. 183.

21. *Complete Works,* Volume I, p. 103.

22. *Ibid.,* Volume II, p. 45.

23. *Ibid.,* Volume II, p. 66.

24. *Ibid.,* Volume I, p. 129.

25. *Ibid.,* Volume I, p. 141.

26. *Ibid.,* Volume I, p. 137.

27. *Ibid.,* Volume XI, pp. 190–91.

28. *Ibid.,* Volume V, p. 239; p. 243. Emerson's emphasis on sentiment explains why certain defenders of Locke were wrong in saying that the Transcendentalist distinction between Reason and Understanding was fully present in Locke. See C. Thompson, "John Locke and New England Transcendentalism", *The New England Quarterly,* Volume XXXV (1962), especially pp. 452–54.

29. For further discussion of Emerson's attitudes toward the American city, see Morton and Lucia White, *The Intellectual Versus The City: From Thomas Jefferson to Frank Lloyd Wright* (Cambridge, Mass., 1962), Chapter III.

30. William James, *Memories and Studies* (New York, 1917), p. 29.

31. *Ibid.,* p. 26.

32. *Ibid.,* p. 24.

33. *Ibid.,* p. 33.

34. *Complete Works,* Volume I, pp. 111–12. The quotation is from "The American Scholar".

35. William James, *Pragmatism* (New York, 1907), pp. 28–32.

36. George Santayana, *Interpretations of Poetry and Religion* (New York, 1922; original edition, 1900), p. 218.

37. *Ibid.,* p. 223.

38. *Ibid.,* p. 225.

39. *Ibid.,* pp. 230–31.

40. *Ibid.,* pp. 220–21.

41. John Dewey, "Emerson—The Philosopher of Democracy", *Ethics* (formerly *International Journal of Ethics*), Volume XIII (1903), pp. 405–6.

42. *Ibid.,* p. 407.

43. *Ibid.,* p. 405.

44. *Ibid.,* p. 409.

45. *Ibid.,* pp. 410–11.

46. *Ibid.,* p. 411.

47. *Ibid.,* p. 412.

48. Matthew Arnold, *Discourses in America* (London, 1889), p. 179.

Chapter 6—Chauncey Wright

1. O. B. Frothingham, *Transcendentalism in New England* (New York, 1886, originally published in 1876), p. viii.

2. See Fiske's *Outlines of Cosmic Philosophy,* Volumes XIII–XVI of *The Writings of John Fiske* (Cambridge, Mass., 1902).

3. See J. B. Thayer's remarks in his edition of *The Letters of Chaun-*

cey Wright (Cambridge, Mass., 1878, privately printed), pp. 137–39; E. H. Madden, *Chauncey Wright and the Foundations of Pragmatism* (Seattle, 1963), p. 21.

4. I say this with full awareness of the fact that Emerson once said, "I hate preaching", J. E. Cabot, *A Memoir of Ralph Waldo Emerson* (Boston, 1887), Volume I, p. 329.

5. See E. H. Madden, *op. cit.*, especially pp. 79–81.

6. *The Letters of Chauncey Wright*, p. 30.

7. For example, James Marsh, as we have seen earlier.

8. Chauncey Wright, "The Faculties of Brutes", bMs Am 1088.5 (misc. 6), Box 11, Norton Collection, Houghton Library, Harvard University.

9. Chauncey Wright, *Philosophical Discussions* (New York, 1877), p. 229.

10. *Philosophical Discussions*, p. 65; *Letters*, p. 109.

11. *Philosophical Discussions*, pp. 126–67.

12. *Letters of Chauncey Wright*, p. 230.

13. *Philosophical Discussions*, pp. 130–31.

14. Edwards wrote: "Anything is said to be contingent, or to come to pass by chance or accident, in the original meaning of such words, when its connection with its causes or antecedents, according to the established course of things, is not discerned; and so is what we have no means of the foresight of", *Freedom of the Will*, p. 155.

15. *Letters*, p. 74.

16. *Ibid.*, pp. 74–75; also pp. 240–46 for a letter to Darwin on related topics.

17. *Letters of Chauncey Wright*, p. 231.

18. J. S. Mill, *A System of Logic* (London, New Impression, January 1947), pp. 79–81 (Book I, Chapter VII, Section 4).

19. *Philosophical Discussions*, pp. 181–82.

20. Following the view of his day, Wright said that it was descended from *Hipparion*.

21. *Philosophical Discussions*, p. 184.

22. *Ibid.* It is of some interest to note that Herbert Spencer says: "By reality we mean *persistence* in consciousness. . . . The real, as we conceive it, is distinguished solely by the test of persistence; for by this test we separate it from what we call the unreal", *First Principles* (6th Edition, New York, 1902), p. 143.

23. *Philosophical Discussions*, pp. 184–85.

24. "*Evolution,*" Spencer says at one place, "*is an integration of matter and concomitant dissipation of motion; during which the matter passes from an indefinite, incoherent homogeneity to a definite coherent*

*heterogeneity; and during which the retained motion undergoes a paral-
lel transformation"*, *First Principles*, p. 367. In his lectures, William
James told his students to learn this formula because "upon this . . . is
based Mr. Spencer's claim to being the greatest genius of his age"; but,
according to Perry, James characteristically proposed the following re-
wording of the formula: "Evolution is a change from a no-howish un-
talkaboutable all-alikeness to a somehowish and in general talkaboutable
not-all-alikeness by continuous sticktogetherations and somethingelse-
ifications", Ralph Barton Perry, *The Thought and Character of William
James* (Boston, 1935), Volume I, p. 482. Perry seems not to have known
that this parody was not original with James. On its history, see Herbert
Spencer, *First Principles*, Appendix B, p. 519.

25. *Philosophical Discussions*, pp. 76–77.

26. *Ibid.*, p. 77.

27. Wright shrewdly observed that Platonists and Transcendentalists
also claim verification of their theories, and that they appeal "to the reason for confirmation of deductions from their theories, which they regard as founded on observation of what the reason reveals to them",
ibid., p. 361; pp. 45–46.

28. *Ibid.*, p. 46.

29. *Ibid.*, pp. 46–47.

30. *Ibid.*, p. 55. It should be pointed out that Herbert Spencer said:
"Inquiring into the pedigree of an idea is not a bad means of estimating
its value". Quoted in John Fiske, *Outlines of Cosmic Philosophy, The
Writings of John Fiske, op. cit.*, Volume XIII, p. 247. Spencer also said
that "all Science is prevision", *First Principles*, p. 15.

31. *Philosophical Discussions*, p. 55.

32. *Ibid.*, p. 56.

33. Madden, *op. cit.*, pp. 79–81.

34. In addition to announcing a very general law to the effect that all
things go through a process of evolution, Spencer maintained that "the
phenomena of Evolution have to be deduced from the Persistence of
Force. . . . This being the ultimate truth which transcends experience
by underlying it, furnishes a common basis on which the widest generalizations stand; and hence these widest generalizations are to be unified
by referring them to this common basis", *First Principles*, p. 369.

35. This is obvious in John Fiske's discussions of the status of the fundamental principle from which, according to Spencer, all so-called derivative truths of the special sciences are derivable—the principle of persistence of force or of conservation of energy. Fiske held that the ground
for accepting this principle is that it is self-evident in a sense closely re-

lated to that in which Locke said that the first principles of natural philosophy are self-evident; but it should be noted that in the first sentence
of the quotation below, Fiske attributes to "Empiricism", and probably
therefore to Locke, the opposite of what Locke held. At one place, Fiske
wrote: "It is indeed a popular misconception,—a misconception which
lies at the bottom of that manner of philosophizing which is called
Empiricism,—that nothing can be known to be true which cannot be
demonstrated. To be convinced that this is a misconception, we need
but to recollect what a demonstration is. Every demonstration consists,
in the first place, of a series of steps in each of which the group of relations expressed in a proposition is included in some other and wider
group of relations,—is seen to be like some other group previously constituted. Now if this process of inclusion is not to be carried on forever,
we must come at last to some widest group,—to some generalization
which cannot be included in any wider generalization, and of which we
can only say that the truth which it expresses is so completely abstracted
from perturbing conditions that it can be recognized by a simple act of
consciousness as self-evident. If, for example, 'we ascribe the flow of a
river to the same force which causes the fall of a stone,' and if, 'in further explanation of a movement produced by gravitation in a direction
almost horizontal, we cite the law that fluids subject to mechanical
forces exert reactive forces which are equal in all directions,' we are
going through a process of demonstration,—we are including a special
fact under a more general fact. If now we seek the warrant for this more
general fact, and find it in that most general fact that force persists, we
are still going through a process of demonstration. But if lastly we in-
quire for the warrant of this most general fact, we shall get no reply
save that no alternative can be framed in thought. That force persists
we are compelled to believe, since the proposition that force can arise
out of nothing or can lapse into nothing is a verbal proposition which
we can by no amount of effort translate into thought. Thus at the end
of every demonstration we must reach an axiom for the truth of which
our only test is the inconceivability of its negation", *The Writings of
John Fiske*, Volume XIII, pp. 91–92.

Fiske said in the same vein: "At the bottom of all demonstration
there must lie an indemonstrable axiom. And the truth of this axiom
can only be certified by the direct application of the test of inconceivability. We are compelled to believe in the persistence of force, because
it is impossible to conceive a variation in the unit by which force is
measured. It is impossible to conceive something becoming nothing or
nothing becoming something, without establishing in thought an equa-

tion between something and nothing; and this cannot be done. That one is equal to zero is a proposition of which the subject and predicate will destroy each other sooner than be made to unite. Thus the proof of our fundamental axiom is not logical, but psychological. And, as was formerly shown, this is the strongest possible kind of proof. Inasmuch as our capacity for conceiving any proposition is entirely dependent upon the manner in which objective experiences have registered themselves upon our minds, our utter inability to conceive a variation in the sum total of force implies that such variation is negatived by the whole history of the intercourse between the mind and its environment since intelligence first began", *ibid.*, Volume XIV, pp. 146–47.

Spencer's view on this matter was criticized by John Stuart Mill in *A System of Logic*, Book II, Chapter VII, Sections 1–4. Mill linked Spencer's views on the "inconceivability of the opposite" as a test of necessary truth with the views of Reid and Stewart. In my opinion, Mill was not sufficiently aware of the similarity between Locke's views and those of the Scottish philosophy on first principles. See, for example, the implication in his essay, "Coleridge", that according to Locke, "there is no knowledge *a priori; no* truths cognizable by the mind's inward light, and grounded on intuitive evidente". See John Stuart Mill, *Dissertations and Discussions*, Volume I, p. 404.

In connection with the views of Spencer on necessary truth, see Chapter 8 on William James, who seems to have been more aware than Mill was of Locke's belief that there are *a priori,* self-evident propositions. When James came to discuss Spencer's view, he was mainly concerned to attack Spencer's Lamarckianism and, indeed, he associated himself with Locke as against Spencer.

36. John Fiske, "Chauncey Wright", *Darwinism, and Other Essays* (Boston, 1894, revised edition), pp. 79–110; see especially pp. 85–87.

37. Writing to his brother Henry in 1875, James said that he intended to tell C. E. Norton that Charles Peirce was willing to write an account of Wright's philosophical ideas for the posthumous volume, adding that "Norton did intend giving it to Fiske, who would make a very inferior thing of it". Peirce never did write anything for the volume. See Perry, *The Thought and Character of William James*, Volume I, p. 363.

38. *Philosophical Discussions*, pp. 199–266.

39. *Ibid.*, pp. 7–8.

40. *Ibid.*, p. 66.

41. *Ibid.*, pp. 65–66; *Letters of Chauncey Wright*, pp. 55–63. See also Madden, *op. cit.*, Chapter 6.

42. *Philosophical Discussions*, pp. 65–66.
43. *Ibid.*, p. 66.
44. *Ibid.*
45. *Ibid.*, p. 342.
46. *Ibid.*
47. *Ibid.*, p. 235.
48. *Ibid.*, pp. 239–40.
49. *Ibid.*, p. 246.
50. *Ibid.*, p. 247.
51. *Ibid.*
52. *Ibid.*, p. 248.
53. *Ibid.*, p. 249.
54. *Ibid.*, pp. 249–50.
55. *Ibid.*, p. 250.
56. *Letters*, p. 103.
57. *Ibid.*, p. 61.
58. *Ibid.*
59. Madden, *op. cit.*, p. 45, and Chapter 2, *passim*.
60. *Letters*, p. 87. Professor Madden has identified "the uninspired disciple" as W. T. Harris on the basis of J. B. Thayer's interleaved copy of the *Letters*. See Madden, *op. cit.*, p. 157.
61. See E. W. Gurney's remarks in *Letters*, pp. 380–81.

Chapter 7–Charles Peirce

1. On Emerson's borrowing habits and his willingness to acknowledge intellectual indebtedness, see the notes in H. A. Pochmann, *German Culture in America* (Madison, Wisc., 1957), p. 587, especially the quotation from Oliver Wendell Holmes, who said of Emerson: "He borrowed from everybody and every book, not in any stealthy or shamefaced way, but proudly, royally, as a king borrows from one of his attendants the coin that bears his own image and superscription".

2. *Charles S. Peirce's Letters to Lady Welby*, ed. I. Lieb (New Haven, 1953), p. 37.

3. *Collected Papers of Charles Sanders Peirce*, eds. C. Hartshorne and P. Weiss (Cambridge, Mass., 1935), Volume VI, Paragraph 102. Hereafter I shall follow the practice of Peirce scholars by making reference to the *Collected Papers* not by page references but by using the number of the volume, followed by a decimal point, followed by the number of the paragraph or paragraphs. On that scheme, the reference in this note would be given by using "6.102".

The Hedge mentioned by Peirce is F. H. Hedge, often described as one of the earliest Transcendentalists, especially because of his essay on Coleridge in *The Christian Examiner* for March 1833 and because he was present at some of the earliest meetings of the Transcendental Club. Indeed, that was often called "Hedge's Club" or the "Hedge Club". See, for example, H. C. Goddard, *Studies in New England Transcendentalism* (New York, 1960; originally published in 1908), p. 33; p. 35. See J. E. Cabot, *Memoir of R. W. Emerson* (Cambridge, Mass., 1887), pp. 244–46. On Peirce's relationship to Transcendentalism, see F. I. Carpenter, "Charles Sanders Peirce: Pragmatic Transcendentalist", *The New England Quarterly*, Volume XIV (1941), pp. 34–48. On the influence of Boehm (as Peirce spells it) and Schelling on Emerson, see R. Wellek, "Emerson and German Philosophy", *The New England Quarterly*, Volume XVI (1943), pp. 42–44; pp. 50–53.

4. *Collected Papers*, 6.102.

5. Thomas A. Goudge, *The Thought of C. S. Peirce* (Toronto, 1950), pp. 5–7.

6. "The fox knows many things, but the hedgehog knows one big thing", Isaiah Berlin, *The Hedgehog and the Fox* (London, 1953), pp. 1–2.

7. *Collected Papers*, 1.1.

8. In his "Historic Notes of Life and Letters in New England", Emerson reports as follows about an earlier Bostonian effort to form an intellectual club: "Dr. Channing took counsel in 1840 with George Ripley, to the point whether it were possible to bring cultivated, thoughtful people together, and make society that deserved the name. He had earlier talked with Dr. John Collins Warren on the like purpose, who admitted the wisdom of the design and undertook to aid him in making the experiment. Dr. Channing repaired to Dr. Warren's house on the appointed evening, with large thoughts which he wished to open. He found a well-chosen assembly of gentlemen variously distinguished; there was mutual greeting and introduction, and they were chatting agreeably on indifferent matters and drawing gently towards their great expectation, when a side-door opened, the whole company streamed in to an oyster supper, crowned by excellent wines; and so ended the first attempt to establish aesthetic society in Boston", *Complete Works*, Volume X (Boston, 1903–4), pp. 340–41. On the Metaphysical Club, see P. P. Wiener, *Evolution and the Founders of Pragmatism* (Cambridge, Mass., 1949), Chapter 2; M. H. Fisch, "Was There a Metaphysical Club in Cambridge?", *Studies in the Philosophy of Charles Sanders Peirce*, Second Series, eds. E. C. Moore and R. Robin (Amherst, Mass., 1964), pp. 3–32.

9. *Collected Papers* (Cambridge, Mass., 1958), 8.378. It should be pointed out that Volumes I–VI of the *Collected Papers* were edited by Hartshorne and Weiss, whereas Volumes VII–VIII were edited by A. W. Burks.

10. William James, "Philosophical Conceptions and Practical Results", *Collected Essays and Reviews* (New York, 1920), p. 410.

11. *Collected Papers*, 5.388–410.

12. *Ibid.*, 2.330. At this place, Peirce says that he is presenting a "precept that is more serviceable than a definition", but elsewhere he speaks of the pragmatic maxim as one that gives rise to definitions; for example in 5.207; also see 6.490, where he says: "Pragmaticism . . . is a theory of logical analysis, or true definition; and its merits are greatest in its application to the highest metaphysical conceptions".

13. *Ibid.*, 5.500; 5.207.

14. *Ibid.*, 5.402, n. 3; 5.438.

15. William James, *Some Problems of Philosophy* (New York, 1911), p. 61. Here James identified concepts with what might better be called propositions.

16. *The Philosophy of John Dewey*, ed. P. A. Schilpp (Evanston, Ill., 1939), p. 527.

17. *Collected Papers*, 6.35–65.

18. *Ibid.*

19. *Ibid.*, 6.39.

20. See A. W. Burks, "Peirce's Two Theories of Probability", *Studies in the Philosophy of Charles Sanders Peirce*, Second Series, pp. 141–50. Burks points out that in later life Peirce spoke of probabilistic "would-be's". This would allow Peirce to say that the statement that a diamond has a disposition might be expressed in some such sentence as "If any normal person were to try to scratch this diamond, his effort would *probably* result in his seeing an indentation on it shortly afterwards". On this view, the pragmatic maxim might be broadened so as to allow lawlike statements of probabilities to be suitable translations of statements like "This diamond is hard".

21. See A. W. Burks' Introduction to his selection from Peirce's writings in M. H. Fisch, ed., *Classic American Philosophers* (New York, 1951), pp. 41–53. It is important to note Peirce's insistence on saying that universals are *real* rather than that they *exist*. For him "exists" means the same as "reacts with other like things in the environment", and universals he does not locate in the environment. He says he defines "the *real* as that which holds its characters on such a tenure that it makes not the slightest difference what any man or men may have *thought* them to be". See *Collected Papers*, 6.495, where he says

that he believes in the reality but not the existence of God. See also 5.503.

22. *Collected Papers*, 4.234.

23. See the passage quoted on p. 154 above.

24. *Collected Papers*, 5.427.

25. See p. 154 above.

26. *Collected Papers*, 8.194. It is worth noting that in the section just cited, Peirce says: ". . . to say that a Jacqueminot rose really is red means, and can mean, nothing but that if such a rose is put before a normal eye, in the daylight, it will look red". In the next paragraph (8.195), Peirce speaks of one meaning of a statement like "This is soft" as "the primary meaning", but this leads me to wonder what the criterion for being a primary meaning is, just as I wonder what the scholastic's criterion is for being an essential, as opposed to a non-essential, predication.

27. On December 6, 1904, Peirce wrote to James: "Thank you very much for your paper 'Humanism and Truth.' You have a quotation from me which greatly astonishes me. I cannot imagine when or where I can have used that language: 'The serious meaning of a concept lies in the concrete difference to some one which its being true will make.' Do tell me at once where I so slipped, that I may at once declare it to be a slip. I do not think I have often spoken of the 'meaning of a concept' whether 'serious' or not. I have said that the concept itself 'is' *nothing more* than the concept, not of any concrete difference that *will* be made to someone, but is nothing more than the concept of the *conceivable* practical applications of it", Ralph Barton Perry, *The Thought and Character of William James* (Boston, 1935), Volume II, pp. 432–33. If one identifies concepts with attributes, then it may be said that Peirce thought of the maxim of pragmatism—in at least some of his writings —as a recipe for providing analyses of attributes which terminate in statements of their identity. This would bring his view of analysis close to that of G. E. Moore in "A Reply to My Critics", *The Philosophy of G. E. Moore*, ed. P. A. Schilpp (Evanston, Ill., 1942), pp. 664–67, though, of course, Moore is not there explaining *pragmatic* analysis. Such a view of analysis would differ somewhat from that which A. W. Burks attributes to Peirce when Burks says the following: "Peirce's pragmatic principle of meaning consists of the following four theses: The set of practical consequences logically implied by a statement has approximately the same meaning as the statement; these practical consequences are superior in clarity and precision to the original statement; to clarify a statement we should analyze it into its practical consequences; and if

two statements imply the same practical consequences, they should be treated as logically equivalent. Note that the first two of these theses are descriptive while the last two are normative", "Peirce's Two Theories of Probability", *Studies in the Philosophy of Charles Sanders Peirce*, Second Series, p. 143. It should be noted that Peirce's insistence in his letter to James that the concepts mentioned in a pragmatic analysis are *identical*, is distinct from the view that his pragmatism involves no more than a recommendation or a "normative statement" that we should *treat* the concepts as logically equivalent. No doubt he held this latter thesis, but it would seem that in defense of it he would say that we should treat them as logically equivalent *because* they are identical. How we find out that they are identical, Peirce never tells us, so far as I know.

It should be added parenthetically that in spite of his protest to James, Peirce *did* often speak of "the meaning of a *concept*" or "of a conception". See, for example, *Collected Papers*, 5.9, 5.465, and 5.467. See also a letter to Christine Ladd-Franklin, quoted in H. S. Thayer, *Meaning and Action: A Critical History of Pragmatism* (Indianapolis, 1968), p. 140.

28. *Collected Papers*, 6.502.

29. *Ibid.*

30. *Ibid.*, 6.503.

31. *Ibid.*

32. *Ibid.*

33. For a brief discussion of Peirce's connection with the Scottish school, see J. Buchler, *Charles Peirce's Empiricism* (London, 1939), pp. 44–49.

34. *Collected Papers*, 6.493.

35. William James, *Pragmatism* (New York, 1928), p. 5.

Chapter 8—William James

1. There is no full-scale historical study which deals both with the ideas of the philosophers of this period and with their lives and times. The closest thing to it is Ralph Barton Perry's monumental *The Thought and Character of William James* (Boston, 1935). James was so central in the period that a study of his life would be bound to cover a great part of the period itself.

The penchant for writing books in the Golden Age is well illustrated by James' remark to Royce: "After all, it's the books that count, not the lectures. . . .", Perry, Volume I, p. 814. Also see James' exclamation to F. S. C. Schiller: "I actually *hate* lecturing", Perry, Volume II, p. 583.

2. Perry, *Thought and Character,* Volume I, p. 165.

3. *Ibid.,* p. 62.

4. "Address at the Emerson Centenary in Concord", reprinted in William James, *Memories and Studies* (New York, 1917), p. 32.

5. *The Principles of Psychology* (New York, 1890), Volume II, p. 617.

6. See Herbert Spencer, *The Principles of Psychology* (London, 1870), Volume I, Sections 189, 205, 208.

7. *The Principles of Psychology,* Volume II, p. 662.

8. See, for example, *ibid.,* p. 661.

9. *Ibid.,* pp. 643–44.

10. *Ibid.,* pp. 647–52.

11. See Chapters 10 and 11 below.

12. *The Principles of Psychology,* p. 665.

13. *Ibid.*

14. *Ibid.,* pp. 666–67. If James thinks that the ideal of natural science is to arrive at a world-formula which will allow us to pass from one of the world's phases to another "by inward thought-necessity", then he may well think that it seeks to achieve what rationalists thought it seeks to achieve, namely, a form in which all propositions may be deduced from axioms seen to be true merely on the basis of detecting the relationships between concepts. I see no other way of interpreting James when he says that as a consequence of our using the wave-theory of light and molecular theory, "the world grows more orderly and rational to the mind, which passes from one feature of it to another by deductive necessity, as soon as it conceives it as made up of so few and so simple phenomena as bodies with no properties but number and movement to and fro", *ibid.,* p. 669.

15. See above, p. 24.

16. *The Principles of Psychology,* pp. 669–70.

17. *Ibid.,* pp. 670–71.

18. Reprinted in *The Will To Believe and Other Essays in Popular Philosophy* (New York, 1898), pp. 145–83.

19. *The Principles of Psychology,* Volume II, p. 672.

20. "The Doctrine of Necessity Examined", *Collected Papers,* 6.35–65.

21. "The Dilemma of Determinism", *The Will To Believe,* p. 151. It is worth noting that in this reprinted version of the essay, James added a footnote to Peirce's "Doctrine of Necessity Examined", which appeared about eight years after "The Dilemma of Determinism" had originally been published. In that essay, Peirce had criticized the idea that the

principle of determinism is a "postulate", without referring to James. See *Collected Papers*, 6.39–42.

22. *The Will To Believe*, p. 152.
23. *Ibid.*, pp. 152–53.
24. *Ibid.*, p. 149.
25. *Ibid.*
26. *Ibid.*, p. 180.
27. *Ibid.*, p. 162.
28. *Ibid.*
29. *Ibid.*, p. 175.
30. *Ibid.*, p. 167, note.
31. *Ibid.*, p. 176.
32. *Ibid.*, pp. 177–78.
33. Quoted by James in the title essay of *The Will To Believe*, pp. 7–8.
34. The bracketed words are those of James.
35. Quoted in *The Will To Believe*, p. 8.
36. *Ibid.*, pp. 1–2.
37. *The Principles of Psychology*, Volume I, p. 295.
38. See Perry, *op. cit.*, Volume II, p. 245, letter from James to L. T. Hobhouse, August 12, 1904.
39. W. K. Clifford, *Lectures and Essays*, eds. L. Stephen and F. Pollock (London, 1901), Volume II, pp. 163–205.
40. *The Will To Believe*, pp. 4–5.
41. *Ibid.*, p. 22.
42. *Ibid.*, p. 23.
43. *Ibid.*
44. *Ibid.*, p. 5.
45. David Hume, *An Enquiry Concerning Human Understanding*, in L. A. Selby-Bigge's edition of Hume's *Enquiries* (Oxford, 1902), p. 165.
46. In his *Dialogues Concerning Natural Religion*, ed. N. K. Smith (Second Edition, New York, 1948). See the editor's introduction, pp. 57–75.
47. *The Will To Believe*, p. 52.
48. *Ibid.*, p. 51.
49. *Ibid.*, pp. 52–54.
50. *Ibid.*, p. 43.
51. *Ibid.*, p. 54.
52. *Ibid.*, p. 3.
53. *Ibid.*
54. *Ibid.*, pp. 54–55.

55. *Ibid.*, pp. 3–4.

56. *Ibid.*, p. 4.

57. *Ibid.*, pp. 5–6.

58. See A. J. Ayer, *The Origins of Pragmatism* (London, 1968), pp. 193–94.

59. *Essay*, Book IV, Chapter XIX, Section 1.

60. See p. 134 of Bertrand Russell, "William James's Conception of Truth", in Russell's *Philosophical Essays* (London, 1910). This article was originally published in the *Albany Review* (January 1908) under the title "Transatlantic 'Truth' ".

61. Bertrand Russell, "Pragmatism", *Philosophical Essays*, pp. 104–5. A view of science similar to Russell's was expressed earlier by Pierre Duhem in *La Théorie Physique: Son Objet, Sa Structure* (Paris, 1906), which brought together a number of articles published serially in 1904 and 1905 in *Revue de Philosophie*. It was translated into English by P. P. Wiener under the title *The Aim and Structure of Physical Theory* (Princeton, 1954). It is worth noting that James calls upon Duhem for support on p. 57 of *Pragmatism* in the course of a defense of the view that "no theory is absolutely a transcript of reality" and that theories "are only a man-made language, a conceptual short-hand . . . in which we write our reports of nature".

62. In the light of James' associating himself with Dewey, it is of interest to observe the following statement by Dewey in a review of pragmatism: "[James'] real doctrine is that a belief is true when it satisfies both personal needs and the requirements of objective things. Speaking of pragmatism, he says, 'Her only test of probable truth is what works best in the way of *leading us,* what fits every part of life best and *combines with the collectivity of experience's demands,* nothing being omitted' (p. 80, italics [Dewey's]). And again, 'That new idea is truest which performs most felicitously its function of satisfying *our double urgency*' (p. 64). It does not appear certain from the context that this 'double urgency' is that of the personal and the objective demands, respectively, but it is probable (see, also, p. 217, where 'consistency with previous truth and novel fact' is said to be 'always the most imperious claimant'). On this basis, the 'in so far forth' of the truth of the absolute because of the comfort it supplies, means that one of the two conditions which need to be satisfied has been met, so that if the idea of the absolute met the other one also, it would be quite true. I have no doubt this is Mr. James's meaning, and it sufficiently safeguards him from the charge that pragmatism means that anything which is agreeable is true. At the same time, I do not think, in logical strictness, that satisfying one of two tests, when satisfaction of both is required, can be said to constitute a belief

true even 'in so far forth.'" See John Dewey, *Essays in Experimental Logic* (Chicago, 1916), pp. 324–25.

63. *Pragmatism* (New Impression, New York, 1928; originally published in 1907), p. 59.

64. *Ibid.*, pp. 59–60.

65. *Ibid.*, pp. 60–61.

66. *Ibid.*, p. 64.

67. *Ibid.*, p. 65.

68. *The Origins of Pragmatism*, p. 201.

69. *Pragmatism*, pp. 216–17.

70. See pp. 84–85 of "Humanism and Truth", originally published in 1904 and reprinted in William James, *The Meaning of Truth* (New York, 1910; original edition, 1909).

71. *The Principles of Psychology*, Volume II, pp. 661–62.

72. *A Pluralistic Universe* (New York, 1912; originally published in 1909), p. 225.

73. *Ibid.*, p. 244.

74. *Ibid.*, p. 212.

75. W. V. Quine, *From A Logical Point of View* (Cambridge, Mass., 1953), pp. 42–43. The passage appears in Quine's essay, "Two Dogmas of Empiricism", in which he explicitly associates himself with the views of Duhem. Note the similarity between Quine's view and that which is expressed in the passage from Russell quoted above and cited in note 61. There, it should be noted, Russell seems to include both mathematics and physics in science when he says that the whole body of facts renders probable the whole body of scientific laws. Also, it is interesting that Quine's phrase "man-made fabric" echoes James' remark, "The whole fabric of the *a priori* sciences can . . . be treated as a man-made product", *The Meaning of Truth*, p. 85. In addition, see my *Toward Reunion in Philosophy* (Cambridge, Mass., 1956), especially Chapters XV and XVI in which I state certain reservations about pragmatism while expressing sympathy with the pragmatic opposition to dualism.

76. Perry, *The Thought and Character of William James*, Volume II, p. 596.

77. *Ibid.*, p. 439.

78. *Ibid.*, p. 440.

79. Justus Buchler, *Charles Peirce's Empiricism* (London, 1939), p. 228.

80. See my essay, "Pragmatism and the Scope of Science", in *Paths of American Thought*, eds. Arthur Schlesinger, Jr., and Morton White (Boston, 1963), pp. 190–202.

81. In his essay, "The Sentiment of Rationality", James said some-

thing about the formation of *philosophical* opinions which he applied in some parts of *Pragmatism* to the formation of *all* opinions: "Pretend what we may, the whole man within us is at work when we form our philosophical opinions. Intellect, will, taste, and passion co-operate just as they do in practical affairs; and lucky it is if the passion be not something as petty as a love of personal conquest over the philosopher across the way. The absurd abstraction of an intellect verbally formulating all its evidence and carefully estimating the probability thereof by a vulgar fraction by the size of whose denominator and numerator alone it is swayed, is ideally as inept as it is actually impossible. It is almost incredible that men who are themselves working philosophers should pretend that any philosophy can be, or ever has been, constructed without the help of personal preference, belief, or divination", *The Will To Believe*, pp. 92–93.

Chapter 9–Josiah Royce

1. Josiah Royce, *The Religious Aspect of Philosophy* (Boston, 1885), pp. 337–38.

2. Peirce frequently credited Berkeley and Kant with having anticipated his views; and sometimes he includes even Spinoza among his anticipators.

3. See Royce's essay, "The Conception of God", in a volume of that title (New York, 1909; original edition, 1897) to which J. Le Conte, G. H. Howison, and S. E. Mezes also contributed, pp. 30–31.

4. *Collected Papers*, 8.194.

5. *The Conception of God*, p. 31.

6. *Ibid.*

7. *Ibid.*, p. 34.

8. *Ibid.*

9. See Chapter IX, "The World of the Postulates", *The Religious Aspect of Philosophy*, for an earlier treatment of this topic. There Royce says something that may be of interest to present-day ontologists who "posit" physical objects: "In short, the popular assertion of an external world, being an assertion of something beyond the data of consciousness, must begin in an activity of judgment that does more than merely reduce present data to order. Such an assertion must be an active construction of non-data. We do not receive in our senses, but we posit through our judgment, whatever external world there may for us be. If there is really a deeper basis for this postulate of ours, still, at the outset, it is just a postulate. All theories, all hypotheses as to the external

world, ought to face this fact of thought. If the history of popular speculation on these topics could be written, how much of cowardice and
shuffling would be found in the behavior of the natural mind before the
question: 'How dost thou know of an external reality?' Instead of simply
and plainly answering: 'I mean by the external world in the first place
something that I accept or demand, that I posit, postulate, actively construct on the basis of sense-data,' the natural man gives us all kinds of
vague compromise answers: 'I believe in the external reality with a reasonable degree of confidence; the experience of mankind renders the existence of external reality ever more and more probable; the Creator
cannot have intended to deceive us; it is unnatural to doubt as to external reality; only young people and fantastic persons doubt the existence
of the external world; no man in his senses doubts the external reality
of the world; science would be impossible were there no external world;
morality is undermined by doubts as to the external world; the immovable confidence that we all have in the principle of causality implies the
fixity of our belief in an external cause of our sensations.' Where shall
these endless turnings and twistings have an end? The habits of the law-
courts as condensed into 'rules of evidence,' the traditional rules of debate, the fashion of appealing to the 'good sense' of honorable gentlemen opposite, the motives of shame and fear, the dread of being called
'fantastical,' Philistine desire to think with the majority, Philistine terror
of all revolutionary suggestions, the fright or the anger of a man at
finding some metaphysician trying to question what seem to be the
foundations upon which one's bread winning depends,—all these lesser
motives are appealed to, and the one ultimate motive is neglected. The
ultimate motive with the man of every-day life is the will to have an external world. Whatever consciousness contains, reason will persist in
spontaneously adding the thought: 'But there shall be something beyond
this.' The external reality as such (*e.g.* the space beyond the farthest
star, any space not accessible, even whatever is not at any moment given
in so far as it is viewed from that moment, in particular every past
event) is never a datum. We construct but do not receive the external
reality. The 'immovable certainty' is not such a dead passive certainty as
that with which we receive a pain or an electric shock. The popular assurance of an external world is the fixed determination to make one,
now and henceforth. In the general popular conceptions of reality we
find then the first use of postulates. We have as yet no justification for
them," pp. 302–4.

   10. *The Conception of God,* p. 35.
   11. *Ibid.,* p. 39.

12. *The Religious Aspect of Philosophy*, p. vii.

13. *Ibid.*, pp. 230–31.

14. Ralph Barton Perry, *Present Philosophical Tendencies* (New York, 1925; original edition, 1912), Chapter VI.

15. *The Conception of God*, p. 41.

16. Josiah Royce, *The Spirit of Modern Philosophy* (Boston, 1892), p. 361.

17. Josiah Royce, *The Philosophy of Loyalty* (New York, 1908), p. 369. With typical brilliance, William James summed up and condemned Royce's absolutism as follows: "Let there be many facts; but since on idealist principles facts exist only by being known, the many facts will therefore mean many knowers. But that there are so many knowers is itself a fact, which in turn requires *its* knower, so the one absolute knower has eventually to be brought in. *All* facts lead to him. If it be a fact that this table is not a chair, not a rhinoceros, not a logarithm, not a mile away from the door, not worth five hundred pounds sterling, not a thousand centuries old, the absolute must even now be articulately aware of all these negations. Along with what everything is it must also be conscious of everything which it is not. This infinite atmosphere of explicit negativity—observe that it has to be explicit—around everything seems to us so useless an encumbrance as to make the absolute still more foreign to our sympathy. Furthermore, if it be a fact that certain ideas are silly, the absolute has to have already thought the silly ideas to establish them in silliness. The rubbish in its mind would thus appear easily to outweigh in amount the more desirable material. One would expect it fairly to burst with such an obesity, plethora, and superfoetation of useless information", *A Pluralistic Universe*, pp. 127–28.

18. *The Religious Aspect of Philosophy*, pp. 432–33. If such skeptics acknowledged that we make false judgments, were they not committed to holding that the negations of those false judgments are true? We may note in passing that Santayana seems to have overlooked Royce's remark that he could have reached his result by analyzing truth. See Santayana, *Character and Opinion in the United States* (New York, 1920), pp. 100 ff. Peirce, on the other hand, was quick to see that Royce could have proceeded in this other way. See Peirce's review of *The Religious Aspect of Philosophy* in *Collected Papers*, 8.41.

19. *The Religious Aspect of Philosophy*, p. 411. Such a view was also held by the neglected American philosopher of science, J. B. Stallo, who regarded it as an "irrefragable truth" that "thought deals, not with things as they are, or are supposed to be, in themselves, but with our mental representations of them. Its elements are, not pure objects, but

their intellectual counterparts", *The Concepts and Theories of Modern Physics* (Cambridge, Mass., 1960; first published in 1881), p. 156.

20. *The Religious Aspect of Philosophy*, p. 418.

21. *Ibid.*, p. 423; *The World and the Individual* (New York, 1899–1901), Volume II, p. 374.

22. *The Philosophy of Loyalty*, p. 369.

23. *The Religious Aspect of Philosophy*, p. 434.

24. See, for example, *The Spirit of Modern Philosophy*, p. 296. It is interesting to observe in this connection that Royce was far more sympathetic to Spencer's disciple, John Fiske, because Fiske was more sympathetic to idealism. See Royce's Introduction to a posthumous reprint of Fiske's *Outlines of Cosmic Philosophy* (Cambridge, Mass., 1902), Volume I, pp. xxi–cxlix. Also see Royce's *Herbert Spencer: An Estimate and Review* (New York, 1904).

25. *The Spirit of Modern Philosophy*, p. 274.

26. *Ibid.*, pp. 274–75.

27. *Ibid.*, p. 277.

28. *Ibid.*, pp. 278–79.

29. *Ibid.*, p. 280.

30. *Ibid.*, p. 281. "Our century" was, of course, the nineteenth.

31. James Harvey Robinson, *The New History* (New York, 1912), especially Chapter II. See also Morton White, *Social Thought in America: The Revolt Against Formalism* (New York, 1949; reprint, Boston, 1957), especially Chapters II, IV, VIII. It should be noted that Robinson gives much credit to Marx for originating the new history, whereas Royce does not mention him. This is partly explained by the fact that Robinson laid stress, as Royce did not, on economic determinism as an ingredient of the new history.

32. In his earliest book, *The Religious Aspect of Philosophy*, Royce spurned the Argument from Design; see Chapter VIII, "The World of Doubt". That is because his God is all-knowing rather than all-causing.

33. *The Spirit of Modern Philosophy*, pp. 284–85.

34. *Ibid.*, p. 285.

35. *Ibid.*, p. 293.

36. *Ibid.*, p. 297.

37. In *Social Thought in America*, especially Chapter II.

38. *The Letters of Josiah Royce*, ed. J. Clendenning (Chicago, 1970), Letter of April 18, 1908, p. 522.

39. See Morton and Lucia White, *The Intellectual Versus The City* (Cambridge, Mass., 1962), especially Chapter XI, "Provincialism and Alienation: An Aside on Josiah Royce and George Santayana".

40. Frederick Jackson Turner, the distinguished historian, expressed his sympathy with certain views of Royce by saying: "It was the opinion of this eminent philosopher that the world needs now more than ever before the vigorous development of a highly organized provincial life to serve as a check upon mob psychology on a national scale, and to furnish that variety which is essential to vital growth and originality. With this I agree", *The Significance of Sections in American History* (New York, 1932), p. 45. The similarity between Turner's views and Royce's has been observed by Ralph Gabriel in his *The Course of American Democratic Thought* (New York, 1940), pp. 275–76.

41. *The Philosophy of Loyalty*, pp. 239–41.

42. *Ibid.*, p. 242.

43. *Ibid.*, pp. 245–46.

44. Henry James, *The American Scene* (New York, 1946; reprint edition), p. 86.

45. *The Philosophy of Loyalty*, p. 247.

46. *Ibid.*, p. ix.

47. *Ibid.*, p. 257.

48. *Ibid.*, pp. 260–61.

49. *Ibid.*, pp. 277 ff.

50. *Ibid.*, p. 302.

51. See note 9 above.

52. *The Philosophy of Loyalty*, pp. 306–7.

53. *Ibid.*, p. 310.

54. In *The World and the Individual*, Royce elaborated the theory of meaning he had presented in *The Religious Aspect of Philosophy*. In the former work he took his point of departure from the traditional theory that certain linguistic expressions have both a connotation and a denotation which are to be distinguished. For example, the great logician Gottlob Frege (whose views Royce did not discuss) held that a phrase like "The evening star" has a "Sinn" (sense) which is the concept we grasp when we understand the phrase and a "Bedeutung" (denotation or reference) which is the physical body we see in the sky. Royce tends to speak of an *idea*—which is for him a state of mind—as having both an internal meaning, the counterpart of Frege's sense, and an external meaning, the counterpart of Frege's denotation. But Royce's fundamental departure from the tradition represented by Frege appears when he says that "in the end, . . . the final meaning of every complete idea . . . must be viewed as wholly an internal meaning". (*The World and the Individual*, Volume I, p. 34.) Royce's opposition to "sundering" internal and external meaning was a consequence of his view that the

internal meaning of an idea viewed as a sign is simply the purpose of the idea, which he regarded as a tool or plan of action (*ibid.*, p. 22; p. 308); and that the external meaning is the "determinate embodiment" of that purpose. Royce goes further and maintains that the determinate embodiment of an idea is always an entire individual life. "This life," he maintains, "is at once a system of facts, and the fulfillment of whatever purpose any finite idea [like my idea of the cat which I say is on the mat] . . . already fragmentarily embodies. This life is the completed will, as well as the completed experience, corresponding to the will and experience of any one finite idea." (*Ibid.*, p. 341.) After having supposedly established that every real thing is a life because a real thing is simply the embodiment of the purpose of any finite idea, he goes on to argue that the Absolute Self contains all such lesser selves like his and those of other human beings as sub-classes. But since each human self is a class of infinitely many thoughts, the question arises as to how each self may form a sub-class of the Absolute Self. His answer, very briefly stated, is that modern mathematics has shown that an infinite class may be a proper sub-class of another infinite class. For example, the class of even integers, though infinite, may be put into one-one correspondence with the class of all integers.

Royce's use of the theory of meaning and especially of the foundations of mathematics illustrates his propensity to bring up heavy guns in order to defend his epistemology and metaphysics, but one may seriously doubt whether he succeeded in showing by this method that his absolute idealism was any less fantastic than it appears to be. To demonstrate this, one would have to devote more time and space than I have at my disposal. In particular, one would have to expound and carefully analyze the "Supplementary Essay" at the end of the first volume of *The World and the Individual*.

Chapter 10—George Santayana

1. See Santayana's essay, "Emerson", in his *Interpretations of Poetry and Religion* (New York, 1922; original edition, 1900), p. 230.

2. See Baker Brownell's interesting comparison of Emerson and Santayana, "Santayana, The Man and the Philosopher", *The Philosophy of George Santayana*, ed. P. A. Schilpp (Evanston, Ill., 1940), pp. 56–61.

3. George Santayana, *Winds of Doctrine* and *Platonism and the Spiritual Life* (two works reprinted together in Harper Torchbook edition, New York, 1957). The former contains "The Genteel Tradition in American Philosophy". For the quotation in question, see p. 188.

4. *Ibid.*, p. 212.

5. *Character and Opinion in the United States* (New York, 1934; original edition, 1920), Chapter IV, "Josiah Royce", p. 98.

6. *Ibid.*, p. 100.

7. See George Santayana, *The Middle Span* (New York, 1945), pp. 166–70.

8. *Winds of Doctrine*, p. 204.

9. *Ibid.*, p. 205.

10. *Ibid.*, p. 206.

11. *Ibid.*, p. 208.

12. *Ibid.*, p. 210.

13. *Ibid.*, pp. 212–13.

14. George Santayana, "A General Confession", *The Philosophy of George Santayana*, p. 6; *The Middle Span*, Chapter VIII.

15. *Character and Opinion*, Chapter III, "William James", p. 96.

16. *The Middle Span*, p. 156.

17. George Santayana, "Brief History of My Opinions", *Contemporary American Philosophy*, Volume 2, eds. G. P. Adams and W. P. Montague (New York, 1930), pp. 244–45.

18. See pp. 138 ff. in *Winds of Doctrine*, Chapter IV, "The Philosophy of Mr. Bertrand Russell".

19. *Reason in Science*, p. 58.

20. *Interpretations of Poetry and Religion*, p. v.

21. *Ibid.*, p. 106.

22. *Ibid.*, p. 107.

23. *Ibid.*, p. 108.

24. *Ibid.*, pp. 108–9.

25. *Reason in Religion*, p. 14.

26. *Interpretations of Poetry and Religion*, p. 91.

27. *Reason in Common Sense*, p. 256.

28. *Ibid.*, pp. 222–23.

29. *Ibid.*, p. 236.

30. *Ibid.*, p. 257. Compare Royce: "Desire is related to developed will in rational agents as sense-data are related to perceptions", Supplementary Essay in *The Conception of God* (by Royce *et al.*), p. 187; also compare James, ". . . *the essence of good is simply to satisfy demand*", p. 201 in "The Moral Philosopher and the Moral Life", *The Will To Believe*, pp. 184–215; and see the discussion of Dewey's ethics below.

31. *Reason in Common Sense*, p. 257.

32. *Reason in Science*, Chapters VI–X, *passim*.

33. *Ibid.*, p. 240.

34. *Ibid.*, p. 33. I do not think that when Santayana spoke of the importance of deduction in natural science, he was merely calling attention to the need for axiomatizing natural science. He was rather adopting a view not unlike that of his teacher, James, who, as we have seen, also held (*pace* Locke) that science aspires to an axiomatization in which the axioms themselves are "rational propositions". We shall see below that even the anti-dualistic Dewey seems to have succumbed to this form of rationalism.

35. *International Journal of Ethics* (later *Ethics*), Volume XVII (1906–7), p. 248.

36. *Educational Review*, Volume XXXIV (1907), pp. 116–29.

37. *Reason in Common Sense*, pp. 10–11.

38. *Ibid.*, p. 13.

39. *Ibid.*, p. 17. Santayana is charitably interpreted as using "mechanics" in a very broad sense as virtually equivalent to "natural science"; and hence as not intending to contest some of the things that J. B. Stallo had maintained in *The Concepts and Theories of Modern Physics* (New York, 1881).

40. *Ibid.*, p. 51.

41. *Ibid.*, p. 61. I take this to mean that we can build our logics on different sets of axioms, but this may be excessively charitable.

42. *Ibid.*, p. 67.

43. *Ibid.*, p. 77.

44. *Ibid.*, p. 95.

45. *Ibid.*, p. 97.

46. *Ibid.*, p. 110.

47. *Ibid.*, p. 124. Perhaps the intermediary was James.

48. *Ibid.*, p. 211. Compare Gilbert Ryle's phrase, "the ghost in the machine", *The Concept of Mind* (London, 1949), *passim.*

49. *Ibid.*, p. 284.

50. *Reason in Society*, p. 35.

51. *Ibid.*, p. 44.

52. *Ibid.*, pp. 52–53.

53. *Ibid.*, p. 81.

54. *Ibid.*, pp. 82–83.

55. *Ibid.*, pp. 142–43.

56. *Reason in Religion*, p. 22.

57. *Ibid.*, p. 39.

58. *Ibid.*, p. 129.

59. *Ibid.*, pp. 156–58.

60. "Apologia Pro Mente Sua", *The Philosophy of George Santayana*, p. 604.

61. *Interpretations of Poetry and Religion*, p. 223; p. 232.

62. In writing about *The Life of Reason*, William James noted a similarity between Emerson and Santayana like the one I have been stressing, but James very acutely noted a difference too: "Santayana's book is a great one, if the inclusion of opposites is a measure of greatness. I think it will probably be reckoned great by posterity. It has no *rational* foundation, being merely one man's way of viewing things: so much of experience admitted and no more, so much criticism and questioning admitted and no more. He is a paragon of Emersonianism—declare your intuitions, though no other man share them; and the integrity with which he does it is as fine as it is rare. And his naturalism, materialism, Platonism, and atheism form a combination of which the centre of gravity is, I think, very deep. But there is something profoundly alienating in his unsympathetic tone, his 'preciousness' and superciliousness. The book is Emerson's first rival and successor, but how different the reader's feeling! The same things in Emerson's mouth would sound entirely different. E. receptive, expansive, as if handling life through a wide funnel with a great indraught; S. as if through a pin-point orifice that emits his cooling spray outward over the universe like a nose-disinfectant from an 'atomizer' ", Ralph Barton Perry, *The Thought and Character of William James* (Boston, 1935), Volume II, p. 399.

63. "His mind is urban in contrast to Emerson's bucolic temperament", says Baker Brownell, *op. cit.*, p. 60.

64. *The Philosophy of George Santayana*, p. 23.

65. *The Middle Span*, pp. 25–26.

66. George Santayana, *My Host the World* (New York, 1953), p. 140.

67. *The Philosophy of George Santayana*, pp. 560–61. See Morton and Lucia White, *The Intellectual Versus The City* (Cambridge, Mass., 1962), Chapter XI, for a discussion of Santayana on the city.

68. Morton and Lucia White, *loc. cit.*

69. V. L. Parrington, *Main Currents in American Thought* (New York, 1927), Volume I, p. vi.

70. *Ibid.*, Volume III, p. 53.

71. *Ibid.*, p. 240.

72. William James "and his brother Henry were as tightly swaddled in the genteel tradition as any infant geniuses could be, for they were born before 1850, and in a Swedenborgian household. Yet they burst those bands almost entirely. The ways in which the two brothers freed

themselves, however, are interestingly different. Mr. Henry James has done it by adopting the point of view of the outer world, and by turning the genteel American tradition, as he turns everything else, into a subject-matter for analysis. For him it is a curious habit of mind, intimately comprehended, to be compared with other habits of mind, also well known to him. Thus he has overcome the genteel tradition in the classic way, by understanding it", *Winds of Doctrine*, pp. 203–4.

Chapter 11–John Dewey

1. See Corliss Lamont, ed., *Dialogue on John Dewey* (New York, 1959), p. 89, where this statement is attributed to Dewey.

2. Jane Dewey, ed., "Biography of John Dewey", in *The Philosophy of John Dewey*, ed. P. A. Schilpp (Evanston, Ill., 1939), p. 12.

3. *Ibid.*, p. 17. In *The Origin of Dewey's Instrumentalism* (New York, 1943), I have examined the impact of absolute idealism on the early Dewey. In connection with this impact, it is of some interest to note that Dewey was a graduate of the university of which James Marsh had been president. It is also of some interest to read in the biography written by Dewey's daughter on the basis of material supplied by him, that although he was taught at Vermont primarily by H. A. P. Torrey, a follower of the Scottish philosophy, Dewey thought that "the rather dry bones of Scotch thought were somewhat enlivened by ideas and topics which persisted from the teachings of the Reverend Professor James Marsh, one of the first Americans to disregard the dangerous reputation of the German philosophers sufficiently to study and teach them", *The Philosophy of John Dewey*, op. cit., p. 12. Dewey published a lecture on James Marsh, previously cited in note 18 of Chapter 4.

4. *The Philosophy of John Dewey*, p. 18; *Origin of Dewey's Instrumentalism*, especially Chapters VIII–XI.

5. In *Reconstruction in Philosophy* (New York, 1920) and *The Quest for Certainty* (New York, 1929), Dewey develops this theme at length.

6. John Dewey, *Democracy and Education* (New York, 1932; original edition, 1916), pp. 392–93.

7. *The Quest for Certainty*, p. 137.

8. *Ibid.*, p. 171.

9. This interpretation of Dewey is mainly guided by his frequent disavowals of subjectivism and idealism. I grant, however, that there are passages which may be difficult to interpret in this way.

10. *Ibid.*, p. 84. The italics are mine.

11. *Reconstruction in Philosophy*, p. 113.

12. See John Dewey, *Art as Experience* (New York, 1934), Chapter III, "Having an Experience".

13. For an expression of Dewey's views on the emotive theory of ethics, see Chapter II of his "Theory of Valuation", *International Encyclopedia of Unified Science*, Volume II, Number 4 (Chicago, 1939).

14. See my article, "Value and Obligation in Dewey and Lewis", *Philosophical Review*, Volume LVIII, Number 4 (July 1949); also C. L. Stevenson, *Ethics and Language* (New Haven, 1944), pp. 253–64. Dewey's views on this question are most clearly expressed in *The Quest for Certainty*, Chapter X.

15. *The Quest for Certainty*, p. 259.

16. See the previous chapter, p. 253.

17. See *The Origin of Dewey's Instrumentalism*, pp. 85–86.

18. Charles Peirce, *Collected Papers*, 8.190.

19. See, for example, *The Quest for Certainty*, Chapter II, "Philosophy's Search For The Immutable".

20. *Reconstruction in Philosophy*, pp. 137–38.

21. John Dewey, *Logic: The Theory of Inquiry* (New York, 1938), pp. 12–14.

22. See, for example, *ibid.*, pp. 283–84.

23. *The Quest for Certainty*, pp. 26–27. I would note that the distinction between "truths relating to the relation of ideas, and 'truths' about matters of existence, empirically ascertained" is an indirect allusion to Hume's distinction.

24. I have developed this in greater detail in "Experiment and Necessity in Dewey's Philosophy", *Antioch Review*, Fall 1959, pp. 329–44. For an allied criticism of Dewey, see M. Brodbeck, "The New Rationalism: Dewey's Theory of Induction", *The Journal of Philosophy*, Volume 46 (1949), pp. 780–91.

25. *Democracy and Education*, pp. 394–95.

26. *Ibid.*, p. 422.

27. John Dewey, "Philosophy of Education", *A Cyclopedia of Education*, ed. P. Monroe (New York, 1925), Volume III, pp. 699–700.

28. *Democracy and Education*, pp. 383–84.

29. *Ibid.*, p. 383.

30. *The Philosophy of John Dewey*, p. 592, n. 57.

Epilogue

1. John Stuart Mill, *Autobiography* (New York, 1924; first published, 1873), p. 158.

2. *Freedom of the Will* (New Haven, 1957), p. 374.

3. For a defense of my views, see *Toward Reunion in Philosophy*, especially Parts III and IV.

4. Richard Hofstadter, *Anti-intellectualism in American Life* (New York, 1963), p. 7. For a point of view like that adopted in the present chapter, see my "Reflections on Anti-intellectualism", *Daedalus,* Volume 91 (1962), pp. 457–68.

5. *Pragmatism* (New York, 1928), p. 81.

6. Here I follow the previously cited important work by the late Richard Hofstadter.

7. Moses Coit Tyler, *A History of American Literature, 1607–1765* (Ithaca, N.Y., 1949), pp. 85–87.

8. "The American Scholar", *Complete Works* (Boston, 1903), Volume I, p. 102.

Index

218, 245, 252; career of, 146, 151-
52; Dewey and, 267, 268, 274-75,
278, 280, 282, 283; "The Doctrine
of Necessity Examined", 160, 181;
education of, 145-47; Edwards and,
159, 166, 168, 169, 298; Emerson
and, 145, 147; essentialism, 161-66;
"How To Make Our Ideas Clear",
150, 152; indeterminism, 159-61;
influence of, summarized, 297-99;
James and, 144-46, 149, 152, 157-
60, 165-66, 169, 181, 215-16, 299,
334-35; meaning, theory of, 152-
59, 161-65; metaphysics, 148-49,
159-66; pragmatism, 149-59, 161-
69, 298; Royce and, 220, 221, 298;
scholastic realism, 161-66; theism,
166-69; Transcendentalism and,
145, 147-48, 169; Wright and, 145-
47, 149, 162

Plato, 33, 269, 277

Pragmatism, 9-10; of Dewey, 267,
280-81; of James, 157-59, 202-16,
307; of Peirce, 149-59, 161-69, 298;
Russell on, 159, 204-5, 208; Wright
and, 122, 133

Quine, W. V., 213, 305, 339

Rationalism: Dewey and, 284-85;
James and, 176-80; of Locke, 15-
16, 18-19, 24, 291, 296; of Santayana, 255-56

Reason: Emerson on, 5-6, 10, 76-77,
98-100, 102-11, 131, 214, 292-94;
Jacobi on, 74-76; Kant on, 74-77;
Locke on, 22-25; in Transcen-
dentalism, 74-78, 81, 86, 131; in
Unitarianism, 72-73

Reid, Thomas, 86, 99, 254, 291; criticism of Locke, 57-62; on Moral
Sense theory, 66-67; Wilson influenced by, 62-64, 66, 315-16

Religion: of Edwards, 30-54; Emerson on, 97-98, 100, 108-9; James
on, 188-201; Locke on, 24-29, 82;
Peirce on, 166-69; Royce on, 218-
20; Santayana on, 246-51, 260-62;
in Transcendentalism, 81-84, 87-

90, 108-9, 166; Unitarianism, 72-
73; Wright on, 136, 140-43

Ripley, George, 78, 95-96, 108, 169,
294-95, 307, 309; on ethics and
utilitarianism, 90-94; on religion,
81-84, 87-88

Robinson, James Harvey, 231, 233,
267, 343

Royce, Josiah, 217-39; mentioned,
5, 143, 247, 253, 296; on the Absolute, 220-29, 232-33, 238; Absolute Idealism, 218-20, 233; The
Conception of God, 220, 228, 242;
Dewey and, 266-68; on evolution,
229-33; at Harvard as teacher, 170-
71, 218; on idealism, 229-33; influence of, 299-300; James and, 218,
230, 234, 236, 342; on loyalty, 234-
39; Peirce and, 220, 221, 298; The
Philosophy of Loyalty, 234, 237;
on provincialism, 234-39; Race
Questions, Provincialism, and Other
American Problems, 219, 234; on
religion, 218-20; The Religious
Aspect of Philosophy, 220, 224-25,
227-28, 238; Santayana on, 241,
243-44; The Spirit of Modern Philosophy, 220, 226; The World and
the Individual, 220

Rush, Benjamin, 317

Russell, Bertrand, 280, 282, 299, 305;
on pragmatism, 159, 204-5, 208;
Santayana's criticism of, 251

Santayana, George, 240-65; mentioned, 5, 143, 178, 285, 296; cultural and social criticism, 256-65;
Dewey and, 266-68, 270, 278, 279;
Dewey on, 256; on Emerson, 111-
12, 115-17, 241, 261-62, 293; Emerson compared with, 241, 246, 256,
260-63, 348; ethics of, 251-56; "The
Genteel Tradition in American
Philosophy", 241-46, 293; at Harvard as teacher, 170-71, 240, 246;
influence of, 300-301; on James and
his brother Henry, 348-49; James
compared with, 255; James on, 348;
The Life of Reason, 247-48, 251-
56, 300; on religion, 246-51, 260-